T0198021

Digital Literacy and Digital Inclusion

Digital Literacy and Digital Inclusion

Information Policy and the Public Library

Kim M. Thompson, Paul T. Jaeger, Natalie Greene Taylor, Mega Subramaniam, and John Carlo Bertot

ROWMAN & LITTLEFIELD
Lanham • Boulder • New York • London

Published by Rowman & Littlefield
A wholly owned subsidiary of The Rowman & Littlefield Publishing Group, Inc.
4501 Forbes Boulevard, Suite 200, Lanham, Maryland 20706
www.rowman.com

16 Carlisle Street, London W1D 3BT, United Kingdom

British Library Cataloguing in Publication Information Available

Library of Congress Cataloging-in-Publication Data

Thompson, Kim M., 1971-
Digital literacy and digital inclusion : information policy and the public library / Kim M. Thompson, Paul T. Jaeger, Natalie Greene Taylor, Mega Subramaniam, and John Carlo Bertot.
pages cm
Includes bibliographical references and index.
ISBN 978-0-8108-9271-2 (hardcover) -- ISBN 978-0-8108-9272-9 (ebook) 1. Information society. 2. Digital divide. 3. Information policy. 4. Electronic information resource literacy. 5. Technological literacy. 6. Information behavior. 7. Libraries and society. 8. Libraries and the Internet. 9. Internet access for library users. 10. Libraries and state. I. Jaeger, Paul T., 1974- II. Taylor, Natalie Greene, 1987- III. Subramaniam, Manimegalai M. IV. Bertot, John Carlo. V. Title.
HM851.T535 2014
303.48'33--dc23
2014009779

∞™ The paper used in this publication meets the minimum requirements of American National Standard for Information Sciences Permanence of Paper for Printed Library Materials, ANSI/NISO Z39.48-1992.

Printed in the United States of America

Contents

Acknowledgments

Developed over many years of research, this book is the result of the support of many friends and colleagues. First, our editor Martin Dillon and the other folks at Rowman & Littlefield deserve credit and gratitude for their support for this project. Martin is supportive, encouraging, and timely—everything an author hopes for in an editor.

We have worked, individually and collectively, with a range of collaborators over the years on work related to this book. Gary Burnett, as the co-creator of the Information Worlds theoretical framework used in this book, is the most notable influence. Additionally, collaborations with Denice Adkins, Waseem Afzal, Elizabeth DeCoster, Ursula Gorham, Renee Franklin Hill, Christie Kodama, Sarah Katz, and Melinda Whetstone have helped us formulate the ideas that are central to the discussions in this book. We also appreciate the information provided by John Stephen Agbenyo, Gifty Boakye, Nitida Carranza, Woojin Noh, Sanghee Oh, and Doris Santos that helped us to understand aspects of and verify the findings of the case studies.

We are grateful for the various forms of support given by all of the other staff members of Information Policy & Access Center—along with the aforementioned Ursula and Christie—at the University of Maryland while we were writing this book: June Ahn, Faith Ambrosini, Frank Bonnevier, Sarah Dammeyer, Jeff DiScala, Kristofer Dubbels, Rebecca Follman, Leahkim Gannett, Karen Kettnich, Jessica Koepfler, Michael Kurtz, Jean Lee, Emily Likins-Hohman, Sheri Massey, Abigail McDermott, Alexis Moses, Johnna Percell, Kaitlin Peterson, Ricky Punzalan, Brian Real, Sophie Reverdy, Lindsay Sarin, Molly Schwartz, Katie Shilton, Beth St. Jean, Amanda Waugh, Ann Weeks, Kim White, and Erin Zerhusen.

We are equally grateful to our families, the assorted spouses, significant whatevers, children, parents, siblings, and pets who were supportive of our writings endeavors for the book. A special thank you goes out to Carol Jaeger—the wonderful mother of one of the authors—for reading and providing feedback on the book manuscript.

Most significantly, we are grateful to the readers of this book for spending time with our ideas.

Figures and Tables

Acronyms

ALA	American Library Association
ARRA	American Reinvestment and Recovery Act
ASCII	American Standard Code for Information Interchange
BTOP	Broadband Technology Opportunities Program
CEIT	Centre of Education for Information Technology (Netherlands)
CIPA	Children's Internet Protection Act
CTC	Community Technology Centers
DCMA	Digital Millennium Copyright Act
DOI	Digital Opportunity Index
EDDI	European Digital Development Index
EIFL	Electronic Information For Libraries
E-rate	Education Rate
EU	European Union
FCC	Federal Communications Commission
GDP	Gross Domestic Product
ICMA	International City/County Management Association
ICT	Information and Communication Technology
IDI	ICT Development Index
IFLA	International Federation of Library Associations and Institution
IMLS	Institute of Museum and Library Services
ISO	International Organization for Standardization
ISP	Internet Service Provider
ITU	International Telecommunication Union
LIS	Library and Information Science
MIC	Ministry of Information and Communication (Korea)
MOOC	Massively Open Online Course
NBN	National Broadband Network (Australia)
NCD	National Council on Disability

NIA	National Information Society Agency (Korea)
NIH	National Institutes of Health
NTIA	National Telecommunications and Information Administration
OCLC	Online Computer Library Center, Inc
OITP	Office of Information Technology Policy
PC	Personal Computer
PLA	Public Library Association
UN	United Nations
UNESCO	United Nations Educational, Scientific and Cultural Organization
USF	Universal Service Fund
VITA	Internal Revenue Service Volunteer Income Tax Assistance
WIC	Women Infants and Children Program

Preface

Education, employment, civic engagement, and other forms of social participation have always depended on information. However, in a world where the technologies required for accessing, using, and understanding information have become increasingly ubiquitous and complicated, the design, implementation, access, and educational components of information and technology produce enormous challenges to inclusion and equity. Information professionals and scholars know that limited digital literacy and inadequate digital inclusion are detrimental to social participation, and libraries engage in a wide array of initiatives to promote equity in these areas. Many governments around the world have also recognized the importance of digital literacy and digital inclusion, taking numerous different approaches to promote digital literacy and digital inclusion among their populations. In most of the nations that are actively engaging with issues of literacy and inclusion, library activities are often recognized or even incorporated into the government efforts.

This book is intended to help information professionals, scholars, students, and policymakers understand the evolution of the concepts of digital literacy, digital divides, and digital inclusion, and the impacts of policy on these concepts. The book highlights the implications that such policy and definitions have on the individuals, communities, libraries, and cultural institutions that serve as pivotal access agents to participation in the dynamic digital society. Although the United States serves as the primary focus of this text, examples from other countries—including detailed case studies of six other nations—are employed to demonstrate the range of library activities and national policies related to digital literacy and digital inclusion. The examples also help to illuminate the breadth of practices and policies being used around the globe, providing more examples that libraries can learn from in developing and improving their own practices.

The Bill of Rights and the Policy Manual of the American Library Association (ALA) and the Internet Manifesto of the International Federation of Library Associations and Institutions (IFLA), among others, present access to, literacy of, and inclusion to information and accompanying information and communication technologies (ICTs) as issues of social justice. The modern practice of librarianship has been one of supporting and promoting social justice in relation to information and ICTs. From the earliest years of the modern public library movement, social justice has been a unifying goal across the evolutions of practice, from the development of children's story time at the dawn of the 20th century to the access and training for the Internet provided today.

In many nations, librarians were far ahead of the curve in recognizing the importance of and supporting digital literacy and digital inclusion. In many public libraries in the United States, access and education programs related to the Internet have been in place for nearly two decades. A number of scholars and practitioners in the field of librarianship have persuasively articulated that Internet access, digital literacy, and digital inclusion should be viewed as human rights issues (e.g., Duffy, 2001; Hoffman, 2001; Jaeger, 2012; Bertot, & Gorham, 2013; McCook & Phenix, 2006; Phenix & McCook, 2005; Stinnett, 2009; Suarez, 2007). The master of library science program at the University of Maryland offers a course entitled Information and Humans Rights to prepare students to deal with equity of access, literacy, and inclusion, linking principles of the academic library science field with the access and education work that public librarians do in practice.

With the steady stream of patrons coming to libraries to use the Internet as their primary or only access point, library professionals have long seen that choices made during design and implementation of online information and services have implications for information access, information literacy, information behavior, intellectual freedom, privacy, security, and freedom of expression, which in turn impact the ability of individuals and groups to participate in education, employment, and civic engagement. However, patrons must first be digitally literate to be digitally included, and libraries are often the only institutions in a community able to teach literacy and provide access. Unfortunately, this reality rarely factors into decisions made by the primary providers of content and services online. Local, state, and national governments now frequently require members of the community to perform activities online that once could be performed in person or on the phone.

Governments, corporations, community organizations, mass media, entertainment venues, and virtually every other facet of society and social interaction now rely on the Internet for key parts of their activities. A significant portion of government-related information found on the Internet is otherwise hard to find and impossible to receive. Many companies and their wares can only be found online; retailers that still exist as physical entities usually offer far fewer choices in their brick-and-mortar locations than on their websites—and this trend is growing at an exponential rate. Facebook, Twitter, Tumblr, Instagram, and innumerable other social media platforms now dominate social interactions for many people. Civic participation, community organizing, volunteering, and dating have also moved into cyberspace.

To not be online means being excluded from a great many activities and opportunities that are essential for an individual's life and growth.

Imagine the difficulty in getting an education, finding a job, participating in a community, or fulfilling basic requirements of citizenship (such as paying taxes) without knowing the skills to effectively use the Internet as a tool or without having the ability to access it at all.

Gaps in access to information have always existed, regardless of the type of technology used in communicating information. As three examples, information disseminated through the written word is unavailable to an illiterate receiver, radio broadcasts do not directly benefit individuals with severe hearing impairment, and television programming in English will be of little use as an information channel to many French-speaking inhabitants of Quebec. The impacts of online exclusion, however, are so large that most people running governments, companies, and other core parts of society miss the fact that not everyone is online. People who lack Internet access and the skills to effectively use the Internet may very well be the most ignored group in society. Although a handful of scholars from a wide array of different disciplines are trying to understand gaps in access and the ways in which to address them, the work largely exists in silos and is mostly ignored by people making the decisions that shape information access.

Under the Affordable Care Act, millions of people—perhaps tens of millions in the United States—were expected to sign up online for health insurance; a great many of them will depend on public library resources and services to do so (Eberhart, 2013). With 15 percent of American adults being nonusers of the Internet (Zickuhr, 2013), much of the work with health-care enrollment will have to begin with basic digital literacy education at the public library. Many of these learners will be additional patrons beyond the 28 million public library patrons who currently use library computers to search for health and wellness information on a regular basis (Pera, 2013). The Department of Health and Human Services stated that it expected considerable support from public libraries to both inform people about options and help them enroll—but expects this service without providing any support to libraries to meet these expectations. As Susan Hildreth, director of the Institute of Museum and Libraries Services (IMLS), noted, "There are no federal funds to support this program" (Eberhart, 2013). Complicating this national service initiative further is the fact that several state governments placed restrictions on the ability of public librarians to help patrons learn about and sign up for health care (Somashekhar, 2013).

President Obama recorded a special video message thanking librarians for helping with the implementation of the Affordable Care Act but only allowed the ALA to show the video once at its 2013 summer convention in Chicago. Members of the public were not allowed to see the video (Morrongiello, 2013). In summary, the national leaders representing public libraries in the ALA and IMLS acquiesced to an enormous new burden to inform and help to enroll millions of uninsured people in a new online government program without receiving additional funding, and with the only public recognition of their assistance trapped in a recorded message that could be played once. Libraries took the responsibility on because no one else could, and the government knew they did not have to provide support or public acknowledgment because there was nothing else the library could do, other than refuse to help their communities. Then, as the culminating insult, the federal government shut down much of its Web presence for most of the month before sign-up was to begin, taking away resources that the libraries would greatly have benefitted from in preparing health literacy training, such as the information from the suspended National Institutes of Health (NIH) sites (Shuler, Jaeger, & Bertot, 2014).

The failure to consider issues regarding the digital inclusion of the people who need to sign up for insurance in this plan—and the casual assumption that public libraries will be able to cheerfully take on teaching digital literacy to and providing sufficient Internet access for millions of more patrons during times of record library usage—demonstrate the utter lack of thought given to issues of gaps in access and literacy at this point.

This situation, though perhaps not at such a scale, is replayed over and over across cultural and national borders. Although some countries certainly have devoted more focus and funding to supporting widespread access and literacy, gaps are present everywhere. In many societies, the gaps in access and literacy are small islands in an ocean of digital inclusion. In some places, these gaps are enormous. The United States provides a telling example of the range of potential causes of gaps in digital access, literacy, and inclusion. Socioeconomic status, education level, geography, disability, age, language, and many other factors can shape levels of access and literacy (Jaeger, Bertot, & Subramaniam, 2013; Jaeger, Subramaniam, Jones, & Bertot, 2011). In spite of the broad differences in the root reasons for gaps in access and literacy, the exclusionary results are quite similar.

To bring greater understanding about the impacts of these issues and the ways in which they might be addressed, this book examines the interrelationships between digital literacy, digital inclusion, and public policy, emphasizing the impacts of these policy decisions on the ability of individuals and communities to successfully participate in the information society and the obligations that these policies create for the social institutions that support digital literacy and inclusion. By drawing upon examples, programs, and policies from around the globe, this book hopes to paint a truly international picture of ways to improve digital inclusion and support the organizations that are essential to digital inclusion.

ONE

Introduction and Overview

The rapid movement of many important social and personal interactions into the digital environment has placed a great deal of importance on the ability to successfully access and use the hardware and software necessary for online participation. The ability to use the Internet to meet information needs is often labeled *digital literacy*, while access to the Internet in order to apply the skills of digital literacy is often discussed in terms of *digital inclusion*. The primary goal of this book is to bring together the dispersed literature related to digital literacy and digital inclusion in order to better understand the impacts of policy decisions about these areas on individuals and communities while also offering policy solutions and recommendations to improve the levels of digital literacy and digital inclusion. These recommendations are geared both toward informing practice in libraries and helping libraries to frame their advocacy for public policies that support literacy and inclusion.

The term *public policy* is used to indicate decisions and actions by the government to address public problems. Policies include "legislation, executive orders, agency memos, rulemaking, signing statements, and a range of other measures at the government's disposal" (Jaeger, Bertot, & Gorham, 2013, p. 62). The discussions in this book draw particular attention to public policies that impact the operations of public libraries and the services and resources they can provide the public. Two central issues for public policy at this time are digital literacy and digital inclusion, as the transfer of many government services to primarily or exclusively online has created a system in which the lack of digital literacy and digital inclusion threatens democratic processes. Decisions in public policy have been key drivers of the move of materials online, from providing financial support for the creation of broadband infrastructure to the economic incentives for e-commerce through regulatory actions or inactions. In the

United States and around the world, obtaining government information, filing taxes, renewing licenses, enrolling children in school, applying for immigration, establishing residency, viewing report cards, paying fines, communicating with a government official, and innumerable other interactions between citizens and governments occur online, with only occasional options of in-person or paper-based access.

National and international policy, evidence of the basic principles by which government is guided, shapes how digital literacy and digital inclusion are promoted or hindered in a society. Changes in policy in liberal democratic government administrations may sway back and forth from ideals of less government intervention to more hands-on governance, or capitalist to socialist leanings. Decisions about funding and other forms of support for institutions that provide the access, assistance, and education to ensure digital literacy and digital inclusion—such as public libraries, public schools, school libraries, and academic libraries—are inextricably linked to these sways in policy guidelines. This can greatly affect the levels of digital literacy and digital inclusion in a community.

For example, the first Finnish Library Act came into force in 1929. This policy emphasized social inclusion through the provision of citizen rights to free service and quality service regardless of financial standing. Services were meant to support the nation's education system and to encourage independent study (Ministry of Education, 2009). As the Finnish welfare state evolved, the Library Act was amended (1961) to reflect the national focus on equitable services to all. State subsidies were allocated to construct library buildings both in urban and in rural areas and to create mobile library services. In 1994, Cable Book Library launched its Knot at the Cable project, offering one Internet workstation for public use. This is believed to be the first Finnish library to offer Internet service to library users (Lounasvuori & Vattulainen, 1996). When digital information resources multiplied in the late 1990s, the Library Act was again amended (1998) to explicitly link public libraries to digital knowledge and to information services, providing additional funding to support this connection. Since then, the Finnish Ministry of Education has elaborated on specific library service objectives in policy publications such as their Library Policy Programme 2001–2004 (Ministry of Education, 2001), the Library Strategy 2010 (Ministry of Education, 2003), Library Development Programme 2006–2010 (Ministry of Education and Culture, 2006), and the most recent library policy release, Public Library Policy 2015 (Ministry of Education, 2009).

The Library Act of Finland (1998) specifically names public libraries as being responsible to

> promote equal opportunities among citizens for personal cultivation for literary and cultural pursuits for continuous development of knowledge, personal skills, and civic skills for internationalisation and

for lifelong learning [and to promote] the development of virtual and interactive network services and their educational and cultural contents. (§2.2)

Prime Minister Jyrki Katainen's Government Programme 2011 (Prime Minister's Office Finland, 2011) adds that "libraries will be developed to meet the challenges of the information society. The opening up of the libraries', museums' and public arts institutions' digitised material for free public access will be promoted" (p. 60). Thus, national policy names public libraries as places of support for digital inclusion and digital literacy.

Another example of public policy affecting public libraries as providers of digital services is the Education Rate (E-rate) program administered by the U.S. federal government. The Federal Communications Commission (FCC) E-rate program provides discounts to schools and libraries for telecommunication services, internal wiring, and computer hardware (Telecommunications Act of 1996). However, the requirements and processes of completing the forms are complex, resulting in many funds going not to the neediest states but rather to those that are best at completing the forms (Jaeger, Bertot, McClure, & Rodriguez, 2007). Different populations in a community can be favored or disfavored by such policy decisions, leaving certain populations—such as the poor, people with disabilities, residents of certain geographic areas, and new immigrants—among the digitally excluded.

Policies can also be in conflict with one another. For example, the U.S. federal government, through recent policy documents such as the 2010 National Broadband Plan issued by the FCC, has called public libraries the cornerstone of digital literacy and inclusion in the nation—and at the same time has reprimanded them for not doing enough in these areas, threatening to take away federal funding. Additionally, the federal government has created DigitalLiteracy.gov as a training site for those lacking digital literacy skills but is relying on libraries to provide access to and guidance in using the site. One may also ask if DigitalLiteracy.gov is developed to be intellectually accessible to all populations (more discussion on this in later chapters).

This book examines the interrelationships among digital literacy, digital inclusion, and public policy, emphasizing the impacts of these policy decisions on the ability of individuals and communities to successfully participate in the information society, as well as the obligations that these policies create for the social institutions that support digital literacy and inclusion—namely, public, academic, and school libraries and public schools. The book uses a tripartite information access model (Burnett, Jaeger, & Thompson, 2008) that examines information access in terms of physical, social, and intellectual factors. As a theoretical framework, the book employs the theory of Information Worlds (Jaeger & Burnett, 2010), which is designed to allow for simultaneous analysis of the social and political aspects of the information behavior of individuals and communities. The model and framework are discussed in the next section.

THE THREE ASPECTS OF INFORMATION ACCESS

Physical access is generally viewed as access to the document or other form embodying information, be it conveyed through print, electronic, verbal, or another means of communication—literally, the process of getting to the information that is being sought (Svenonius, 2000). The vast majority of discourse on information access tends to focus on physical issues, such as the physical structures that contain information, the electronic structures that retain and distribute information, and the paths that are traveled to get to information (Jaeger & Bowman, 2005). Issues of physical access relate to the location and format of the entity containing information, and the conditions, technologies, or abilities required for reaching that entity. Such issues are often readily identifiable and revolve around the questions of whether people can get into the location that houses the information and then reach the specific information that they seek.

Physical access to information is primarily an institutional issue, depending on formalized structures that exist to ensure that the information is located somewhere and is theoretically available. This location can be physical or virtual, and the availability is not necessarily wide or egalitarian. The effectiveness of structures in facilitating the storage and retrieval of information is shaped by how well those structures function as intended, how easy they are to use, and how accessible they are for users with different physical abilities. Physical access, however, also depends on knowing that the information is stored and retrievable. At the individual level, to achieve physical access the user has to know that the information exists, where it can be found, and how to navigate the institutional structures to reach it. Individual factors that can affect physical access include technology, economics, geography, and disability. Lack of necessary funds, substantial distance from or inability to use an information source, or inability to enter a location housing an information source can all create barriers to physical access.

Physical access is of utmost importance; without it, no other type of access is possible (Jaeger & Bowman, 2005). However, while it is a necessary prerequisite, mere physical access is not sufficient for full access. For instance, "it is a common, but mistaken, assumption that access to technology equals access to information" (McCreadie & Rice, 1999, p. 51). The ability of a user to get to information and the ability of that user to employ information to accomplish particular goals are very different (Culnan, 1983, 1984, 1985). As a result, the physical aspects of information access cannot be considered without also considering the intellectual aspects of information access.

Intellectual access can be understood as the accessing of the information itself after physical access has been obtained (Svenonius, 2000). It revolves around the ability to understand how to get to and, in particular, how to understand the information itself once it has been physically obtained. Much less research has examined issues of intellectual access than of physical access. Issues of intellectual access involve understanding how the information is presented to people seeking information, as well as the impact the presentation has on the process of information seeking.

> Intellectual access to information includes how the information is categorized, organized, displayed, and represented. Studying intellectual access can reveal the best ways to make information accessible when people act to retrieve the information and to bring the information seeker and the information together in the most efficient manner possible through representation of the available information sources. (Jaeger & Bowman, 2005, p. 67)

Intellectual access can only occur when an individual has sufficient information to engage in critical thinking (Pitts & Stripling, 1990). It has been discussed in terms of a number of specific forms of information, including images, classification, catalogs and archives, government materials, periodicals, software, digital documents, and library services (Aschmann, 2002; Bednarek, 1993; Cary & Ogburn, 2000; Chen & Rasmussen, 1999; Comaromi, 1990; Deines-Jones, 1996; Dilevko & Dali, 2003; Gilliland, 1988; Intner, 1991; Mandel & Wolven, 1996; Neville & Datray, 1993; Rankin, 1992).

Intellectual access to information, at a more conceptual level, "entails equal opportunity to understand intellectual content and pathways to that content" (Jaeger & Bowman, 2005, p. 68). As a result, for an item to provide information equally to all, it must be able to produce similar outcomes or results for any user, regardless of any disadvantages that the user might have. Intellectual access to a particular item of information, however, is often not equally available.

Many individual issues unique to each user influence intellectual access, since it hinges on the user understanding the information once it has been physically accessed. Factors that can affect intellectual access can include information-seeking behavior, language, dialect, education, literacy, technological skill, cognitive ability, disability, vocabulary, and social elements, like norms and values. Each of these factors has the potential to influence whether an information seeker can access the information contained in a source. Intellectual access requires the ability to understand the information in a source, which, in turn, requires the cognitive ability to understand the source, the ability to read the language and dialect in which the source is written, and the knowledge of the

specific vocabulary that is used. Intellectual access also requires knowledge of the use of any necessary technology to access a source, such as
telephones, computers, mobile devices, search engines, electronic databases, or the Internet.

In many cases, the discussion of information access ends with physical
and intellectual access to information. Many assume this means the individual should have no problem becoming fully informed. However, in
terms of actual information access, this overlooks one additional layer
that is omnipresent although too often overlooked: *social information access*. This third and most abstract aspect of information access captures
the idea that simply because one *can* physically and intellectually access
needed information, it does not necessarily follow that one *does* access
that information or that all readers, listeners, or touchers interpret the
information in the same way. The social layer of information access has
been well established in research, such as studies of the influences of
social trust, social motivation, and social inclusion on information behavior (e.g., Chatman, 1987, 1990, 1991; Dervin & Greenberg, 1972; Rogers,
1995); social and cultural norms that influence information availability
and use within the social context (e.g., Burnett, Besant, & Chatman, 2001;
Chatman, 1996, 1999, 2000); social grounds or locations where information is accessed through interpersonal interactions (e.g., Fisher & Naumer, 2005); social networks and information access (e.g., Granovetter, 1973,
1983); and studies of information access in terms of the normative behavior and the social sphere, such as Paul T. Jaeger and Gary Burnett's (2010)
theory of Information Worlds. Jaeger and Burnett's framework in particular incorporates micro, meso, and macro perspectives of social information access, which is why this framework is used here to further the
discussion of social information access as it relates to the tripartite information access model.

Information behavior is normative as a day-to-day activity, occurring
within specific social contexts, and the value of information is not universal but is rooted within the norms and attitudes of a particular social
group.

> While one might, for instance, make use of some tidbit of information
> from the larger world for casual conversation with a neighbor or
> friend, the purpose might simply be to measure the overall soundness
> of the world "out there," to maintain a connection, or to engage in
> "small-talk." (Burnett, Besant, & Chatman, 2001, p. 537)

The social contexts of information occurring within and between members of social groups and communities interact with the physical and
intellectual aspects of information access. *Small worlds* are created, wherein "insiders" share social norms, social values, and social behaviors.
These social elements influence information value, or what information is
seen to be permissible for members of a group or community to access,

and what kinds of information will be perceived as acceptable (Jaeger & Burnett, 2010). Additionally, normative information behavior defines the appropriate mechanisms and activities involved in information access.

Overall, the importance of social access is often recognized, even if it is not actually articulated. For example, a United Nations (1986) report noted, "Perhaps the most fundamental part of information is a perception" (p. 1). Thus, efforts emanating from society at large impact information use and access at the local level, and social access issues even occur in the making of information available for access. "Anyone who assigns subject categories or descriptors to a piece of recorded information is in part trying to guess the modes of access that might be found useful at some future date" (Swanson, 1979, p. 11). As such, the act of creating categories and identifiers is based on the social perceptions about access by the person making the information available and guessing how best to make it findable for those seeking access.

Studies of the acceptance of government agricultural information by rural farmers provide a telling example of physical, intellectual, and social access to information in action. Prior to the widespread usage of information and communication technology (ICT)—including radio, television, and the Internet—to distribute government information, government agencies relied on people—specially trained government employees—as the primary means of communication to specific groups. Though people are clearly constrained by limitations of knowledge, presence, physical ability, and cultural barriers, they were still the best option to get needed information to groups like rural farmers with little formal education (Woods, 1993). Studies of these programs in a number of nations demonstrated that the most effective people as communicators of government information—such as agricultural information to help rural farmers—took into account the social considerations of the members of the society they were trying to communicate with, offering practical information explained in a holistic manner that the groups could relate to based on their daily experiences (Woods, 1993).

In other words, the government agents put the new agricultural information into a form that would be understandable and acceptable—in sync with the social norms, social types, information behavior, and information value of the rural farmers—leading them to accept and apply the information from someone outside of their small world and to share the new information within their small worlds and across the boundaries of their small worlds. The government agents traveling to the rural areas provided physical access, and the efforts of the government agents to provide the information within the known contexts of the farmers promoted intellectual access. Finally, by accounting for the social considerations of the rural farmers, the agents promoted social access to the information.

A very simple illustration of the tripartite information access model may be an equilateral triangle. At the three corners of the equilateral triangle are the concepts of physical, intellectual, and social information access as described above. The model represents how all three areas of information access must be considered when discussing any information problem, barrier, or context. Having physical access alone is of little good if the information cannot be understood or shared. Understanding the social value of information is of limited help if the information is not physically accessible. Not only are the three types of access highly inter-related, but all three elements are necessary for meaningful access to be achieved.

For example, the ability of persons with cognitive impairments to use an educational website depends on all three aspects of access (Jaeger, 2012). The site must be programmed so that it works with the assistive technologies that users might rely on, such as screen readers, text en-largement, or alternate color schemes, to ensure physical access to the educational content. To promote intellectual access, it must be designed and organized to enable the users to understand the content at the level it is written, through the ways the ideas are organized, and by the way in which navigation occurs. Finally, social access will then rely on the content being useful within the users' lives, providing educational information that they share with others in their small worlds, as well as content that will be accepted as valid by the people with whom they interact.

THE INFORMATION WORLDS FRAMEWORK

Throughout this book, this model of access is situated within the theory of Information Worlds. This theory marries Elfreda A. Chatman's social conceptualization of the information small world—in which information is managed through social typing, normative information behavior, and allotment of value to information based on social norms and a common social worldview—with Jürgen Habermas's concept of the lifeworld, or the larger sociopolitical mosaic of information within which the small worlds exist. The small world focuses on the micro level, "the shared understandings of small groups of people living and working together in definable and bounded cultural worlds," and the lifeworld brings togeth-er these small worlds in a macro-level understanding of social informa-tion access, since the individual can "at different times, [be] a member of multiple worlds" and even "act as intermediary—or gatekeeper—be-tween those worlds" (Jaeger & Burnett, 2010, p. 34–36).

Individuals create boundaries and limitations within their small worlds, separating themselves from information that is not deemed rele-vant to them socially or culturally, for example, possibly rejecting or completely avoiding information that does not sync with the political, ethnic, religious, and/or family values and ideals with which they identify. The information small world is always influenced by the larger lifeworld, manipulated by public-sphere organizations such as libraries and schools, that "exist specifically to ensure that information continues to move between [populations] and that members of each small world are exposed to other small worlds" (Jaeger & Burnett, 2010, p. 38). Thus, social access to information relies on social and cultural norms, both in the small world and the lifeworld, which affects both physical access to information and one's intellectual processing of and acceptance or rejection of information.

DEFINING DIGITAL INCLUSION

To match the current policy language, digital inclusion is defined here as outreach as a means to empower underserved and marginalized populations. Rather than distinguish between the digitally excluded, the digitally unengaged, digital inequality, and so forth, this book discusses digital inclusion in terms of the means developed by governmental and nongovernmental entities to close the digital divide and promote social inclusion and digital literacy. In terms of the tripartite framework, digital inclusion would work within the lifeworld and the intermediaries to affect the information access of the small worlds.

When reviewing the literature related to information literacy, information inclusion, information practice, information access, and so forth, it is not difficult to see that many have discussed these concepts in terms of a physical, intellectual, and social attributes, even though only a few have explicitly done so. The idea that information access is expressed in multiple forms is well documented. Of particular note to the model used in this book is Mark Warschauer's (2003) *Technology and Social Inclusion: Rethinking the Digital Divide*. In Warschauer's discussion of access, he presents "device," "conduit," and "literacy" (pp. 31–48) models for understanding access to new technologies. The device model, he writes, focuses on physical access to end-user information technology—for example, providing a laptop to every child in school. Warschauer notes that policies and programs that focus on the device model of access do not take into consideration the ongoing expenditures needed to maintain reliable access (e.g., electricity, broadband Internet service, costs of software, and general upkeep of hardware) or the cognitive factors needed to adequately use the devices available (what is identified above as intellectual access). They build infrastructure but neglect the needs of the actual users.

Warschauer then describes what he calls the conduit model. This model incorporates an element of social perspective into the discussion of physical access by focusing on information channels providing information, such as telephone, radio, television, and cable; the resources needed to sustain these information channels, such as electricity, wiring, and satellites; and the sociopolitical question of who provides these to ensure equitable distribution worldwide or even within the boundaries of a single nation or state. Warschauer notes that the shortfall of this model is that it still does not acknowledge the need for end users to be information literate.

Finally, the literacy model Warschauer describes weaves together elements of literacy (intellectual access), the need for physical access (which he labels as access to physical and digital resources), and human and social resources (social access). While this model touches upon some of the same terms and topics discussed in the tripartite model, Warschauer's focus remains on access to technology (accurately delimited in the title of his book) rather than the information the technology delivers. In other words, he seems to be saying that if one does not have intellectual or social means or resources, one cannot physically access information technologies, which fits with the conceptual approach that underlies the arguments in this book. However, the model extends beyond this because ensuring physical access to information technology is only one angle of information access; even when physical access to information-bearing entities is nonproblematic, one may not be able to intellectually access the information therein contained or one may still choose to reject the information available because of social norms. The tripartite model of information access broadens the scope to include not only the factors that create barriers to physical information access but also barriers to intellectual and/or social information access.

Another model that is similar to the tripartite model is Annemaree Lloyd's (2006) "holistic view of information literacy," which suggests that information literacy analyses need to include understanding of "textual," "physical," and "social" contexts (p. 184). Lloyd uses these terms to describe information (e.g., textual information, social information, physical information) and the ways individuals process text within the context of physical surroundings (e.g., workplace, home, school, library) and social context (i.e., communities of practice) to become information literate. As with Warschauer's model, this model is narrower in scope than the tripartite model of information access used in this book. It is important to emphasize that this discussion is about full access to information—not only the ability to reach or obtain the information (physical access) and then understand and use that information (intellectual access), but also to access and use information without barriers created by social context (social access).

STRUCTURE AND CONTRIBUTION OF THIS BOOK

This book is intended to make several unique contributions to the literature. First, work on digital literacy and digital inclusion is widely spread among many fields—library science, information, communication, public policy, sociology, political science, evaluation, and education, among others—that are not sharing ideas and findings well, resulting in fragmented and disjointed discourse about major social and political concerns. Second, digital literacy and digital inclusion have not been adequately analyzed as policy issues, both being driven and regulated by policy, often in conflicting ways. This book provides the first large-scale consideration of digital literacy and digital inclusion as policy problems. Third, the book draws on a wealth of original research conducted by the authors using different quantitative and qualitative data-collection approaches on four different continents when analyzing these issues, providing unique examples, cases, and perspectives. Fourth, the theoretical framework employed in the book—which was co-created by one of the authors—allows for important insights about these issues at individual, community, and political levels.

The authors of this book have been individually and collectively involved in this research space for many years, contributing many pieces of the existing scholarly discourse in a number of different areas of the discourse. This experience provides a broad view across the literature and problems, as well as across national perspectives. This book is designed to bring the various areas of discourse on these topics together, engaging all of the fields listed above and more while also attempting to make the subject comprehensible to specialists and generalists, regardless of their field. This breadth of work in these areas allows the book to offer comprehensive policy recommendations, solutions, and best practices for an area that is currently extremely fragmented in discourse, practice, and policy.

Although there are a dozen or more titles, including government and professional association reports, that provide practical exploration of the concepts of digital literacy or digital inclusion, provide digital-literacy training materials for Internet novices, or discuss the impact of information policy on social inclusion, no book to date matches digital literacy and digital inclusion with information policy and libraries. This first chapter has provided an overview of the tripartite information access model and the theory of Information Worlds that is used as a framework for analysis.

Chapter 2 focuses on the social implications of the digital age and the implications for the disadvantaged, underserved, and underrepresented as a result of policies related to digital literacy and digital inclusion. The chapter explores how policy in this area favors certain stakeholders and disfavors others; populations in the latter category then face higher barriers to digital literacy and digital inclusion than other populations. The resulting information poverty and digital exclusion affect many populations based on age, race, language, geography, disability, socioeconomic status, education level, and other factors.

Chapter 3 examines and compares definitions applied to the terms *digital literacy* and *digital inclusion* by nations, government agencies, and nongovernmental organizations, and the implications of these various definitions. Special attention has been given to the approaches to digital literacy and inclusion advocated by and implemented in libraries and the ramifications of these approaches. The chapter also reviews the existing definitions about digital literacy and digital inclusion that have been collected and analyzed across academic disciplines, examining the implications of these definitions for the discussion at hand and as revealing the perspectives on digital literacy and digital inclusion held by various disciplines.

The fourth chapter collates and examines the policies, laws, regulations, and other instruments of government related to digital literacy and digital inclusion, tracing the historical development of these instruments. The instruments are explored in terms of the various ways in which they promote or hinder digital literacy and digital inclusion, as well as the impacts of these policies on physical access, intellectual access, and social access to information. The ramifications of these policies on libraries and schools as providers of digital literacy and inclusion are examined. Efforts to promote digital literacy and digital inclusion by governments are also discussed.

Chapter 5 describes the institutions that promote digital literacy and digital inclusion. Some of these institutions are international organizations, some are government agencies, and some are local entities. In the United States, public libraries have become the primary guarantor in society of Internet access, assistance, and education, with both local communities and the national government expressly relying on public libraries to meet these needs. However, other types of libraries, as well as schools and nonprofit organizations, also play important roles in digital literacy and digital inclusion. This chapter illustrates ways in which these institutions work together to provide physical, intellectual, and social access in the United States, offering specific examples of exemplary programs that serve these access areas.

Each of chapters 6 and 7 presents three detailed case studies of the intersections of policy, literacy, inclusion, and libraries as they relate to specific nations. The goal of these chapters is to provide an exploration of the variety of ways national policy and programming influence the physical, intellectual, and social facets of digital literacy and digital inclusion.

Chapter 8 considers the ways in which the promotion of digital literacy and digital inclusion through policy can serve to increase equality and social progress in the information society, as well as the roles of libraries and other social institutions in ensuring that digital literacy and digital inclusion are available to all members of the public. This chapter introduces a set of policy recommendations to improve the creation and implementation of policy instruments that promote digital literacy and digital inclusion. This chapter also offers policy, practice, and advocacy recommendations for supporting libraries and other institutions that foster the access, assistance, and education needed to ensure that all members of society have opportunities to achieve digital literacy and digital inclusion. The recommendations in this chapter are based on best practices and lessons learned from research in the United States and internationally. The chapter also explores digital literacy and digital inclusion as part of the broad view of information as a human right and the related roles for policy. Finally, the chapter considers the research questions and opportunities raised by the theory of Information Worlds for the future study of and design of policies related to digital literacy and digital inclusion.

TWO

The Evolution of the Digital Society

The term *digital* is centuries old and relates literally and simply to the use of whole numbers, or digits, from 0 to 9. In the 1800s, analog machines allowed for slide-rule and cashier calculations, the representation of time (e.g., clocks), the remote sending and receiving of sound waves (e.g., radio), typewriting, and printing, and used such devices as punch paper cards to create "preprogrammed" loom settings for weaving patterns, computational mathematics, and so forth. In the 1930s and 1940s, these early computers were modified using Claude Shannon's digital electronics, going digital, so to speak, by using binary data in the form of series of 0s and 1s to create computational meaning (Ifrah, 2001). Analog and digital computational devices were created as means to both organize and transform data. The first computers were used to enhance human ability with regard to computation and calculation (hence the name "computer"), but the American Standard Code for Information Interchange (ASCII) and other codes later allowed computers to process letters, characters, punctuation, and other symbols in addition to numerical figures, creating a system wherein text could also be organized and manipulated.

One remarkable attribute of digital bits and bytes is that they are capable of creating virtual representations of physical objects without occupying the amount of space the actual object requires. Because of this, immense amounts of data can be represented in bits and bytes that can be stored in devices smaller than one's thumb. In fact, the ability to create smaller and smaller storage devices with greater and greater memory capacities has allowed digital technology to permeate modern society, appearing in kitchen appliances, automobiles, mobile telephones and other pocket-sized digital devices, audio recorders and amplifiers, medical technologies, educational materials, video devices, and even smart

15

eyewear. Digital technologies allow humans to moderate and acclimatize the spaces in which they reside; create and modify art; perform scientific work; communicate across vast distances; and store, share, and manipulate data in ways that were not possible 100 years ago or even last month.

In recent years, "digital" has been merged rhetorically to constitute whole institutions—or at least new labels—such as "digital university" (Hazemi, Hailes, & Wilbur, 1998), eras such as "digital world" (Collis, 1996) and "digital age" (Borgman, 2007), populations such as "digital natives" (Bennett, Maton, & Kervin, 2012; Prensky, 2001) and "digital youth" (Subrahmanyam & Smahel, 2011), technology references such as "digital technology," and access impediments such as "digital divide" (Gunkel, 2003). The emergence of these composite terms and the relevant discussions of how each of these terms emerged are neither distinct nor linear (Bennett, Maton, & Kervin, 2012; Gunkel, 2003; Jaeger, Bertot, Thompson, Katz, & DeCoster, 2012). However, the emergence of these terms, especially the ones that constitute institutions, eras, and technology, brings attention to the discussion of all aspects of this "digital life": leisure, education, work, and home.

Digital gadgets allow individuals and communities to play, work, study with, and observe each other in an increasing variety of ways, incorporating visual, oral, aural, and even tactile elements. The popularity of digital devices does not stem from the dissolution of communication and the stunting of the upcoming generation that is often debated on television and radio talk shows and lamented in the opinion column of the local newspaper; rather, the widespread adoption of digital technologies is a reflection of the enrichment digital formats lend to society. Digital cameras allow photographers to know instantly whether the image they took is optimally composed, well lit, and if all subjects in the shot had their eyes open. As digital cameras have advanced, the quality of digital photographs is equal to—if not of higher quality than—negative-based photography. If there is a problem with the digital shot and another cannot be snapped immediately, the digital image can be modified, enhanced, or distorted to create the artistic effect desired before even printing the photograph. In fact, the photograph need never be printed, as digital images can reside in perpetuity in digital-only format.

The same is true with digital video and audio recordings. Digital music and video editors simplify the editing process to a level where even children can edit and produce music and movies for entertainment and even sometimes for profit. Digital word-processing software and publication templates allow students, educators, researchers, and other writers to produce submission- and/or market-ready products. Digital databases and portals provide access to entire libraries of books, journals, documents, websites, and other digitized or born-digital resources. Digital tools, products, and resources create efficiencies that can simplify and minimize processes and procedures and at the same time provide platforms that allow individuals and society to create an increasingly complex and robust civil life.

This is not to say that digital resources are fundamentally necessary for a healthy life or for social inclusion or that digital information or products are better than analog or any other information or products. This also does not mean there are not new issues related to security, privacy, and social inequity. Rather, digital technologies allow information to be presented in a new format that is faster, more portable, sharable, transferable, and, once the receipt of digital information is acquired and understood, offers more free or affordable access to information and information resources than previously available in history. It is this digital information access that is the point of discussion in this chapter.

The question is not whether governments need to provide equitable access to cutting-edge information tools. It is, rather, whether governments are responsible for maintaining an infrastructure that allows citizens, at the very least, basic means by which to reach the necessary information for employment, education, business, and government engagement. In today's information-enabled and information-dependent environment, this basic digital-information access is becoming essential to functional participation in society.

DEMOCRACY AND INFORMATION

The idea that information holds social value is, of course, not new. The recording of information in writing for many centuries was a means to preserve and store information, indicating value. Technologies from chisels to carbon paper, from linotype to photography, have aided in the creation, preservation, copying, and sharing of information. The ideal of government supporting the flow of information between citizens and the government is also not new. Sweden's 1766 Freedom of the Press Act is heralded as the first freedom of information policy in modern times, abolishing political censorship of public documents, ensuring right of access to public documents, and underscoring the right of anyone to publish written documents. The U.S. Declaration of Independence (1776) and Constitution (1789) enshrined a range of freedom of information policies in the foundation of a government, from freedom of assembly and freedom of the press to establishment of a national postal delivery system. Finland (Act on the Openness of Public Documents of 1951), the United States (Freedom of Information Act, 1966), Mexico (constitutional amendment to include right of information, 1977), and at least 64 other countries currently have freedom of information legislation, and similar legislation is pending in several additional countries.

Universal access and service policies have been enacted in many democratic countries to provide equitable access to information and communication infrastructures and technologies needed for all members of the society to have access to needed information. Public education policies likewise promote literacy and other cognitive skills and abilities and the social training needed for full information access and use. In addition, universal service and public education are basic means to ensure a reasonable information exchange between a government and its governed members. Radio, television, print media, and, more recently, the Internet are mass media that can deliver government decisions, laws, changes in policy, safety and security updates, and warnings to the people. Postal services, telephones, and the Internet provide means for citizens to send information about interests and local needs to representatives in government.

So if a healthy democratic system relies on the communication of information, barriers to information exchange are problematic. Information barriers on the side of governments lead to uninformed political governance and legislation, and information barriers on the side of the citizenry lead to disenfranchisement and the collapse of democracy. One way these barriers have been presented in the information studies literature is through discussion of what is termed *information poverty*. An overview of the concept of information poverty provides context for discussion of the social, political, and economic problems that can arise when information problems are not resolved.

INFORMATION POVERTY

Although early predictions of the rising importance of information in society was not solely an American phenomenon (e.g., Umesao, 1963), the concept of "information poverty" grew from the American dialogue during the second half of the 20th century when serious attention was given to both poverty and information. Researchers such as Daniel Bell (1960) and Fritz Machlup (1962) had recently demonstrated that white-collar information-related services were quickly overtaking blue-collar industrial labor as the mainstays of economic strength in the United States and elsewhere. The American context at this time seemed to be one of surplus. Information storage and retrieval had advanced rapidly post–World War II and had created a rich information environment where more information could be accessed by more individuals than any time previously in history, and news and educational resources were available in more formats than ever. Print, radio, and television streamed information to households, workplaces, and community institutions (see Table 2.1). Education (see Table 2.2) and literacy (see Table 2.3) rates were the highest in American history. The United States was already one of the wealthiest and most powerful nations in the world (see Table 2.4), and 62 percent of Americans were homeowners, an increase from 55 percent in 1950 and 44 percent in 1940 (U.S. Census Bureau, 2003).

Because of this unprecedented prosperity, it was deeply troublesome when a book published by sociologist Michael Harrington (1962), *The Other America*, revealed that within this apex of bounty, nearly one in four Americans was still living in abject poverty. The federal government researched the situation more carefully and adopted a new instrument for measuring economic poverty, a poverty line, based on economist Molly Orshansky's (1963, 1965) use of Engel's law to assess the minimum income needed for an individual to be able to meet basic nutritional needs for one year. This new poverty line calculated that, indeed, nearly 20 percent of Americans were living at poverty levels. President Lyndon B. Johnson (1964a, 1964b) declared a "War on Poverty" in the United States, and researchers and scholars began serious investigation of how there could be this level of poverty when so many resources were generally available. Fifty years later, the war continues, as still 16.1 percent of Americans live in poverty (U.S. Census, 2013).

POVERTY, INFORMATION, AND SOCIAL INCLUSION: A CULTURAL/BEHAVIORAL APPROACH

Some scholars, political figures, and media commentators saw lack of opportunity as the primary barrier to economic inclusion, while others claimed that cultural behaviors passed from one poor generation to the next kept individuals in poverty. Still others asked if perhaps the problem might be that the poor did not know how to navigate the changing

Table 2.1.   Mass media distribution from 1920 to 1970, by percentages of households.

Year	Telephone service	Radio	Television	Daily newspaper circulation (in millions)
1920	35.0	NA	NA	27.8
1930	40.9	39	NA	39.6
1940	36.9	73	NA	41.1
1950	61.8	91	9.0	53.8
1960	78.3	94	87.1	58.9
1970	90.5	95	95.3	62.1

Source: Data from U.S. Census Bureau, 2003

Table 2.2.   Educational attainment from 1900 to 1970

Year	Percentage of 17-year-olds who were high school graduates
1920	16.8
1930	32.1
1940	50.8
1950	59.0
1960	67.9
1970	75.9

Source: Data from U.S. Census Bureau, 2003.

information environment in a manner that would allow them to prosper. Radios and televisions were in almost every home, meaning the costs and distribution of the prime information technology of the day was already surmounted. Research showed that the low-income populations relied quite heavily on television for both entertainment and information (Greenberg & Dervin, 1970a). News and educational programming were broadcast at times that were scheduled to reach the greatest potential audience. In fact, by 1960, 47 percent of Americans reported that they were using television as a primary source of news (Kimmelman, 1989). But the poor seemed to benefit less from this broadcast information than the general population. Researchers pointed to the *increased* use of mass media as the information problem.

For example, communications researchers Bradley S. Greenberg and Brenda Dervin (1970a, 1970b) showed that television played a distinct role in the lives of the poor of all ages. Their data indicated that 53 percent of low-income individuals watched more than 4 hours of television a day and 27 percent watched 8 hours a day or more. In contrast, of the general population, only 17 percent watched 4 hours or more and only 5 percent watched 8 hours or more a day. Greenberg and Dervin suggested that the heavy reliance on television as the primary information resource resulted in the poor using fewer information access points, thus restricting the breadth of information accessed. Soon thereafter, sociologist James S. Coleman (1972) described these modern changes in information channels as being detrimental to social inclusion as well. He wrote,

> The emergence of electronic methods of communication such as television has shifted the balance between direct and vicarious experience toward vicarious experience for all of us, and it has done so most strongly for the young. Instead of information poverty they now confront information richness. (Coleman, 1972, p. 72)

Table 2.3.   Literacy rates from 1900 to 1979

Year	Percentage of persons 14 years old and over who were able to read or write in at least one language
1920	94.0
1930	95.7
1940	97.1
1950	96.8
*1959	97.8
*1969	99.0

Source: Data from Snyder, 1993
*National Center for Educational Statistics literacy data collected in the ninth year.

Coleman's perspective was that information-rich was not a better situation than information-poor. He described the "information-poor societies of the past" wherein the school system had a "very powerful effect on [a student's] values," and contrasted these past societies with the "information-rich, open societies" of 1972 that seemed to be creating a generation of "action-poor" youth who relied too heavily on vicarious information channels, thus missing out on experiences that would help them become productive, self-supporting human beings (p. 74). In other words, it was not the information that was problematic, rather, the problem was the channel through which the information was transmitted (technological versus social channels) and the way the technology created passive information experiences that lacked the social contexts that provide the values that help the individual interpret and use distributed information. Societies were depending on information technology to replace the socialization of information, leading to isolation and social exclusion.

This idea was reexamined and re-emphasized with a 1975 study of more than 720 reports and other publications about information and the poor conducted by library and information scientist Thomas Childers, with the assistance of Joyce A. Post. Their publication, entitled *The Information Poor in America*, observed that, according to the body of literature of the day, the information-poor were found to have low information-processing skills. This disadvantage included low literacy or language ability, physical disability, or poor social communication skills. Mainstream information behaviors were "not conventional knowledge for them" (1975, p. 32). Second, the information-poor did not feel a part of the larger society but rather occupied a closed subsystem "harboring an inordinate amount of unawareness and misinformation (myth, rumor, folklore). While they do have information contacts with the rest of soci-

Table 2.4. Real gross domestic product per capita in 1960 (in 2011 US$)

U.S.	U.K.	Australia	Canada	W. Ger.	Swe.	Den.	Austria	France
17,747	11,879	15,320	14,733	12,352	13,936	14,926	11,432	11,272

Source: Data from U.S. Bureau of Labor, 2012.

ety, these contacts are very often one-way information flows, via the mass media, from the greater society" (p. 32). And third, they noted that "report after report portrays the various disadvantaged populations as despairing, fatalistic people with a pervasive sense of helplessness" (p. 34). Thus, according to Childers and Post, information-processing skills, subcultural behavior, and personal attitude are the three factors that affect one's information wealth or poverty, directly reflecting one's level of social inclusion.

The "culture of poverty" approach to information poverty was supported by other poverty research of the time (e.g., Lewis, 1959, 1961) but quickly became unpopular, as it seemed to blame the poor for their poverty rather than examine the infrastructural issues that marginalized and disadvantaged these groups, begging the question of whether the information behaviors led to the poverty situation or the poverty situation resulted in the passive information behaviors. Childers and Post (1975) had identified nine socially disadvantaged groups: Mexican Americans and others with Spanish as a first or primary language, American Indians and Eskimos, poor blacks and whites, Appalachians, poor farmers, migrant workers, aging adults, prisoners, and the blind or deaf. At this time in American history, many if not each of these groups faced clear social segregation or disadvantages related to race, language, educational opportunities, geographic location, or disability.

POVERTY, INFORMATION, AND SOCIAL INCLUSION: AN INFRASTRUCTURAL/ECONOMIC APPROACH

Parallel to this series of reporting the sociocultural behaviors of the poor that diminished their access to, use of, or understanding of information and the changing information environment was another view of information poverty. This second view argued that while there could be some cultural behaviors that excluded certain groups from obtaining full access to needed information, it was more likely that there was a dimension of poverty that was based on a "poverty of information" or "a lack or scarcity of information about resources or opportunities available within and outside one's community" (McClure, 1974), and that this type of information poverty required an infrastructural/economic approach to address concerns.

Studies showed that when greater quantities of information reached public awareness, the public became more informed and participated in civic duties such as voting (Campbell, 1960; Dhillon, 1980; Zukin & Snyder, 1984). Information poverty as seen through this lens depended on access to information and indicated that improved access to information could lead to greater social inclusion, which could lead to more civic engagement as well as greater economic opportunity for the disadvantaged. While television and radio did indeed distribute important information, they were neither sufficient nor were they the only information resources in place. Schools, libraries, and other community centers and resources provided both information and the expertise and training needed to help the public understand how to navigate that information in the social context. Still, those in remote areas or who could not access information services in their primary language or those who were physically unable to or socially discouraged from using public information services because of race or national origin, age, or disability still could not enjoy the benefits these information resources afforded. Edwin B. Parker and Donald A. Dunn (1972) posited that "if access to . . . information services is not universally available throughout society, then those already 'information-rich' may reap the benefits while the 'information-poor' get relatively poorer," potentially creating "social tensions" because, they wrote, information gaps contribute to gaps "in economic and political power" (p. 1396).

Much of the information poverty literature of the late 1970s and then the 1980s focused on evening out the physical distribution of information (e.g., Branscomb, 1979; Buckley, 1987; Companie, 1986; Dhillon, 1980; Dubey, 1985; Gannett Center, 1987; Lang, 1988; Menou, 1983; Murdock & Golding, 1989; Scherer, 1989; Zukin & Snyder, 1984) and provision of training in the intellectual skills needed to obtain and use the information available (e.g., Childers & Post, 1975; Duran, 1978; Dubey, 1985; Mason, 1986; Orman, 1987). By the end of the 1980s, much of the information-poverty literature was directed at a new potential schism in information service and access: the unequal distribution of computational information technology.

INFORMATION POVERTY AND INFORMATION TECHNOLOGY

The first commercial computers appeared in the 1970s; then, soon enough, spreadsheets and word-processing software began showing up in offices and homes, leading to questions about the social effects that follow sweeping changes in information technology. Edwin B. Parker

(1970, 1973–1974) observed that new information utilities or technologies create an information divide between technology haves and have-nots. This precursor to digital divide rhetoric synced with Everett Rogers's (1995) *Diffusion of Innovation* theory—first articulated in 1962—that showed how new technology is first adopted by those with higher incomes, as they can afford the risk should the technology turn out to be a dud. When the technology turns out to be beneficial, the early adopters reap the benefit of the technology before later adopters, creating additional economic division.

Communications researcher Natan Katzman (1974) advanced a similar argument, focusing on how uneven access to new information technologies creates detrimental information disparities because of lack of access to the information technology afforded to those with more economic means and greater levels of information skill. Katzman's argument is laid out in the structure of six premises as follows:

- Premise 1: The adoption of new communication techniques and technologies tends to increase the amount of information transmitted and received by individuals. . . .
- Premise 2: All individuals receive more information after the adoption of a new communication technology. . . .
- Premise 3: With the adoption of new communication technology, people who already have high levels of information and ability will gain more than is gained by people with lower initial levels . . . [thus widening] the gap between the "information-rich" and the "information-poor" in society. . . .
- Premise 4: Humans have a limited capacity to process information and a limited capacity to store information. . . .
- Premise 5: Compared to humans, machines now have unlimited capacity to process and store information. Training and access, providing the ability to command new technological phenomena, give the information-rich a different type of advantage over the information-poor. It is not just a case of people having seen, read or heard more than other people. Rather, the advantaged group has a staggering amount of potential information available that the disadvantaged group cannot begin to tap. . . .
- Premise 6: New communication techniques and technologies create new information gaps before old gaps close. . . . The children of the information-rich use techniques their parents never dreamed of, while the children of the information-poor fall farther behind (although they are above the levels attained by the earlier generations in their own group). (pp. 125–129)

In short, as new technologies are adopted and as the infrastructure develops to support these new technologies, the distribution of information available throughout a society changes. Those able to keep up with the changes benefit from the advances while those who cannot keep pace fall behind, creating cases of relative information poverty in the underclass. Populations without access to new technologies such as computers and training in the skills needed to use them would become "information-poor communities" (Martin, 1973, p. 568). At that time, information-poor communities would have included the socioeconomically marginalized, individuals with disabilities, and individuals who had low levels of educational attainment or, because programming and the majority of the software was available only in English, those who were not literate in English.

The introduction of the Internet to popular culture in the early 1990s increased the elation/concern over the impact of digital technology on global societies and information access. Worldwide marketing of online services through the mass media already in place (i.e., television and radio) helped speed along the diffusion of this new information technology (Leiner et al., 2012). But prices for online connections were expensive and computer costs were high. The software and hardware needed to maintain a well-equipped computer were luxury costs that many around the world or those with lower incomes in richer countries could not afford. Because the Internet began as a U.S. military project, all the coding was English based and the materials presented online were almost exclusively in English only, thus making early Internet Web pages and other distributed information primarily accessible only by individuals with English proficiency (see Figure 2.1). This spearheaded concern that those described as information-poor were becoming even more so in comparison to those who could afford the latest information technologies. Researchers began to illustrate how this digital divide and limits an individual's ability to fully participate in a democratic society (Barber, 1997; De Cindio, Gentile, Grew, & Redolfi, 2003; Nicholas, 2003; Norris, 2001; O'Neil & Baker, 2003; Sawhney, 2003; Servon, 2002; Stanley, 2003; Strover, 2003; Thompson, 2008; van Dijk & Hacker, 2003; Warschauer, 2003; Wresch, 1996). Many of these concerns continue to this day; for example, as can be seen in Figure 2.1, the English continues to be the most commonly used language online.

There are two major organizations that provide information on access and use of information in the United States: the U.S. Department of Commerce's National Telecommunications and Information Agency (NTIA) and the Pew Internet & American Life Project. Then beginning in 1995, NTIA performed a series of national surveys on American use of the Internet. These reports analyzed the influence of demographics such as gender, age, race, level of education, economic status, and geographic location within the United States (NTIA, 1995, 1998, 1999, 2000). Beginning around the year 2000, the Pew Charitable Trusts began funding studies of American use of the Internet as part of a new Pew Internet &

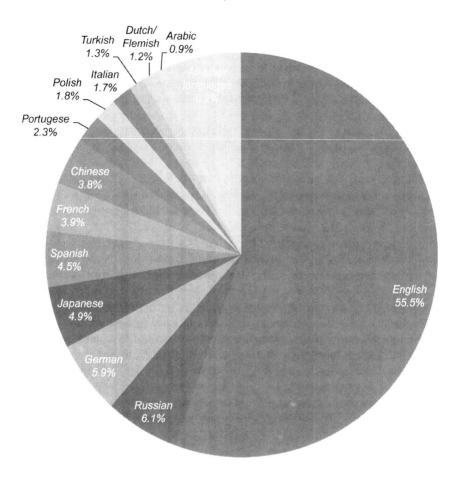

Figure 2.1.   Languages on the World Wide Web in 2013 *Source: Data from W3Techs.com, November 16, 2013*

American Life Project. Both these organizations provided great insight to the access and use (and lack) of information.

By the start of the new millennium, only slightly more than half of the American population (55 percent) had reliable Internet access (NTIA, 2002), but by December 2002, Pew studies reported the Internet to be "a mainstream information tool" that 84 percent of Americans expected could provide them needed information on "health care . . . , services from government agencies, news, and commerce" (Horrigan & Rainie, 2002a, p. 7). Although not all households had computers or Internet connections, research indicated that the American public was logging on in greater numbers for a greater variety of information and services. Legislation was passed to facilitate community and public access to technology (Bertot, 2003); for example, the NTIA Technology Opportunity Program and the Department of Education Community Technology Centers (CTC) programs provided grants to support community technology projects and the Federal Communications Commission's (FCC) E-rate program provided discounts to schools and libraries for telecommunication services, internal wiring, and computer hardware (Telecommunications Act of 1996).

The NTIA (2002) study, entitled *A Nation Online*, shifted focus from lamenting "have-not" problems of the digital divide, and applauded instead the number of Americans who now *had* access. Internet access in public libraries and community technology centers subsidized by the U.S. government ostensibly diminished digital divide problems by ensuring equal Internet availability to all. Around this time, digital divide studies shifted away from concentrated focus on simple physical access to information tools and technologies, redefining the digital divide as a phenomenon that must take into account technological skill, information literacy, and social and economic opportunities beyond simple computer ownership (Fink & Kenny, 2003; Horrigan & Rainie, 2002a, 2002b; Kommers & Rainie, 2002; Larsen & Rainie, 2002; Mossberger, Tolbert, & McNeal, 2008; Mossberger, Tolbert, & Stansbury, 2003; Strover, 2003; van Dijk & Hacker, 2003).

Much as early poverty literature had explored the noneconomic factors leading to poverty lifestyles, digital-divide-based information poverty studies had begun to focus on elements affecting information access such as gender (Nath, 2001), geographic location (Bertot & McClure, 1999; Jue, Koontz, Magpantay, Lance, & Seidl, 1999; Nicholas, 2003), community networks or barriers (De Cindio, Gentile, Grew, & Redolfi, 2003; Gurstein, 2003; O'Neil & Baker, 2003), disability (First & Hart, 2002; Jaeger, 2012), social factors (Burnett & Jaeger, 2012; Jaeger & Thompson, 2003, 2004; Thompson, 2008; Thompson & Afzal, 2011; Wood, 1993), education level (Hendry, 2000; NTIA, 1999), psychosocial barriers to information (Stanley, 2003), and income (Warschauer, 2003). Even so, use of the term *digital divide* consistently emphasizes the binary nature of the digital gap (Gunkel, 2003; Selwyn, 2004). People either have access technology or they do not; they use technology or they do not; they understand technology or they do not. This view fails to acknowledge the continuum of use, access, and understanding in which people actually exist. Numerous scholars have called for a better way of classifying the divide, taking into account the range and types of uses in which people engage (Gunkel, 2003; Livingstone & Helsper, 2007; Selwyn, 2004). These scholars suggest that looking at ranges of online behavior may point to additional inequalities that a dichotomous view is not able to highlight.

Related to this need to look further into degrees of use (and access), scholars also criticize the idea that simply having access implies usage (Bertot, 2003; Gil-Garcia, Helbig, & Ferro, 2006; Selwyn, 2004). There are a variety of reasons that access may not yield use. Content may be irrelevant for certain populations, or these populations may not understand what the relevance to their life is, even if the content is in fact applicable (Selwyn, Gorard, & Furlong, 2005). Users may also lack the necessary literacies and skills to use the technology even if physical access is met. There is a wide range of literacies necessary to engage with digital content. The latter part of this chapter discusses this issue in more detail, but it is important to remember that in addition to digital literacy, users may need to use traditional literacy (reading and comprehension), language literacy (if the content is not in the user's native language), civic literacy (particularly relevant to e-government, as users may not know where to look for information relating to such life needs as paying taxes or registering their child for school), and more. The binary digital-divide approach does not address the range of knowledge that users may or may not have.

Finally, some critics argue that traditional digital-divide literature ignores underlying social issues and the fact that technology might actually exacerbate existing inequalities (Servon, 2002; Stevenson, 2009). Instead of focusing on different ways to help specific populations use technologies to better their lives, a binary view sees a universal way that users access and use technology. Bryne (2006) describes "zones of silence" to describe "the unseen, seemingly quiet, technology-sparse spaces of the digital divide" and voices that are unconnected to widespread communication networks. This view addresses the need to listen to the digitally (and socially) excluded in policy and infrastructure decisions. This link between social exclusion and the digital divide has indeed become one of the defining characteristics of digital exclusion (which is discussed in the next chapter) because of the strong link between those traditionally marginalized and those negatively affected by increasing reliance on technology.

CURRENT GAPS IN ACCESS, LITERACY, AND INCLUSION

Using the United States as an example, the evolution of the groups seen as affected by gaps in digital access, literacy, and inclusion can be seen as paralleling the evolution of Internet technologies and Internet-related policies. Overall, equal access to the Internet is an issue where the disadvantaged are those "who have fought for civil rights in other areas of our society" (First & Hart, 2002, p. 385).

From the beginning of the explosion of popular usage of the Internet, there have been many proclamations that the Internet would quickly become an all-inclusive, completely egalitarian medium that eliminates many societal differences and provides opportunities for everyone. Such wildly optimistic projections have never approached accuracy, with many populations being left behind in the availability and usage of the Internet, due to a range of factors. Often, "the problems of Internet access are common to the problems of access to other communication and information technologies" (Norris, 2001, p. 66). Yet, a decade after that observation, nearly 40 percent of U.S. homes still lacked Internet access, with the percentage of households without Internet access jumping to 62 percent in rural communities; among homes with Internet access, 45 percent lacked broadband access, while 10 percent continued to rely on dial-up Internet service (Horrigan, 2008, 2009). In 2012, 30 percent of America households did not have home Internet access, and, unsurprisingly, public libraries are the primary option for Internet access among those who do not otherwise have access (NTIA, 2013).

In 1995, the first NTIA *Falling through the Net* report documented the gaps in access to the Internet in the United States, in the process popularizing the term *digital divide* among the media and the public (NTIA, 1995, 1998, 1999, 2000). Under the George W. Bush administration, two more reports in the series were issued under the much more optimistic name of *A Nation Online* (NTIA, 2002, 2004). The more optimistic title, however, poorly hid the fact that the numbers had not changed all that much from 2000 to 2002 (Bertot, 2003; Fairlie, 2005; Jaeger & Thompson, 2003, 2004).

Over the course of the reports, the groups that were on the wrong side of the digital divide did change, due in part to the reports figuring out the appropriate areas to focus on (Kinney, 2010). The 1995 report identified urban and rural poor, urban and rural minorities, older adults, young adults, and those of lower education levels as the groups being left behind. Three years later, the 1998 report identified the groups on the wrong side of the divide as rural poor, rural and urban racial minorities, young households, and female-headed households. The 1999 report found the disadvantaged groups to be identifiable by education level, income level, certain racial and ethnic groups, and rural and urban households. The final *Falling through the Net* report in 2000 highlighted growing Internet access among most populations, though the report also noted clear divides based on education, income, age, and disability. The 2002 and 2004 *A Nation Online* reports avoided the use of the term *digital divide* and instead focused on *digital inclusion*. The reports emphasized the growing adoption of the Internet among the groups already using it, sidestepping the groups not being included in the growth of Internet access and usage.

By not considering the larger social contexts and the reasons for gaps in access, the reports painted a fairly limited picture of gaps in access and the ways to address them (Bertot, 2003; Stevenson, 2009; Warschauer, 2003). However, across the reports, they did demonstrate a clear trend that groups that are disadvantaged in other ways in society—such as lower socioeconomic status, lower educational achievement, disability, and rural residency—were also the most likely to have difficulties in accessing and using the Internet. Other studies have demonstrated that the gender, racial, and ethnic disparities that the reports identified were actually far more tied to economic differences (Hoffman & Novak, 1998; Lenhart, Rainie, Fox, Horrigan, & Spooner, 2000; Organisation for Economic Co-operation and Development, 2000; Spooner, Meredith, & Rainie, 2003). Additionally, nations with the largest economic disparities tend to have those disparities reflected in socioeconomic gaps in Internet usage (Booz Allen Hamilton, 2002).

There are also key reasons for divides that are not addressed in the reports. Lower levels of availability of non-English materials related to the United States have hindered Internet use for many Americans who do not speak English. For example, 32 percent of Latinos in the United States who do not speak English use the Internet, but 78 percent of Latinos who speak English use the Internet (Fox & Livingston, 2007; Livingston, 2010). Similar language-related differences can be found in other groups (Fairlie, 2005; Spooner, Rainie, & Meredith, 2001). Additionally, lower levels of formal education are typically linked to lower levels of technological literacy—the understanding of how to use technologies like computers and the Internet (Jaeger & Thompson, 2003, 2004; Powell, Byrne, & Dailey, 2010).

People with disabilities have the lowest levels of Internet usage of any group in the United States and in most other nations as well (Jaeger, 2012). Dobransky and Hargittai (2006) found that 30.2 percent of people with disabilities use a computer at home, 33 percent live in a household with Internet access, 26.0 percent use the Internet at home, and 30.8 percent use the Internet at any location; each of these percentages is less than half of the equivalent percentages for the rest of the population. Persons with disabilities can be limited in their access to and use of the Internet by a wide range of factors, including accessibility problems with Internet service providers (ISPs), the ability to afford the hardware, and Web browsers that are not compatible with vital assistive technologies (Fox, 2004; Fox & Madden, 2005; Jaeger & Bowman, 2005; University of California–Los Angeles, 2003). For persons with disabilities, the barriers they face are not necessarily as fixable by intermediaries as the barriers faced by other groups, since these barriers to access are commonly found in the design of computing technologies, the infrastructure to reach content, and the content itself (Jaeger, 2013; Lazar & Jaeger, 2011; Wentz, Jaeger, & Lazar, 2011).

This gap for persons with disabilities will also become larger as the number of older adults, and thereby the number of people with disabilities, increases as the baby boom generation ages. This rise in the number of older adults has paralleled the time in which the Internet has become an important—even essential—new platform for information and communication in contemporary societies (Fox, 2004; Fox and Madden, 2005). Like persons with disabilities, older adults are much less likely to regularly use the Internet—and are more likely to limit Internet usage—than many other populations as a result of these barriers to initial access (Loges & Jung, 2001; Jaeger & Bowman, 2005; Xie & Jaeger, 2008). Older adults are the group most likely to not use the Internet entirely by choice (Horrigan, 2008, 2009).

The availability of access is not the only issue. On an Internet dominated by social media, streaming audio and video, and other bandwidth-intensive applications, the level of access is as important as the presence of access. Nonbroadband connections are "minimally useful" and becoming "increasingly strained" as the content on the Internet becomes richer (Boyd & Berejka, 2009, p. 7). Levels of access now present some very significant access gaps. In April 2008, only 55 percent of American adults had home broadband access (Horrigan, 2008). Rural Americans are least likely to have home broadband access (38 percent), as compared to suburban (60 percent) and urban (57 percent) Americans. Higher educational attainment and higher income levels correlate to higher home broadband penetration. For example, whereas 85 percent of Americans earning over $100,000 per year have home broadband access, only 25 percent of Americans earning less than $25,000 per year have home broadband access. Many current users of lower-speed connections would not be able to switch due to issues of cost (Horrigan, 2009). These gaps in access speed are now being paralleled by gaps in access to mobile Internet-enabled technologies, as more and more development of Internet content is likely to focus on such mobile technologies that are owned by high-income, highly skilled users (Horrigan, 2009).

Another issue that is generally ignored in discussions about the gaps in Internet access is the literal availability of access. In a nation in which phone service is still not available in some rural areas, the availability of the Internet cannot be taken for granted. In fact, a large range of factors—including physical geography, levels of urbanization, condition of infrastructure, corporate priorities, local politics, and success in applying for government funding—affect the levels of access, availability, and affordability of the Internet in any location (Gabel, 2007; Grubesic, 2008; Jaeger, Bertot, McClure, & Rodriguez, 2007; Jaeger, McClure, & Bertot, 2005; Mack & Grubesic, 2009; Mandel, Bishop, McClure, Bertot, & Jaeger, 2010; Sgroi, 2008; Yu, 2002). In some communities, Internet access is limited to low-speed access or is not available at all because the areas are so rural, while in other locations the same access scenario occurs because the area has a high poverty level and telecommunications companies do not feel it economically worth their time to provide service (Gabel, 2007; Grubesic, 2008; Mack & Grubesic, 2009; Sgroi, 2008). And yet, telecommunications carriers fought aggressively to prevent municipalities from creating low-cost or free municipal networks in noncovered areas as inappropriate encroachment into telecommunications markets (*Economist*, 2013). Some telecommunications carriers are installing community wi-fi networks in selected areas, but access is for those who subscribe to their services (*Economist*, 2013).

In other cases, the combination of geography and federal funding has created regional differences in quality of access. The monies to support Internet access by the federal Universal Service Fund (USF) have not been evenly distributed based on population size or need. Instead, the application process, and thereby the distribution of funds, have favored certain states and regions of the country (Jaeger, McClure, & Bertot, 2005). Ironically, some of the most successful states in receiving these funds have been among the wealthiest states, while some of poorest and least connected states have received limited benefits, resulting in areas such as the Gulf Coast having much lower levels of access than the national average (Jaeger, Bertot, McClure, & Rodriguez, 2007; Jaeger, McClure, & Bertot, 2005).

The recession of recent years has led many people to drop their home Internet access, considering it to be a luxury that can be cut to save money in harsh economic times (Horrigan, 2008). This recession has exacerbated the situation, as those of lower socioeconomic status were already the least likely to use the Internet, have Internet access, or to use advanced online tools (Horrigan, 2008). A great many people who no longer can afford home Internet access have turned to the free Internet access made available in public libraries (Carlton, 2009; Nicholas, Rowlands, Jubb, & Jamali, 2010; Van Sant, 2009; Yates, 2009). In most communities in the United States, the public library is the only source of free Internet access (Bertot, McClure, & Jaeger, 2008). To meet these needs, public library branches average 14.2 workstations for public use, a number that has increased from last year, and 82.2 percent of public libraries now offer free wireless access for patrons (ALA, 2010). Among those using libraries for Internet access, 52.4 percent do not own a computer, 42.4 percent lack access both at home and at work, 40 percent are there because access is free, and 38.1 percent rely on the assistance of librarians (Gibson, Bertot, & McClure, 2009). It is worth noting that these gaps in access are not uniform across socioeconomic strata. Households making less than $50,000 a year, and especially households making less than $30,000 a year, are far more likely to use the library and consider it more important to their families than do those in higher income households (Zickhur, Rainie, & Purcell, 2013).

ADDRESSING INFORMATION POVERTY AND DIGITAL EXCLUSION

In the current prolonged economic downturn, use of public libraries and library computers for applying for unemployment benefits and social services, seeking employment, and other e-government activities has increased substantially (Bertot, 2009; Bertot, Jaeger, McClure, Wright, & Jensen, 2009; Jaeger & Bertot, 2010, 2011; Powell, Byrne, & Dailey, 2010). In 2012, 73 percent of unemployed and 52 percent of underemployed Internet users went online to look for work (NTIA, 2013). Such increases should not be surprising as jobs are scarce and, according to a 2009 survey, 63 percent of people have reduced their entertainment spending during the recession (Gibbs, 2009). The ALA (2010) found that 99 percent of public libraries in the United States provide free Internet access, 90 percent of public libraries have Internet training courses for patrons, and more than that offer informal assistance with the Internet whenever patrons need it. In spite of these levels of Internet access available, 73.5 percent of libraries still have insufficient workstations some or all of the time (ALA, 2010). In 2009, 75.7 percent of libraries reported increased usage of workstations over the previous year, while 71.1 percent reported an increase in wireless usage (ALA, 2010). Additionally, 45.6 percent of libraries reported increases in usage of electronic resources and 26.3 percent had increases in requests for training services; to manage the scope of access demands, 92.3 percent of public libraries have established time limits for access to workstations (ALA, 2010).

For all of those groups, the challenge is one of access to the Internet, be it overcoming cost, education, or availability issues. As fewer users are excluded from a technology, the costs to those excluded rise exponentially (Tongia & Wilson, 2007). With more than 16,500 public libraries covering the United States, free Internet access and training are available to those who need it in most cities and towns in the nation. However, "this is not the same as having automatic access via high-speed connections at home and at the office" (Norris, 2001, p. 92). A core challenge for public policy and public libraries and other community institutions is finding ways to resolve the major problems related to digital access, inclusion, and literacy that continue to affect many groups in society. Solving these problems, though, hinges on reaching an agreement on what the problems actually are; as the next chapter reveals, this dilemma remains unresolved.

THREE

The Struggle to Define Digital Literacy and Digital Inclusion

This chapter traces the emergence of the terms *digital inclusion, digital exclusion,* and *digital literacy* by tracking their evolution from the introduction of the terms (and surrounding events) to their current state and use. The focus is on comparing the various definitions that are available from different nations, government agencies, and nongovernmental organizations, and the implications of these various definitions in practice. It is not the intent of this discussion to analyze the specific connotations of each of these terms, as there are other scholars who have already done so (e.g., Goodfellow, 2011; Whitworth, 2009). Additionally, the need for consistent usage of these terms across government entities, libraries, schools, and other organizations to avoid confusion and conflict in terms of policymaking, adoption, and implementation has been discussed in previous works (e.g., Jaeger, Bertot, Thompson, Katz, & DeCoster, 2012).

The review of definitions in this chapter is meant to be thorough but introductory, as it establishes a baseline for discussion on the approaches to digital literacy and inclusion advocated by and implemented in libraries and the ramifications of these approaches in the chapters to come. Hence, in this chapter, these terms *digital inclusion, digital exclusion,* and *digital literacy* are presented from perspectives of top-down government policymaking, and they are used throughout the book to highlight the ramifications of such definitions in policymaking processes. The chapter also reviews the definitions of these terms that stem out of bottom-up approaches whereby scholars from various academic disciplines coin, frame, or use these terms based on sociological, cultural, and ethnographic perspectives. Because of the importance of examining the various nuances of these concepts, this chapter is necessarily denser than the previous chapters and those that follow. Later chapters emphasize the policies

and programmatic examples that demonstrate these concepts and definitions in practice.

DIGITAL INCLUSION AND EXCLUSION IN
SCHOLARLY LITERATURE

As was detailed in earlier chapters, the rhetoric around the term *digital
divide* was widely criticized for a variety of limitations, particularly an
emphasis on access as a binary problem. As a result, the conceptualization of the divide evolved into one where gaps are recognized as occurring on multiple dimensions (Bertot, 2003; Gil-Garcia, Helbig, & Ferro,
2006; Klecun, 2008; Tsatsou, 2011; Yu, 2011). Vehovar, Sicherl, Hüsing,
and Dolnicar (2006) suggest the problem with current digital-divide conceptualizations is how to operationalize the issues and challenges that
have been identified. But despite this reconceptualization, the term is still
somewhat constrained by its historical link to access. The terms *digital
inclusion* and *digital exclusion* to describe the gap between users and nonusers have emerged as a response to the criticisms of the binary dichoto-
my that the early digital-divide literature expounded as discussed in
Chapter 2. This section discusses the ways that both academics and
governments define these terms.

There are several common factors that are considered by academics to
define the terms *digital inclusion* and *digital exclusion*. Common themes
that emerge from a review of literature from a variety of fields include
accessibility (e.g., physical access), literacy (e.g., intellectual access), and
cultural factors (e.g., social access). A review of the academic literature
finds that *digital inclusion* is defined by various scholars to varying degrees of detail. Wong, Law, Fung, and Lam (2009) describe the term as
"the extent to which the disadvantaged segments of a society can have
equal opportunity to take part in the information society" (p. 61) and
outline five factors of inclusion that affect both access and usage: affordability, ICT skills/literacy, availability, sociocultural factors, and content/
application. While this analysis of digital inclusion focuses on problems
of inclusion that result from economic disadvantages, other works connect digital inclusion with social inclusion (which may or may not rely on
economic parity), calling for a shift from an equipment-focused view of
ICT integration to one of a more robust integration that includes the
broader physical, digital, human, and social factors (e.g., Warschauer,
2003).

Other definitions agree with these factors and discuss implications of
the way in which these factors are applied. Powell, Byrne, and Dailey
(2010) view digital inclusion

from the perspective of marginalized people who have difficulty in gaining and maintaining access to broadband, and whose efforts to gain access to employment, education, and government services—either online or offline—are not well understood or represented in policy debates. (p. 164)

This approach considers the fact that excluded groups often want access, and it disregards the notion that groups not using technology are doing so by their own choice, despite the existence of people who deliberately do not want to use the Internet and related technologies.

Seale, Draffan, and Wald (2010) define digital inclusion as "a phenomenon whereby marginalized people . . . are able to access and meaningfully participate in the same learning, employment, social and citizenship activities as others, through access to and use of digital technologies such as computers" (p. 445). These authors further break down this conceptualization into two strands of inclusion, one based on technology, personal, and contextual factors and the other based on resources and choices. This second strand—resources and choices—is how the factors in the first strand are practically applied to behavior.

Helsper's (2012) corresponding fields model takes this behavioral element further, asserting that "access, skills and attitudes mediate influence of offline social exclusion fields on digital exclusion" but do not create a state of digital inclusion in and of themselves (p. 410). She identifies social exclusion fields, from which one can be excluded both offline and online, as economic, cultural, social, and personal. For example,

the economic field of inclusion (offline) consists of income, employment, and educational resources, which can be operationalized—to take the case of education—through questions about the level of education of the head of the household, the years of schooling, and the highest completed degree. The corresponding economic digital field consists of financial and commercial uses, as well as information and learning digital resources, which can be operationalized through questions about participation in online shopping, selling, and banking, and questions about distance learning and online information seeking. (Helsper, 2012, p. 404)

Helsper notes a difference between technology usage and the social outcomes that follow such as "whether the nature of their use enhances their life" (p. 410). All of these definitions consider a wide range of life circumstances as factors impacting digital inclusion. They also reflect the move away from a binary "have and have-nots" to the idea that there are degrees of digital inclusion and, in Helsper's (2012) model, different areas of digital life in which to be included to various extents.

Related to these ideas of digital inclusion is the term *digital exclusion*. Warren (2007) defines social exclusion as having "a variety of roots and potential meanings, but is commonly used to denote a bundle of factors that combine to marginalise the individual from collective processes and benefits" (p. 378) and suggests that this exclusion "leads to digital exclusion, which in turn perpetuates and exacerbates that social exclusion" (p. 379). Discussions of digital exclusion often focus on the barriers to adoption, such as van Dijk and Hacker's (2003) typology that includes mental access (related to motivation, confidence, and attractiveness of the human–technology interface); material access (opportunity to use technological interfaces and connect to networks); skill access; and usage access (relating to the use of sophisticated information and communication processes as opposed to basic tasks, entertainment, etc.). This type of conceptualization is similar to how digital inclusion is defined. By focusing on factors that relate to being either included or excluded, the terms can encompass the wide range of aspects to the idea of this digital gap.

Social or economic marginalization is a correlate of digital exclusion, but some academic studies have sought to understand whether offline marginalization always results in digital exclusion. Longley and Singleton (2009), for example, suggest that the term *digital exclusion* is pejorative and instead use *digital unengagement* to describe "the outcome of processes that fail to engage significant proportion of the population in the use of ICTs" (p. 1277). Longley and Singleton studied neighborhoods in England, looking for correlations between economic and social deprivation and digital exclusion. The researchers found a strong correlation between material deprivation and digital exclusion, but they were surprised to find a number of neighborhoods that were not deemed materially deprived that they identified as digitally unengaged. In other words, digital engagement relies on factors other than economic wherewithal or marginalization.

Yu (2011) suggests a similar disconnect between economic exclusion and digital exclusion, using *digital inequality* to describe the concept of the "multifaceted disparity between individuals, communities or nations in mobilizing society's information resources for the benefit of their lives and development" (p. 660). By and large, however, *digital inclusion* and *digital exclusion* are most widely accepted as terms to be practically applied to issues around the gap in digital use and access.

These academic definitions are often echoed in policy rhetoric, though the frequency of which actual policy decisions are based on these understandings is far less common. This disjunction is discussed in greater detail in subsequent chapters.

DIGITAL INCLUSION AND EXCLUSION IN NATIONAL POLICIES

In the United States, digital inclusion has historically been viewed through the lens of access and the binary conceptualization of the digital divide. The NTIA *Falling through the Net* report released in 2000 asserts that "overall, [the United States] is moving toward full digital inclusion," but also acknowledges that "a digital divide still remains" (p. iii). The report focuses on gaps between groups of citizens and on how Americans access technologies. While there is some discussion of how Americans are using certain tools, the focus is not on how these activities benefit their lives. There are some signs that this access-driven focus is changing, however. The 2013 report *Exploring the Digital Nation: America's Emerging Online Experience* asserts that "universal Internet use in the United States is a critical national policy objective," but also asks " *why* does Internet use matter, and what makes adoption by all Americans an appropriate goal for policymakers?" (NTIA, 2013, p. 4). This shift to asking how citizens' Internet use benefits them reflects a move from the top-down ideology of past digital-divide policy rhetoric to a more bottom-up approach. This shift suggests that the way future policies will define digital inclusion may reflect more than just the access element of bridging gaps.

The IMLS—the federal government agency in the United States that collects library data—also uses broader language in conceptualizing inclusion, defining the term as

> the ability of individuals and groups to access and use information and communication technologies . . . encompass[ing] not only access to the Internet but also the availability of hardware and software; relevant content and services; and training for the digital literacy skills required for effective use of information and communication technologies. (2011, p. 1)

The agency further describes what digital inclusion means for a community, including understanding of the benefits, equitable and affordable access, and the ability for members "to take advantage of the educational, economic, and social opportunities available through . . . technologies" (2011, p. 1).

In England, the Department for Communities and Local Government has commissioned a variety of reports that highlight various aspects to digital inclusion, including "the amplification of existing social divides . . . the creation of new types of inequality caused by developments in technology . . . and more positively, the emergence of new opportunities" (CapGemini, 2008, pp. 5–6). The benefits of inclusion are categorized as the user having "information about public services; choice of public services; access to public services; information about private services; choice of private services; access to private services; efficiency and value for money; voice; social activities; fulfillment and identity" (Office for Public Management Ltd., 2008, pp. 20–26) and the common factors to those digitally excluded are listed as "inappropriate market provision . . . lack of skills . . . [and] lack of support" (pp. 6–7). This report calls attention to the fact that support is often too focused on information technology skills and not enough on life skills, referring to the academic literature on inclusion that describes all the various mediating factors of social exclusion on digital behavior.

In Scotland, a report commissioned by the Scottish Executive Office in 2004 called for an increased focus on "'intangibles' (such as training and education and community portals) rather than 'tangibles' (such as computers)" (DTZ Pieda Consulting, 2004, p. i), suggesting a shift away from access-driven digital-divide policies. A later report by the Scottish Executive (2007) defines digital inclusion as "social inclusion in the knowledge and information society," and identifies a variety of areas to address such as awareness, access, basic information technology training, and community involvement (pp. 6–7), again suggesting an acknowledgment of the link between social and digital inclusion/exclusion and the wide range of factors involved in eliminating the digital gap.

In 2006, 34 ministers of the European Union endorsed six "e-Inclusion" targets aimed at reducing gaps in usage, increasing physical access to broadband, making websites accessible, focusing on digital literacy and skills, and encouraging further recommendations on standards by 2010 (European Commission Press Room, 2006). While these targets seem to shift the conceptualization of digital inclusion toward a more access-based approach, the addition of digital literacy and skills acknowledges other factors in the gap. The more recent Digital Agenda for Europe (targeted for 2020) includes enhancing digital literacy, skills, and inclusion as one of the seven main goals (European Commission, 2013). Within this goal, the commission calls for a variety of actions, such as increased focus on accessibility, the development of frameworks to assess ICT skills, and increased education in the areas of ICT skills and new media. In this policy, the European Commission both equates inclusion with accessibility and strongly connects it to digital literacy.

In the developing world, a central characteristic of digital inclusion definitions is the influence of nonprofits (often U.S. based) into policy and infrastructure development. Examples of this include the numerous global projects funded by the Bill & Melinda Gates Foundation. This influence has meant that Western developed ideas of inclusion permeate the global landscape. Thus, as U.S. and Western European definitions have evolved from primarily access-based to broader ideas of the components of digital inclusion, globally the idea of inclusion has also expanded. One example of a global nonprofit that emphasizes a broader definition of inclusion is the Center for Digital Inclusion, a nonprofit organization founded in Brazil in 1995 with a presence in 12 countries that aims to bring both computers and digital education to communities. One of their main projects is the development of community-based Centers for Digital Inclusion, which are "informal spaces for teaching computer science and citizenship, sheltered by partner institutions within communities" (n.d.), suggesting an understanding of inclusion as influenced by community characteristics, such as social values, access, and digital skills. However, just as is often the case in Western countries, there remains a strong underlying emphasis on broadband capabilities and infrastructure in many non-Western countries' definitions of digital inclusion. This is further emphasized in international organizations' conceptualizations of digital inclusion.

In 2012, the Broadband Commission for Digital Development published a report on the international state of broadband and was aimed eponymously at "achieving digital inclusion for all." The commission itself was established in 2010 by the International Telecommunication Union (ITU), one of the United Nations' (UN) specialized agencies, and the United Nations Educational, Scientific and Cultural Organization (UNESCO) to "boost the importance of broadband on the international policy agenda" and in response to the UN secretary-general's goals of "stepp[ing] up UN efforts to meet the Millennium Development Goals" (Broadband Commission for Digital Development, n.d.). The 2012 report focuses almost exclusively on infrastructure and broadband access issues, "expand[ing] awareness and understanding the importance of broadband networks, services, and applications for generating economic growth and achieving social progress" (p. 4) and frequently references the digital divide (Broadband Commission for Digital Development, n.d.).

There are, however, acknowledgments of needs beyond hardware and infrastructure in these international organizations. For example, the Development Sector of the ITU defines digital inclusion as "empowering people through information and communication technologies" (n.d.). The ITU specifically mentions information and communication technology accessibility and targets several populations as focuses for their programs, including indigenous peoples and those in rural areas; persons with disabilities; women and girls; and youth and children. This conceptualization echoes the goals of the seminal ITU World Summit on the Information Society meetings held in 2003 and 2005 with the intention of bringing together countries to develop a global strategy to address the information needs arising from the developing information society. Early goals emphasized access and connectivity but also acknowledged the need for relevant content, utilization of local information agencies such as libraries, and information and communication technology literacy and education (World Summit on the Information Society, 2003).

Another international organization, the International City/County Management Association (ICMA), worked with IMLS and the University of Washington Information School on their report, *Building Digital Communities: A Framework for Action* (2012), which defines inclusion in a much broader way, specifically mentioning things like relevance of information and digital literacy skills. Although these government reports, agencies, and organizations use a more inclusive definition of the digital divide, most policies still focus on access as the major obstacle to universal inclusion. For this reason, the terms *digital inclusion* and *digital exclusion* are used as ways to differentiate between the idea that access is the only barrier to usage and the idea that there is a multiplicity of reasons for a person to not be fully engaged in digital society.

OVERVIEW OF DIGITAL LITERACY

The ecology of literacy is ever expanding, and various aspects of literacies' meanings, exclusiveness, similarities, and relationships to each other continue to be debated in the scholarly and practical literature. There are literacies that are termed *foundational literacies* such as reading, writing, and numeracy, and which still remain the core focus in education around the world. However, acknowledgment by scholars and governments that digital forms of information and communication are transforming what it means to work, study, research, and live entitles digital literacies to coexist alongside reading, writing, and numeracy literacies (Littlejohn, Beetham, & McGill, 2012). As a result of the ubiquitous nature of digital communication, there is recognition that new competencies are required to interact with digital information and communication, and many governments, their agencies, and higher education are investing heavily in digital competence development (Jaeger, Bertot, Kavanaugh, Viselli, & Nassar, 2012; Littlejohn, Beetham, & McGill, 2012; Sefton-Green, Nixon, & Erstad, 2009).

A thorough examination of the literature on the evolution of literacies reveals that new literacies are created from the emergence of "social [and cultural] practices" that are introduced for "making and exchanging meanings" (Littlejohn, Beetham, & McGill, 2012, p. 548) in specific social and cultural contexts, such as in an academic discipline, country, organization, workplace, school, etc. (Koltay, 2011). "Literacy was never a context-free or neutral skill, rather the mastery over the processes that culture and society made significant" (Park, 2012, p. 89). Many societal trends impact the need for new literacies—such as the transformation of workplaces to knowledge-driven communities; the increased complexity of work problems that require workers to be lifelong learners, constantly updating their expertise and career tracks; the dispersed communities of expertise that require the need to learn across sites; and the overhauled process of learning based on all the above changes (Littlejohn, Beetham, & McGill, 2012; Park, 2012; Sourbati, 2009).

Online education, for example, is a trend that stemmed out of the changing workforce that demands lifelong learning (Yuan & Powell, 2013) and the emergence of people seeking such education that is convenient, meets their career needs, accommodates health or disability issues, and provides flexibility and cost effectiveness. This trend of educational entrepreneurship is growing at an exponential rate, with a dramatic increase in completely online universities, public and private educational institutions offering online programs and courses (in addition to on-campus programs), and the most recent offerings of Massively Open Online Courses (MOOCs). In fact, many programs and courses are gradually being moved to online platforms, necessitating the learning of skills that allow one to function successfully in these virtual learning environments. Cultural and societal demands for transparency have also made speed and efficiency important in online services for civic engagement provided by governments, such as taxation, immigration, voting, welfare, etc. (Jaeger, 2012).

The above-mentioned societal trends are only a subset of those changes happening in society that are intimately linked to the development and use of technologies that support and mediate these trends. As a result of these emerging societal trends, the use of digital forms of information and communication is also transforming, changing from simple communication such as sending a text, instant message, or e-mail to more complex interactions such as the need to find resources and information or to analyze, evaluate, aggregate, recombine, create, and distribute information and knowledge online (Littlejohn, Beetham, & McGill, 2012). With newer ways to access, use, and interpret information via these technologies, the ecology of literacies needed to function in the digital environment is changing. Literacy "is a socially defined concept that is bound to specific technologies" (Park, 2012, p. 90), and there is a need to consider the technological changes that influence the development of these emerging literacies and create a working definition for such literacies that is appropriate for the time and age (Gunkel, 2003; Park, 2012).

Physical access to information and communication technologies is vital, but physical access alone is not sufficient; digital literacy skills are required to function in digitally inclusive communities (ALA, 2013a; Institute of Museum and Library Services, University of Washington & International City/County Management Association, 2012). What the necessary skills are—and the ways in which such skills can ensure fair and quality participation in social, political, and economical opportunities—is neither clear nor well articulated. The challenge of defining the competencies for the new form of literacy arises primarily from the multiple forms of digital information and communication that are being used and by the complexity of norms of the society and culture of which an individual is a part.

THE EMERGENCE OF DIGITAL LITERACY

The concept of digital literacy was popularized by Paul Gilster (1997) through his seminal book, *Digital Literacy*. Gilster was not the first to coin the phrase, as it had been used since the 1990s to represent the ability to read and comprehend hypertext documents (Bawden, 2001; Koltay, 2011). For example, Lanham (1995) treats the term as synonymous to multimedia literacy when he argues that digital literacy means the ability to decipher information (such as images, sounds, text, etc.) however presented. Gilster (1997) expanded Lanham's view of digital literacy, building relationships to the area of information retrieval and information management by providing a definition of digital literacy that includes "the ability to understand and use information in multiple formats from a wide range of sources when it is presented via computers" (p. 33). Gilster's definition of digital literacy also "involves being able to understand a problem" (p. 33) or one's information need. Through means of searching for and evaluating information resources online, the digitally literate individual can resolve that information need.

There has been some controversy surrounding Gilster's seminal work on digital literacy. Subsequent scholars criticized the definition as being restrictive, saying that he was simply equating digital literacy with Internet literacy (Bawden, 2001, 2008; Koltay, 2001). This is not quite true. Gilster's work was written in the very early days of commercial (dial-up, narrowband) Internet use and so obviously does not include coverage of the range of digital platforms and utilities available today; still, Gilster's book indicates that he does consider non-Internet tasks as well, such as backing up traditional forms of content with networking tools (Bawden, 2001). As Bawden (2001) notes, a close examination of Gilster's book provides an itemized list of suggested competencies for digital literacy that includes:

- The ability to make informed judgments about what is found online, which he equates to "the art of critical thinking," the key to which is "forming a balanced assessment by distinguishing between content and its presentation"
- Skills of reading and understanding in a dynamic and nonsequential hypertext environment
- Knowledge assembly skills; building a "'reliable information horde' from diverse sources, with 'the ability to collect and evaluate both fact and opinion, ideally without bias'"
- Searching skills, essentially based in Internet search engines
- Managing the "multimedia flow," using information filters and agents
- Creating a "personal information strategy," with selection of sources and delivery mechanisms

- An awareness of other people and the expanded ability [through networks] to contact them to discuss issues and get help
- Being able to understand a problem and develop a set of questions that will solve that information need
- Understanding of backing up traditional forms of content with networked tools
- Wariness in judging validity and completeness of material referenced by hypertext links (pp. 247–248)

It is vital to note that Gilster's definition of digital literacy did not affiliate itself with a specific type of technology (although Internet and computers were mentioned), but Gilster took a broader approach that the term is "about the ideas and mindsets, within which particular skills and competencies operate," allowing his definition to be "adaptable to changing times and concerns" (Bawden, 2008, pp. 19, 23).

Gilster's (1997) definition set the initial agreed-upon parameters for digital literacy. However, scholars have debated the nature of the core competencies of the digital literacy skills in Gilster's definition, as he did not specify which competencies are fundamental (Bawden, 2008) but merely listed these competencies in context of an "impressionistic and anecdotal" context (Bawden, 2001, p. 247). Discussion about the differences between digital literacy and other literacies, and continued discussion about refining the definition of digital literacy, began to take place soon after this seminal work was produced (Bawden, 2001; Koltay, 2011; Kope, 2006; Martin, 2006a; Williams & Minnian, 2007). It is beyond the scope of this book to present a lengthy discussion on the differences and similarities between *digital literacy* and other terms such as *information literacy* and *new media literacy*. Although these terms are sometimes used interchangeably, scholars such as Bawden (2001) and Koltay (2011) have made marvelous attempts to compare and contrast these terms. Koltay (2011) stipulates that digital literacy is distinct from the other literacies mentioned above, as it is composed of different sets of literacies, thus there is "no need to search for similarities and differences with other types of literacy" (pp. 216–217).

There are many substantive definitions of digital literacy—particularly stemming from government agencies who feel the need to ensure that citizens are competent to access the information and services that are provided by them and academic disciplines that continue to debate the differences between digital literacy, information literacy, media literacy, participatory literacy (and the list goes on). Exploring these definitions of digital literacy evidences some highly contrasting definitions, with these definitional differences (and similarities) tied to disciplinary and governmental perspectives and contexts.

DIGITAL LITERACY AS LIFE SKILL

Active discussions among scholars have resulted in two main approaches to describing digital literacy: (1) extending Gilster's definition or crafting "Gilster-like" definitions that designate digital literacy as a life skill, and (2) framing digital literacy as a list of competencies needed to master formal education in schools or higher education. This distinction has influenced a range of subjects, though most of the references in this section come from the library and information science (LIS) field, reflecting the richness of such discussion in the LIS field.

Perhaps the most straightforward introductory definition of digital literacy has been provided by Wilson (1998), wherein digital literacy is described as "literacy appropriate for the Internet age; it therefore extends the boundaries of traditional literacy" (p. 190). Wilson then agrees with Gilster's definition of digital literacy, summarizing it as "gaining the ability to understand and use information in multiple formats from a wide range of sources when presented via a computer" (p. 193). Wilson discusses how literacy in the Internet age demands agility with skills that extend beyond basic literacy. Rather than use a collection of information resources selected and acquired by a trained information professional or educator, the Internet and other digital resources require that the user create his or her own collection of materials, selecting, acquiring, evaluating, deselecting, sharing, and organizing information. As such, digital literacy is essentially self-efficiency in information access and use.

Others have discussed this same view of digital literacy, naming it as a necessary life skill in the information age. For example, echoing Gilster, Martin (2006b) writes that digital literacy is

> the awareness, attitude and ability of individuals to appropriately use digital tools and facilities to identify, access, manage, integrate, evaluate, analyze and synthesize digital resources, construct new knowledge, create media expressions, and communicate with others, in the context of specific life situations, in order to enable constructive social action; and to reflect upon this process. (p. 156)

Martin further describes that a digitally literate individual is able to execute fruitful digital actions in everyday life activities such as work, learning, and leisure; identify his or her own digital literacy needs for a particular life situation; self-identify as a digitally literate person; and reflect and track his or her own digital literacy development (Martin, 2008). Martin (2006b, 2008) further states that digital literacy consists of three stages that correspond to skills that an individual needs to learn and develop over time. The first stage is the digital literacy that is needed for carrying out tasks in an individual's digital life context such as e-filing his/her taxes, completing an online job application, obtaining day-to-day information for work, and many similar activities. The next stage consists of digital literacy needed in order to belong to a community or a specific domain such as participating in community-based virtual sharing spaces and online education. The third and most advanced stage, according to Martin (2006b), is digital transformation, which denotes that one has advanced the digital skills needed to be creative and innovative, such as participation in group-based virtual computing spaces, virtual learning spaces where one is able to create and share media, and so on. Although Martin claims that there is no specific progression between these stages (Knutsson, Blasjo, Hallsten, & Karlstrom, 2012), the mere designation of these as "stages" represents progress in the development of digital literacy skills for an individual, but they are not sequential, as one can be involved in all these three stages at one period of time.

This perspective on digital literacy as a life skill is reflected in national reports such as the Canadian SchoolNet National Advisory Board, which stresses the ability to use digital literacy in "appropriate circumstances":

> Digital literacy presupposes an understanding of technical tools, but concerns primarily the capacity to employ these tools effectively. Hence, digital literacy begins with the ability to retrieve, manage, share, and create information and knowledge, but it is consummated through the acquisition of enhanced skills in problem solving, critical thinking, communication and collaboration. (Martin, 2008, p. 165)

Furthermore, a report entitled *Digital Horizons*, written by a team of scholars from New Zealand, also makes clear references to digital literacy as life skill:

> Digital literacy is the ability to appreciate the potential of ICT to support innovation in industrial, business and creative processes. Learners will need to gain the confidence, skills, and discrimination to adopt ICT in appropriate ways. Digital literacy is seen as a "life skill" in the same way as literacy and numeracy. (quoted in Martin, 2008, p. 165)

The ALA Office of Information Technology Policy (OITP), via their OITP Digital Literacy Task Force, recently convened a group of literacy experts and librarians from academic and public libraries to explore the challenges and opportunities of digital literacy to cultural institutions and discuss digital literacy–related policy and its ramifications on facilities and services offered or that should be offered in libraries. Similar to the *Digital Horizons* report (Martin, 2008), ALA points out the importance of traditional literacies (such as basic writing and reading skills) in the acquisition of digital literacy (ALA, 2013a), to ensure that one has what it takes to become a lifelong learner. The task force defines digital literacy as "the ability to use information and communication technologies to find, understand, evaluate, create, and communicate digital information, an ability that requires both cognitive and technical skills" (ALA, 2013a, p. 2). This task force envisions a digitally literate person as a person who can execute the following tasks (and their associated skills):

- Find, understand, evaluate, create, and communicate digital information in a wide variety of formats (have cognitive and technical skills to execute these tasks)
- Search and retrieve information, interpret and evaluate search results (be able to use diverse technologies appropriately and effectively to conduct these tasks)
- Understand the stewardship of information and lifelong learning (be able to protect personal privacy and take cybersecurity measures to protect confidentiality)
- Communicate and collaborate with family, friends, and public (using the skills mentioned above)
- Participate actively in civic society and contribute to a vibrant, informed, and engaged community (using the skills mentioned above) (ALA, 2013a)

The latter points made by the OITP Digital Literacy Task Force indicated above exemplify an emphasis on life skills, similar to Gilster.

DIGITAL LITERACY AS EDUCATION OUTCOME

Littlejohn, Beetham, and McGill (2012) define digital literacy as

> capabilities required to thrive in and beyond education, in an age where digital forms of information and communication predominate. Digital forms of communication are ubiquitous and wide ranging, from relatively simple communication via email or instant messaging to more complex forms of scholarships that involve sourcing, using, evaluating, analyzing, aggregating, recombining, creating and releasing knowledge online. (p. 547)

They further elaborate that:

> digital literacy extends beyond technical competence, such as the ability to form letters in writing, or use a keyboard. Digitally based knowledge practices are meaningful and generative of meaning: they depend on the learner's previous experiences . . . , on dispositions such as confidence, self-efficacy and motivation . . . , and on qualities of the environment where that practice takes place, including of course the available digital technologies . . . digital literacies are both constitutive of and expressive of personal identity. (p. 551)

From a rather different angle, one that characterizes digital literacy as technical competencies for formal education, Eshet-Alkali (2004) and Eshet-Alkali and Amichai-Hamburger (2004) describe digital literacy as a coalescence of five other "literacies": photo-visual literacy (the understandings of visual presentations); reproduction literacy (creative reuse of existing materials); information literacy (concerned with the evaluation of information); branching literacy (essentially the ability to read and understand hypermedia); and social-emotional literacy (now known as the cybersecurity skills in cyberspace). This echoes Wilson's definition of digital literacy as the ability to evaluate Internet resources, and differentiates it from the skills required to evaluate print materials (Wilson, 1998). These definitions simply point out the technical competencies needed to navigate digital materials in schools but do not indicate the applicability of these skills beyond formal education. Perhaps these authors feel that the applicability of these competencies in life skills is inherent.

Although the definitions of digital literacy discussed above can be separated between perspectives of scholars who either view it as life skill or as skills needed for formal education, it is evident that some of these definitions are an amalgamation of both or value one perspective only slightly more than the other. The emphasis in the perspectives may be a result of the audience for which they are writing (e.g., the ALA-OITP report was for librarians and information policymakers) or as a response to a specific task to which they have been assigned (e.g., Martin's definitions were crafted as part of the DigEuLit project that he was heading). Bawden (2008) expresses the flux in digital literacy definition as:

> touch[ing] on and includ[ing] many things that it does not claim to own. It encompasses the presentation of information, without subsuming creative writing and visualization. It encompasses the evaluation of information, without claiming systematic reviewing and meta analysis as its own. It includes organization of information but lays no claim to the construction and operation of terminologies, taxonomies and thesauri. (p. 26)

DIGITAL LITERACY AND POLICY

As a response to the digital divide and in an expression of their commitment to promote digital inclusion, government agencies around the globe have begun to define and develop digital literacy frameworks to ensure citizens are able to acquire the necessary skills to participate in the 21st-century knowledge economy and to fully participate in society. Indeed, as technology becomes more ubiquitous, these frameworks increasingly reflect a recognition by government agencies that access is only the beginning; there is a need for education, training, and public engagement (ALA, 2013a, 2013b; Clark & Vissner, 2011; ICT Digital Leadership Council, 2010; Knight Commission, 2009; New York State Universal Broadband Council, 2011). The digital inclusion dialogue has evolved in recent years to focus more on the need for the development of technical and cognitive skills for citizens to be digitally included.

This examination of adoption of digital literacy definitions and frameworks by government agencies reveals that these agencies typically embrace digital literacy framework using two approaches. One, the top-down government policy dissemination approach, which is often motivated by civic and economic aspirations, aims to devise and implement a range of policies and curriculum initiatives that fits the needs of the digital age. The second, the bottom-up approach, expects digital literacy frameworks and movements to develop in social contexts among citizens (commonly nonprofit organizations) and for the findings from these sociological and ethnographic studies to inform or push the policy reforms that need to be in place (Sefton-Green, Nixon, & Erstad, 2009). Thus, the definitions of digital literacy by government agencies can be viewed through both of these above-mentioned lenses. Surprisingly, many countries do not define digital literacy in their manifesto documentation or white papers (even though they do define digital inclusion or exclusion explicitly in their policy documents), but do substantially reference the need to develop digital literacy among their citizens (Organization for Economic Cooperation and Development & Hungarian Ministry of Education, 2004; U.K. Department of Communities and Local Government, 2008).

A common approach in these policies is the use of top-down definitions. In the United States, two major federal initiatives, the National Broadband Plan and the Broadband Technology Opportunities Program (BTOP), brought national attention to digital inclusion and to the need to educate citizens in digital literacy. In the National Broadband Plan released by the Federal Communications Commission (2010) in the United States, digital literacy is defined as:

> a variety of skills associated with using ICT (information and communication technology) to find, evaluate, create, and communicate information. It is a sum of the technical skills and cognitive skills people employ to use computers to retrieve information, interpret what they find and judge the quality of that information. It also includes the ability to communicate and collaborate using the Internet—through blogs, self-published documents and presentations and collaborative social networking platforms. (p. 174)

But even prior to these two federal initiatives to promote digital inclusion, as a response to legislation such as the No Child Left Behind Act of 2001 and the related Enhancing through Technology Act (which dictates that all children must have a measurable level of digital literacy by the end of eighth grade), K–12 educational government and state agencies had been developing standards and assessments, such as the Framework of the Partnership for 21st-Century Learning, National Educational Technology Standards from the International Society for Technology in Education, and the Common Core State Standards that inherently make references to the mastery of digital literacy skills to become informed and engaged citizens.

The European Union (EU) continues to struggle with defining digital literacy for its policy decisions, speaking in terms of "the ability to use ICT and the Internet" (Martin, 2008, p. 165) and acknowledge not being able to reach this consensus in its policy documents dated as far back as 2001 (Martin, 2008; Rantala & Suoranta, 2008). In a white paper, the Ministry of Education and Research in Norway articulated a national reform, Program for Digital Literacy, that calls for a national curriculum reform of Norwegian schools; Norway is one of the first countries in the EU with a curriculum on digital literacy skills (Soby, 2008). This white paper defines digital literacy as

> the sum of simple ICT skills, like being able to read, write and calculate, and more advanced skills that make possible creative and critical use of digital tools and media. ICT skills consist of being able to use software, to search, locate, transform and control information from different digital sources, while the critical and creative use of ICT refers to the ability to evaluate, to make critical use of sources, to interpret and analyse digital genres and media forms. In total, digital literacy can be seen as a very complex competence. (Sefton-Green, Nixon, & Erstad, 2009, p. 115)

An example of the bottom-up approach is the collaboration between the IMLS, University of Washington, and the ICMA. Their Building Digital Communities project (referenced earlier) built a framework for digital communities by soliciting input of more than 100 organizations and individuals with profound knowledge about public access to technology and the diverse information needs of communities. Community and leadership forums were held around the country and a survey was conducted to solicit feedback on their proposed framework. In building this framework, one of the adoption principles identified was digital literacy:

> Digital literacy skills, including the ability to find, evaluate, and use information to achieve goals, are a necessary pathway to digital inclusion. Digital communities meet the needs of their members for learning about technology and maintaining the skills necessary to take advantage of the opportunities enabled by it. (Institute of Museum and Library Services, University of Washington, International City/County Management Association, 2012, p. 25)

The suggested framework comes with specific goals for digital literacy adoption and sample individual, library, business, and community strategies to facilitate the mastery of digital literacy.

Analyzing closely the definitions of digital literacy shared in this chapter and mapping them to the three levels of access described in the theory of information worlds—physical access, intellectual access, and social access—within the context of the digital information age, digital literacy can be seen as the ability of the individual to access and use digital information with enough effectiveness to allow him or her to engage physically, intellectually, and socially in the micro, meso, and macro information world.

For one to be able to access digital information physically, the individual must be able to identify, find, retrieve, and manage digital information in various formats. For one to be able to access digital information intellectually, the individual must be able to integrate, evaluate, analyze, and synthesize digital information and construct new knowledge based on the information found. In addition, the individual must have the competence to develop a personal information strategy, develop questions that will solve information and knowledge needs, use relevant information to solve the information problem at hand, and protect his or her privacy and confidentiality while seeking, retrieving, and sharing information. For one to be able to access digital information socially, the individual must be able to communicate digital information with others, determine constructive social actions based on the information received, and reflect upon this process. The individual must also be able to participate actively in civic engagement using the information at hand, self-identify as a digitally literate person, and track his or her own digital literacy development.

A digitally literate person who does all of the above successfully will have the skills to actively contribute to a digitally inclusive society. In practice, however, digital literacy and inclusion among individuals and communities is heavily dependent on decisions made in public policy that often do not account for these types of lessons about supporting and promoting digital access, literacy, and inclusion or that fail to even consider the existence of implications of policy decisions for digital access, literacy, and inclusion.

FOUR

Public Policy, Literacy, and Inclusion

Some of the policies, laws, regulations, and other government macro-level decisions have been focused on promoting digital literacy and digital inclusion; others have been intended to limit digital literacy and digital inclusion; and a great many have generated unintended impacts on digital literacy and digital inclusion. These types of governmental instruments can be found in nations with high levels of technology usage and in nations struggling to create technology infrastructure. Along with the underlying policy goals, several factors unrelated to the instruments themselves shape the effectiveness of the instruments at promoting digital literacy and digital inclusion, including structure of government, homogeneity of population, income, education level, geography of the nation, and transparency and openness, among other factors. A deeper exploration of these factors is included in the case studies in chapters 6 and 7 of this book.

Using examples from around the world to offer perspectives on the range of policy goals and other influences on these goals, the current chapter presents a snapshot of the intersection of policy, literacy, and inclusion internationally. Particular attention is given to the impacts of the policy goals and governmental instruments on the ability of public libraries to provide services and training that promote digital literacy and digital inclusion.

PROMOTING DIGITAL INCLUSION

Although digital inclusion and digital literacy are directly tied to the Internet, the root ideas significantly predate the Internet in the United States (Jaeger, Bertot, Thompson, Katz, & DeCoster, 2012). The legislative roots of digital inclusion can be traced to the Communications Act of 1934 in which Congress established the precedent of unifying telecommunications and broadcasting standards to promote widely available nationwide wire and radio communication services in an affordable and nondiscriminatory manner. Though subsidies or other forms of support to the disadvantaged were not provided, it did establish the precedent that telecommunications should be provided in an inclusive manner.

In the early 1990s, policies in the United States—along with the United Kingdom and France, among others—shifted toward viewing technology as a means of promoting social inclusion (Selwyn, 2004). The Telecommunications Act of 1996 was a comprehensive update and expansion of telecommunications laws, including promoting universal service to people in low-income, rural, insular, high-cost, and other disadvantaged areas to make telecommunications more affordable. This law was based in the notion of trying to increase access broadly to telecommunications at the point in which Internet access was dependent on affordable access to telephone lines. The attention paid to universal service to telecommunications was based on the focus of the Clinton administration on the demographics of Internet access, with the series of *Falling through the Net* reports detailing the levels of Internet access available to different populations in the United States. These reports were reminding legislators and members of the public that:

> [Some people] have the most powerful computers, the best telephone service and fastest Internet service, as well as a wealth of content and training relevant to their lives. . . . Another group of people don't have access to the newest and best computers, the most reliable telephone service or the fastest or most convenient services. (NTIA, 2000)

Similarly, the passage of the new telecommunications law also coincided with the beginning of a serious academic focus on "information haves" and "information have-nots" (Bertot, 2003; Wresch, 1996).

The Telecommunications Act of 1996 could not foresee the advent of broadband as a defining communication medium; the language of the law, however, anticipated that there would continue to be advancements in this area and included nonspecific text to allow for promotion of access to future technologies (Gilroy & Kruger, 2002). As telecommunications companies increasingly focused on developing and marketing Internet services, then broadband, and then mobile technologies, the disparities between Americans who could access the infrastructure and those who could not became more pronounced, leading to what is now a key challenge to digital literacy and digital inclusion. The creation of the NTIA itself in the 1990s demonstrated the widespread embrace of addressing issues of digital inclusion and digital literacy in the U.S. government.

The most important way in which the Telecommunications Act of 1996 worked to improve digital literacy and digital inclusion was through the creation of the Universal Service Fund (USF). The USF is a mechanism by which schools, libraries, and rural health-care providers receive financial assistance (under what is known as the E-rate program) to ensure that Internet connectivity is available to those institutions. Over time, the E-rate program has been enormously important in the development of Internet infrastructure and connectivity in schools and libraries, providing billions of dollars over the course of a decade and a half (Jaeger, Bertot, McClure, & Rodriguez, 2007; Jaeger, McClure, & Bertot, 2005). Currently, virtually all public schools and about half of public libraries benefit directly from E-rate funds (Jaeger & Yan, 2009). For people who lack any other means of Internet access or have only insufficient Internet access, the E-rate program has been vital in helping libraries in particular become the societal guarantor of Internet access in the United States. In about two-thirds of communities, public libraries are the only source of free public Internet access, particularly in rural and economically disadvantaged areas (Bertot, McClure, & Jaeger, 2008).

After the passage of the Telecommunications Act, the FCC implemented several programs beyond the E-rate program to assist individuals on the adverse side of the digital divide. The Link-Up America program was designed to help low-income households pay for the installation costs required to initiate telecommunications services, and the parallel Lifeline Assistance program was designed to help low-income households pay monthly telecommunications bills. According to the program website, USF funds were also designated for promoting "reasonable comparability of telecommunications services rates to limit underserved areas from having lesser access or higher costs." The FCC also created a series of Community Technology Centers (CTCs), which were funded to create an environment that would provide public computer access in communities where it was lacking (Strover, 2003). The CTC program quickly failed, however, since they usually did not offer available assistance and training and lacked a tradition of being trusted by communities (Jaeger & Fleischmann, 2007). Instead, people turned to their public libraries for access and training.

The FCC's National Broadband Plan (2010), the IMLS Proposed Framework for Digitally Inclusive Communities (2011), the multiagency DigitalLiteracy.gov site, and many other government policies and statements all rely on public library technology and training in different ways to achieve a more digitally inclusive society, though few adequately acknowledge the significant cost-shifting onto libraries to fill these gaps (e.g., immigration services in many states are entirely online and agencies refer individuals to the public library to access and fill out immigration forms) (Gorham, Bertot, Jaeger, & Taylor, 2013; Jaeger & Bertot, 2011). Such reliance occurs because public libraries are uniquely equipped to support these efforts with hardware, Internet connections, trained staff, and significant resources available online and in print to support lifelong learning and skills development (Jaeger & Bertot, 2011; Jaeger, Bertot, Thompson, Katz, & DeCoster, 2012). In fact, this role will likely grow as reductions of funding for school libraries result in students needing another outlet for homework resources, given that public library computers are already heavily used by youth to complete homework (Becker et al., 2010).

After the Telecommunications Act of 1996, the next major bill related to digital inclusion and digital literacy was the American Reinvestment and Recovery Act (ARRA), commonly called the Stimulus Bill. Primarily intended to build infrastructure, ARRA provided $7.2 billion in funding for loans and grants to be offered and administered by the NTIA and the U.S. Department of Agriculture's Rural Utilities Service (RUS). The majority of the funding ($4.7 billion) was to be used to build broadband infrastructure in underserved and unserved areas, with $2.5 billion specifically for rural areas (White House, 2009).

NTIA created the Broadband Technology Opportunities Program (BTOP) as its grants-funding arm. In its first round of funding, BTOP provided $293 million to 56 grantees, one each from the 50 states, five territories, and the District of Columbia, for a variety of state-level programs intended to increase the level of broadband access and therefore encourage digital inclusion (http://www.broadbandusa.gov). Additionally, BTOP committed funds for states to gather data "twice a year on the availability, speed, and location of broadband services, as well as the broadband services that community institutions, such as schools, libraries and hospitals, use" (n.p.). In collaboration with the FCC, the data collected were used to develop the National Broadband Map, which launched in 2011 at http://broadbandmap.gov. RUS, operating its own funding program, primarily through loans, as the Broadband Initiatives Program (BIP), provided funding for 285 last-mile projects (providing access to customers), 12 middle-mile awards (transmissions lines for large areas), four satellite awards, and 19 technical assistance awards in 45 states and one territory (U.S. Department of Agriculture, 2011).

In February 2010, the FCC released its National Broadband Plan, consisting of recommendations to "guide the path forward through the rule-making process at the FCC, in Congress and across the Executive Branch" (n.p.). The FCC's plan attempts an umbrella approach to the issue of broadband availability and addresses development, economic market forces, policy reform, and policy creation, among other subjects. With regard to digital inclusion, the FCC emphasizes creating incentives to promote digital inclusion, which the report views as the combination of sufficient broadband service, affordable broadband service, and the availability of opportunities to develop digital literacy needed to use broadband. Perhaps recognizing the broad scope of the above-mentioned inclusion efforts, the FCC couches its recommendations in terms of "should," not "must"—a less effective but infallible strategic move should none of the methods suggested come to fruition.

In the plan, several new programs are suggested. Of relevant interest is the Connect America Fund and the proposed method of financially supporting it (FCC, 2010). The FCC recommends transferring at least a decade's worth of monies invested in the USF to expand broadband access. When considering acting upon the ideas of digital inclusion and thereby bridging the digital divide, divesting the E-rate program presents a paradoxical approach. Schools and libraries offer Internet services to communities and constituencies who are likely to fall within the Stimulus Bill's mandate of making broadband accessible to unserved and underserved populations. Defunding the program obviously will lead to a loss of Internet access in the physical structures where it has been most readily available to the largest number of people who need access. Defunding the E-rate program also presents another challenge, including loss of public access to those who have no wish for Internet in their homes but still wish to perform e-government Internet-only functions, such as filing taxes.

In 2010, 60 percent of American adults used broadband connections at home (Rainie, 2010), which means that nearly 125 million Americans do not use broadband at home. This could mean in some cases that Internet access exists in the home but people are using slower-access technologies, such as dial-up service. Two recent surveys, one by the NTIA (2010) and one by the Pew Foundation (Zickuhr & Smith, 2012) present a staggeringly large number—20 percent to 30 percent of all persons in the United States—who do not use the Internet anywhere, while a 2013 study suggested that 15 percent of American adults were nonusers of the Internet (Zickuhr, 2013). Even if the lowest numbers presented in these surveys is closest to accurate, that is an extraordinarily large number of people who are disconnected from the Internet. For certain populations, such as persons with disabilities, the percentage of nonusers of the Internet is even higher (National Council on Disability, 2009). In the case of persons with disabilities, the nonusage is directly linked to the laws related to infrastructure and digital inclusion providing explicit permission for providers of access and content to not include persons with disabilities in their services (Jaeger, 2012; Lazar & Jaeger, 2011).

With respect to digital inclusion and broadband capabilities, the NTIA survey emphasized four major reasons for the high number (40 percent) of those not using broadband at home (NTIA, 2010):

- People did not feel they needed broadband;
- People felt broadband was too expensive;
- There was a lack of or insufficient end-point equipment (i.e., computers); and/or
- There was a lack of service availability, particularly in rural areas.

The NTIA study demonstrates that absence of infrastructure for physical access—hence the goal of ARRA to ensure access to broadband capabilities for all—is not the only obstacle to fostering digital inclusion and creating a digital nation and might not even be the main complication.

Beyond the wide range of activities at the national level, state and local governments in the United States have also devised their own programs and services to promote digital literacy and digital inclusion. Many of these programs and services are the creations of public library systems. As the next chapter discusses in detail, public libraries serve as the societal guarantor of digital literacy and digital inclusion in the United States. Some local governments have developed policies promoting other kinds of efforts, as well. A particularly interesting recent trend in the United States has been the creation of online platforms to community-source solutions to problems that the government can identify but cannot solve (Jaeger, Bertot, Kavanaugh, Viselli, & Nassar, 2012). The state of Virginia, for example, has these platforms in communities such as Alexandria, Blacksburg, and Arlington, among other places. The goals of these platforms include improving digital literacy and digital inclusion in communities by creating partnerships between the local government efforts and the efforts of local nonprofits and community service groups.

HINDERING DIGITAL INCLUSION

Despite a series of government programs that promote digital inclusion and the widespread use of mobile technologies, many populations—based on socioeconomic status, education, age, geography, language, literacy, and disability—experience gaps in access to the Internet and training in digital literacy skills (Jaeger, Bertot, Thompson, Katz, & DeCoster, 2012). Education, employment, civic participation, social engagement, and many other foundational elements of an economically and socially successful community now often require widespread access to the Internet. This increases the importance of digital literacy and of digital inclusion skills for all members of the community. Thus, the importance of the public library as the community anchor guaranteeing Internet access, services, training, and support continues to grow exponentially, particularly for those without access to mobile, personal, or at-work computers and Web access. Yet, while the governmental instruments in the United States directly related to the Internet are generally meant to promote digital inclusion and digital literacy, the past two decades have also seen an explosion of federal laws and policies related to information. This unprecedented level of regulation of information access and usage has led to many significant consequences, mostly unintended and unforeseen, for public libraries and their ability to support digital inclusion and digital literacy (Jaeger, Bertot, & Gorham, 2013).

The recent growth of federal policies related to information means that federal policy has much greater relevance to public libraries than at any time in the past, though public libraries are rarely considered in policy debates. In the past 15 years or so, federal policy affected public libraries by establishing the following mandates:

- The USA PATRIOT Act and the rights of government agencies to collect a wide range of libraries' physical and electronic records and observe a wide range of patron behaviors in libraries
- The Homeland Security Act, with its capacities for government agencies to limit the government information available and to take information out of library collections
- The Children's Internet Protection Act (CIPA) requiring the filtering of Internet access for all library computers—and thereby reducing the information patrons can access—in order to receive certain types of funding
- The Digital Millennium Copyright Act (DCMA), raising serious issues for libraries in providing electronic resources through their own services and through interlibrary loan
- The E-rate funding program, which while generally very helpful, requires libraries to complete a byzantine application process in order to receive support for library technology
- The E-Government Act, which ultimately encouraged many government agencies to offload the training and support for use of their online services to public libraries
- The aforementioned FCC Broadband Plan from 2010, which suggests defunding libraries to promote private-sector growth of broadband access

These policies—particularly the first three—were primarily produced in reaction to ideas that were extremely popular in the political arena. For public libraries, the impacts of policies—by limiting information available, channels of information access, and ways to use and exchange information—fall extremely heavily on the ability to provide digital literacy and digital inclusion to those who otherwise are limited in their abilities to participate online.

A major government initiative of the past 15 years has also served as a confounding factor for policies intended to promote digital inclusion and digital literacy. By strongly encouraging agencies to move information, communication, and services online, the federal, state, and local governments of the United States have created a situation where engagement with government depends in most cases on being able to go online and use e-government. Unfortunately, it has been evident from the early years of e-government that many members of the public lack the appropriate technologies and/or the necessary skills to effectively engage in e-government (Bertot & Jaeger, 2006; Jaeger & Thompson, 2003, 2004). As the usage of e-government to deliver information, communication, and services to members of the public has become commonplace, the demand in public libraries for access to and assistance using e-government has skyrocketed, creating sizeable new demands on libraries (Jaeger & Bertot, 2009). Libraries receive no additional support from governments for taking on these e-government education and assistance roles, in spite of the fact that some government agencies have gone so far as to put instructions on their websites instructing people to seek help using their websites at the local public library (Jaeger & Bertot, 2011).

Not only do the people without Internet access in the home come to the public library for access to e-government, but many people with home access also use library computers for e-government access because they either lack sufficient access speeds at home to accomplish their tasks or because they lack government literacy to find what they are searching for without help (Bertot, Jaeger, Langa, & McClure, 2006a, 2006b). Reliance on the public library for access is not evenly distributed across society, as 51 percent of African Americans and 41 percent of Latinos who use the Internet rely on public libraries for access (FCC, 2010). Of the 169 million visitors to public libraries, 45 percent use the Internet as part of their visits (Becker et al., 2010). A key reason for this usage is e-government. Among patrons using e-government in libraries, 52.4 percent do not own a computer, 42.4 percent lack access both at home and at work, 40 percent are there because access is free, and 38.1 percent rely on the assistance of librarians (Gibson, Bertot, & McClure, 2009).

In addition to a wide range of recent laws and policies that impact the ability of public libraries in the United States to provide digital literacy and digital inclusion, funding decisions by governments in the past five years have also created major constraints on the activities of public libraries. Overall, public services have been hit very hard by budget cuts in the latest recession. Based on 2012 Bureau of Labor Statistics (BLS) data, 584,000 public-sector jobs in the United States were lost between June 2009 and April 2012, or 2.5 percent of the local, state, and federal government jobs that existed before the prolonged economic downturn began. In previous recessions, public sector employment has traditionally increased (Hatch, 2004). According to the Center on Budget and Policy Priorities (2012), state budget shortfalls have ranged from $107 billion to $191 billion between 2009 and 2012, and current projections place state budget shortfalls at $55 billion for 2013. Some states—Florida, Nevada, and Arizona, for example—have fared much worse. This current situation stands in stark contrast to other recessions of the past several decades, during and after which the number of public-sector jobs actually increased. Certain public-sector areas have been hit particularly hard in this prolonged economic downturn, with 20 percent of the public health workforce losing their jobs since 2009 (Kliff, 2012).

State and public libraries have not been untouched in these cuts. According to the 2012 Public Library Funding & Technology Access Study (Bertot, McDermott, Lincoln, Real, & Peterson, 2012), public library funding has stagnated or declined since 2009, resulting in reduced hours open and reduced staff at some libraries. In addition, 40 percent of states reported reduced state aid funding for public libraries over the past three years. In at least one state (Texas), state aid was completely cut, which—if not reinstated in the next legislative session—will result in a loss of federal Library Services and Technology Act funds. Overall, budgets for public libraries, public schools, public health services, and other state and local government agencies devoted to the public good have been cut substantially since the recession began, greatly limiting their ability to serve their communities in many cases. These cuts have had enormous impacts on public library systems and individual libraries.

The library systems in such cities as Boston, Chicago, Detroit, Los Angeles, Miami-Dade, Philadelphia, and Seattle have experienced a combination of staffing cuts, service reductions, and even branch closings in some cases. In Chicago, the union representing library employees voted to accept a 10-percent pay cut and the elimination of 120 part-time positions to preserve more jobs (Pensa, 2009). In just 2012, the Miami-Dade system lost 30 percent of its budget and 25 percent of its staff, while the Detroit system closed four branches, and the Seattle system closed the entire system for one week and employees were not paid (Kelly, 2012). These are just examples of large systems that have received attention in the national media and library discourse. In Los Angeles, however, community members rallied to limit drastic cuts imposed by city leaders that had led to staff cuts from 1,156 to 828 in one year and all libraries being closed for two days a week (Kelly, 2011, 2012). Citizens of many other communities have not been as successful in fighting cuts; though most citizens support library funding and will vote in favor of ballot initiatives for library funding, they often do not get a chance to express their support (Dempsey, 2009, 2010).

The impacts on medium- and small-sized systems—particularly systems of one library—are not as large in real dollars but can be far greater proportionally. The Charlotte-Mecklenburg Library, a public library system that serves the city of Charlotte and the County of Mecklenburg in North Carolina, is an example of an entire library system that has suffered repeated dramatic cuts, reducing it to a mere shadow of its former self (Bethea, 2011). In 2006, that library system was visited by then–first lady Laura Bush to honor it for its innovative outreach and community programs; in 2011, it had lost one-third of its staff, closed branches, cut most programs, and slashed hours in half at the remaining libraries.

Additional examples are seen in such diverse settings as Colton, California, where the city manager walked into the two library branches one day in 2009 and informed everyone who worked there that they were fired and that the libraries would be closed indefinitely (Goldberg, 2009), and in Jackson County, Oregon, all 15 libraries were closed for 7 months, laying off 100 library employees in the largest library closing in U.S. history (Battistella, 2010). By 2012, most libraries and systems of all sizes were "furiously treading water," with libraries reporting an overall average of 2.7 fewer employees than the year before (Kelly, 2012). Governments have been telling libraries around the country to make across-the-board cuts, reduce staffing, cut materials budgets, close facilities, reduce hours, raise fees and fines, and/or seek private funding (LaRue, 2009). Not surprisingly, these economic cuts have enormous implications for library services and training.

As their budgets are being slashed, public library usage has been driven upward by the long-term economic crisis, resulting in the untenable pairing of dramatically rising usage and precipitously declining funding. During the downturn, use of public libraries and library resources for job-seeking activities, social services, e-mail access, entertainment, and other purposes has increased substantially. Public libraries have long experienced that economic downturns lead to increased usage of the library and its services, with references to this relationship dating back to as early as 1880 in library discourse (James, 1985). This relationship is now known as the Librarian's Axiom and has been demonstrated to be true through numerous studies and, more importantly, many years of library operation during times of economic crisis (Davis, 2009, 2011; James, 1986; Lynch, 2002).

During the Great Depression, library services and materials were "eagerly sought" and "contributed something to the lessening of social ills during a difficult period" (Herdman, 1943, p. 334). The demand for library books and for reference services skyrocketed; between 1930 and 1932, circulation at libraries around the country jumped by 25–30 percent annually, though those averages were down to 14 percent by 1935 as libraries had fewer materials left for patrons (Herdman, 1943; Waples, Carnovsky, & Randall, 1933). The increased demand coupled with budget decreases left many libraries with decimated collections by the end of the Depression (Kramp, 1975/2010). The needs of patrons during the Depression also led to expansions of services for unemployed adults and of children's services, creating "a broader concept of community service" that continues to this day (Ennis & Fryden, 1960, p. 253). Yet a lack of funds drove libraries to stop buying materials and hiring new employees—a whole generation of library school graduates had to take jobs without pay simply to be able to work in their chosen fields (Shera, 1933). Subsequent recessions have increased demands for library services, though even in the best of economic times, libraries are a vital resource for individuals in economic distress (Berman, 1988; Nyquist, 1968).

The current prolonged downturn has been no exception. Libraries in communities with long-term economic difficulties typically have more limited resources for patrons (Constantino, 2005). Yet, between 2006 and 2008, the number of Americans with library cards increased by 5 percent, in-person library visits increased by 10 percent, and library website visits increased by 17 percent (Davis, 2009, 2011). "These increases in use translate into 25 million more in-person visits, 11 million more uses via computer, and about 4 million more uses by telephone" (Davis, 2009, p. 13). On average, circulation in libraries rose 5.6 percent between 2007 and 2008 alone (Hoffert, 2009). In 2009, more than 14 million people were considered regular users of library computers for Internet access (C. Hill, 2009). In individual libraries, the impacts can be overwhelming, with some systems seeing a 25-percent increase in visits in one year or a 500 percent increase in computer usage over a three-year period (N. M. Hill, 2009). In 2010, 50 percent of the computer users in Wichita public libraries were using them for job and career purposes and more than 10 percent were using the computers to apply for unemployment benefits (Urban Libraries Council, 2010).

The need for use of technology to access social services is particularly acute and an area in which digital inclusion and digital literacy support are often the most needed. In the United States, millions of people now rely on government-provided social services to meet basic needs: Medicaid (57.8 million people in 2006), food stamps (over 33 million in 2009), the Women, Infants and Children (WIC) program (9 million in 2009), Social Security's Supplemental Security Income (over 7 million in 2009), and many others (U.S. Centers for Medicare and Medicaid Services, n.d.; U.S. Office of Retirement and Disability Policy, 2009; U.S. Supplemental Nutritional Assistance Program, n.d.; U.S. Women, Infants and Children Program, n.d.). In addition to these federal services, each state provides a range of local services that cover health, family, employment, and other social services. With one in six Americans living in a household where there is difficulty feeding the members of that household and nearly half of older adults facing poverty, many Americans who have never previously applied for social services now find themselves seeking government support (Chen, 2010; Reuters, 2010). Most of these support services must now be applied for online, and a great many of the people applying for these services online lack the necessary digital literacy to apply successfully on their own (Bertot & Jaeger, 2012; Jaeger & Bertot, 2011; Sigler et al., 2012).

Along with a muddled policy and economic approach that serves to hinder digital literacy and digital inclusion, the policy approach to actively promoting digital literacy and digital inclusion in the United States is also contradictory and problematic. In an attempt to address the issues of the digital divide and create a more digitally inclusive infrastructure, several government agencies collaborated to create DigitalLiteracy.gov as an instructional website to "serve as a valuable resource to practitioners who are delivering digital literacy training and services in their communities" (DigitalLiteracy.gov, n.d.). In accordance with this statement, one of the main menu categories is entitled "Find Educator Tools." However, the lack of a clear audience creates some inconsistencies in the website's approach. While providing educational tools, materials, and guides for individuals and entities, such as libraries, that are attempting to bridge the digital divide, the site also attempts to speak directly to the have-nots of the digital world. An in-depth review of the site shows that the majority of the website appears to speak directly to those very people who do not have Internet or prefer not to go online. Within the Digital Literacy Initiative Fact Sheet, the push–pull complications of digital inclusion are perfectly represented by two sequenced bullet points:

- There are notable disparities between demographic groups: people with low incomes, disabilities, seniors, minorities, the less-educated, non-family households, and the non-employed tend to lag behind other groups in home broadband use.
- Although there is no single solution to closing the broadband adoption gap, increasing digital literacy skills among non-users is key to bringing them online and opening doors to opportunity.

Identifying underrepresented groups is absolutely necessary in order to target those in the most need of education, attention, and access. But not offering solutions, approaches, best practices, or other means to resolve the disparities (as seemingly evinced by the second bullet point) is problematic.

Additionally, devoting resources to an entire "Learn the Basics" section assumes that the people needing to gain digital literacy will somehow intuitively find the site if they manage to find Internet access. As a lack of government literacy is frequently tied to a lack of digital literacy, there are several flaws in this approach to the site (Jaeger & Thompson, 2003, 2004). A more fruitful approach would perhaps be to design the site's content with and for those community institutions (e.g., libraries and schools) that are best positioned to help meet the challenges of digital exclusion within their communities. Also, the "In the Community" section discusses online training and digital literacy resources for people with disabilities, yet the website suffers from a clear lack of accessibility for users with different disabilities. Adding to the missing facets of digital inclusion not addressed by DigitalLiteracy.gov is that it exists only in one language, yet language barriers are one of the three key drivers—along with income and education levels—of racial disparities in Internet access and usage in the United States (Chinn & Fairlie, 2007). These oversights are especially problematic, as persons with disabilities and non-

English-speaking persons are two of the groups facing the greatest barriers to digital inclusion (Jaeger, 2012; Livingston, 2010). These gaps in inclusion can have tremendous consequences for individuals on the wrong side of the gaps. For example, Latinos seek online health information at one-third the rate the white Americans do (Lorence, Park, & Fox, 2006).

Another institution attempting to define, address, and implement a viable plan for digital inclusion is the IMLS. As requested in the National Broadband Plan, IMLS created a Proposed Framework for Digitally Inclusive Communities (IMLS, 2011). IMLS defines the goals of digital literacy as falling within the following categories:

- All members understand the benefits of advanced information and communication technologies.
- All members have equitable and affordable access to high-speed Internet-connected devices and online content.
- All members can take advantage of the educational, economic, and social opportunities available through these technologies.

The IMLS framework identifies a total of 11 principles "for focusing efforts in the areas most important for making the entire community digitally inclusive now, for planning for the future, and for identifying areas where special effort will be required." Five of these principles are defined as "foundational principles," with the other six defined as "targeted principles." By initiating the five foundational principles, the remaining six targeted principles ostensibly will be achieved. While the framework is a more coherent approach to digital literacy and inclusion than that of DigitalLiteracy.gov and is mostly in line with the current administration's goals, it is not a plan that is mandated, enforceable, or funded (Jaeger, Bertot, Thompson, Katz, & DeCoster, 2012).

INTERNATIONAL APPROACHES TO POLICY

Although the United States has the longest engagement between government policy and issues of digital literacy and digital inclusion, most nations have had to deal with these issues as policy problems since the advent of the World Wide Web. At this point, issues of digital literacy and digital inclusion have become central to global economic competitiveness; without sufficient telecommunications infrastructure and digital literacy among the populace, an entire nation faces being excluded from much of international commerce (Ferro, Helbig, & Gil-Garcia, 2011). The ability of nations to use policy levers to promote digital inclusion and digital literacy, however, is contingent on a range of factors, from the composition and size of the population to established regulatory structures and level of government centralization to the geography of the nation. Each of these factors is a significant part of the equation.

Nations that have more centralized governments are usually more effective at implementing information policies, from openness and transparency to social media usage (Bertot, Jaeger, & Grimes, 2010, 2012; Bertot, Jaeger, & Hansen, 2012; Bertot, Jaeger, Munson, & Glaisyer, 2010; Jaeger & Bertot, 2010). South Korea's strong central government has been the key to its rapid adoption of broadband and spread of access and usage of the Internet among the population. Nations like Sweden and Finland have strong central governments and have used the growth of the Internet and the increasing number of government services available online as an opportunity to consolidate the centrality of the public library as a social institution by expanding the funding, resources, services, and access to government agencies in public libraries (Helling, 2012; Landoy & Zetterlund, 2013).

The same holds true for the ability to implement policies promoting digital inclusion and digital literacy and is a point of departure between the United States and many other highly industrialized nations. The United States has a federated national government with weak central authority on many issues, which makes the imposition of national standards of digital inclusion much harder than in countries with a heavily centralized government. Other major differences between the United States and most other highly industrialized nations include the vast geographic size and wide variation of topography of the United States, which creates substantial infrastructure challenges, and the enormously diverse population of the nation, which creates many additional issues of language and culture in promoting digital literacy and digital inclusion.

Several recent economic studies have shed light on the policy barriers to digital inclusion and digital literacy across nations. Internationally, per capita income level, the presence of regulations that promote private sector competition, and the extent of telecommunications infrastructure are the biggest determinant of the diffusion of Internet access and usage in a country (Chinn & Fairlie, 2007). The regulatory issue seems especially important. Countries—even those among the nations that the World Bank designates as low-income countries—with economic policies that promote private-sector competition, economic growth, and consumer choice have wider levels of diffusion of Internet access than nations that are similarly situated in economic terms (Dasgupta, Lall, & Wheeler, 2007). Policies that promote usage of the Internet have been successful internationally. Initial studies on users of technology in the United States, for example, show that low-income individuals who gain access spend more time online than users from higher income levels, and a majority of people who are currently digitally excluded and lacking digital literacy indicate that they would likely use the Internet extensively if given the opportunity (Goldfarb & Prince, 2008).

Several indexes have been developed to measure cross-national differences in digital inclusion and digital literacy. The Digital Opportunity Index (DOI) is relied upon by governments, telecommunications companies, and international organizations to gauge levels of ICT access and usage in countries. It is based on the data collected by the International Telecommunication Union (ITU) from these same groups that rely on the index. The higher the ranking, the more widespread the opportunities are for digital inclusion in the nation. South Korea, Japan, Denmark, Iceland, Singapore, the Netherlands, Taiwan, Hong Kong, and Sweden are the current top nine countries on the index. These countries that rank highest on the DOI tend to be countries that have high levels of per capita income and high levels of education, exist in a small geographic area, and have a homogenous population; in addition, most have a highly centralized national government. The ITU also provides the ICT Development Index (IDI) to benchmark the countries moving at the fastest rates of ICT development and implementation. The top nations on this list—South Korea, Sweden, Denmark, the Netherlands, Iceland, Norway, Luxemburg, Switzerland, and Finland—parallel many of the leading nations and their characteristics on the Digital Opportunity Index.

Another relevant measure, the Digital Inclusion Risk Index (DIRI), has been created using ITU by the international consulting firm Maplecroft. The DIRI measures just ICT indicators: access to computers, Internet access, broadband access, fixed line telephone infrastructure, wireless infrastructure, and the like. As the focus of the DIRI is on the nations where digital inclusion and digital literacy are most lacking, nations in Africa, South America, much of Asia, and Russia rank as having the highest risks for perpetuation of digital inequalities, while North America, Western Europe, and Australia are rated the areas of lowest risk. The DIRI also spotlights programs that are designed to alleviate digital inequalities. In the nations that rank as high or extreme risk, the majority of the programs are the work of either the private sector or international aid organizations, not of the governments.

In addition to the United States, two other nations that have engaged digital inclusion and digital literacy as broad policy issues are South Korea and the United Kingdom. South Korea, which is ranked no. 1 on both the DOI and the IDI, may have had the greatest success in fostering digital inclusion through government initiatives. South Korea embraced broadband early in its availability and has remained one of the leading nations in terms of broadband connectivity through national government initiatives that mandated near-ubiquitous access to top-level broadband speed across the nation, a sharp contrast to the U.S. government, which has merely been able to encourage diffuse access to low-end speed broadband (Mandel et al., 2010). The South Korean government also established the Korea Agency for Digital Opportunity and Promotion, a national agency devoted to promoting comprehensive digital literacy in the

South Korean population. This agency created education programs, outlets for access and training, online training sites and materials, research into closing the digital divide, and programs to distribute computers donated by members of the public and private sector groups to those without computers, among much else.

In the United Kingdom, the efforts have been closer to those of the United States. These parallels are not surprising; while the United Kingdom is much smaller than the United States, the population of the United Kingdom is more diverse and the form of government is more decentralized than that of South Korea. In 1999, not long after the United States created the NTIA, the government of the United Kingdom created the Office of the e-Envoy to shape the creation and usage of e-government in the nation. Part of this mission was the establishment of access points to e-government throughout the country and training programs for digital literacy. The national government has since commissioned several studies of digital exclusion across the nation and ways to foster digital inclusion. Echoing some of the problems encountered in the United States, the network of "UK Online Centres" that offer free public Internet access and assistance using the Internet were not all placed in areas where they would be needed, and a great many of the locations are not physically accessible to people with disabilities (Clear & Dennis, 2009).

It should be noted that not all countries that have tried public computing centers in communities have struggled, though, as the nations that have situated them in places that people would naturally congregate have had far more success. Government-sponsored information technology cafés have been successful in Sweden, as the computers were added to already existing cafés that had established clientele and roles in the community (Ferlander & Timms, 2006). The Sao Paulo, Brazil, government launched widely used computer centers focused on digital literacy and access to government services in established community spaces, such as fast food restaurants (Jacobi, 2006; Reinhard & Macadar, 2006; Sacchi, Giannini, Bochic, Reinhard, & Lopes, 2009).

Digital inclusion efforts have also been made at the lower levels of government in the United Kingdom. In Scotland, for example, the regional government began its own efforts in 2002 to create tools to aid members of the public in becoming digitally literate, from establishing new public access points to the Internet and mapping existing public access points to creating education programs and call centers for support. Other governmental initiatives in the United Kingdom include local governments creating their own public computing facilities and implementing digital literacy programs in public housing (Liff & Stewart, 2001; Newhome, Keeling, McGoldrick, Macaulay, & Doherty, 2008). Other programs have focused on bridging digital literacy and digital inclusion gaps in specific groups, such as trying to increase the participation of women online (Faulkner & Lie, 2007; Rommes, 2002).

Also paralleling the United States, other political choices by the government in the United Kingdom have inhibited some of the policy goals for digital literacy and digital inclusion. In the years that Margaret Thatcher was prime minister and the years since, the concept of providing free public access to information has grown more contentious in the United Kingdom. In the 1980s, for example, public libraries were attacked in the political discourse by some conservatives for the crime of "daring to order books in the name of the public" (Webster, 2005, p. 283). Extending to the area of Internet access, this political resistance to public goods has manifested prominently in the recent wave of privatization of public libraries and other places of public computer access. It demonstrates a trend of government moving away from taking a large interest in digital literacy and digital inclusion as policy objectives (Jerrard, Bolt, & Strege, 2012). A democratic government withdrawing from responsibilities related to digital access, literacy, and inclusion, however, is failing to support its own social institutions and its own democratic processes.

POLICIES AND INFORMATION WORLDS

As was described in chapter 1, the theory of information worlds is designed to provide a framework through which the multiple interactions among information, information behavior, and the many different social contexts within which they exist—from the micro (small worlds) to the meso (intermediaries) to the macro (the lifeworld)—can be understood and studied (Jaeger & Burnett, 2010). The theory argues that information behavior is shaped simultaneously by both immediate influences—such as friends, family, co-workers, and trusted information sources of the small worlds in which the individual lives—as well as larger social influences, including public sphere institutions, media, technology, and politics. These levels, though separate, do not function in isolation, and to ignore any level in examining information behavior results in an incomplete picture of the social contexts of the information. The theory of information worlds argues for the examination of information behavior in terms of the small worlds of everyday life, the mediating social institutions of the public sphere, the lifeworld of an entire society, and the hegemonic forces that shape the lifeworld. These social structures constantly interact with and reshape one another.

Policy decisions about information, information access and usage, freedom of expression, intellectual property, privacy, regulation of media, physical communication structures, and the support of education, research, and innovation all shape the parameters and the health of the public sphere in a society (Starr, 2004). The amount of information that is available to develop, articulate, and communicate opinions on social and political issues is key to democratic participation and to the functioning of the public sphere. "Public affairs in a democracy is, among other things, a stream of collective consciousness in which certain actions . . . come to be noticed and remembered. . . . They are observed by politically aware citizens trying to size up events in their environment" (Mayhew, 2000, p. 5).

In the terms of the theory of Information Worlds, the most important information value in a democracy is the broadly agreed-upon belief that open access to information is not only a virtue but also is a necessity if a democratic information world is to succeed. Such success depends on information behaviors that emphasize attention and action as a result of the information access—participation in democratic processes, community engagement, and civic activism. As a result, few policies related to information are more important than the promotion of digital inclusion and digital literacy to ensure that all members of the lifeworld can participate in the democracy.

As one of the largest influences on the lifeworld, the choices of governments have major impacts on information.

> The rules established by the government in relation to information are the most significant drivers of the amount of information available to a society and the ways in which that information can be accessed and exchanged, whether across the full lifeworld, or within or between individual small worlds. (Jaeger & Burnett, 2010, p. 121)

These choices can serve to promote information access and usage by the constituent small worlds within a lifeworld or to control and constrain access and usage. In the case of the United States, the array of national government policies related to digital literacy and digital inclusion serve variously to both promote and constrain digital literacy and digital inclusion in the lifeworld and in individual small worlds.

Although policy decisions related to information have an effect on the entire lifeworld, the policies related to digital inclusion and digital literacy are primarily aimed at changing the state of behavior in certain small worlds, those in which levels of access and usage are far more limited than the rest of the population. Thus, these policies tend to be about offering opportunities to and changing information behavior of specific small worlds that are on the wrong side of the digital divide. In some cases, the small worlds are currently digitally excluded due to lack of sufficient income to afford access or the infrastructure is not available where they live, with the policy interventions then focusing on providing access and training and connectivity. In other cases, the small worlds do not view digital literacy as an important or acceptable aspect of their information behavior, with the social norms, types, and values not finding value in the small world for Internet usage. In these cases, the policy interventions focus on educating the members of the small world about the importance of access and making them comfortable as users of the Internet.

The examples of the places in which members of the public will or will not use free public computers and Internet access encompass both of these cases. To the former issue, the success of Internet access points in cafés, mass transit stations, and restaurants that people already frequent in Sweden, Brazil, and Colombia—and the struggles with CTCs in the United States and UK Online Centres in the United Kingdom—demonstrate the importance of policies based on situating Internet access in places that are easy to access and part of the established patterns of the activities of small worlds in the communities. In terms of the latter issue, the widespread reliance on the public library as the provider and educator about the Internet for those with no access, limited access, or limited skills in the United States demonstrates the importance of policies embracing community institutions that are already trusted by small worlds that are socially marginalized. This point is reinforced beyond digital literacy and digital inclusion programs, as public libraries are increasingly used as the trusted community access point to reach disadvantaged small worlds with a range of social services related to unemployment, child welfare, immigration, homelessness, food insecurity, and other major life issues (Bertot, Jaeger, Gorham, Taylor, & Lincoln 2013; Gorham, Bertot, Jaeger, & Taylor, 2013; Taylor, Gorham, et al., in press; Taylor, Jaeger et al., 2014).

When a policy impacts a lifeworld, it also impacts the constituent small worlds and the ways in which they use information, ultimately affecting the public sphere. Public libraries in the United States, as central institutions of the public sphere, have been dramatically impacted by the policies intended to promote digital literacy and digital inclusion. These policies have greatly increased reliance on public libraries for the computer and Internet access, education, and support that underlie digital literacy and digital inclusion. The next chapter explores at length the interrelationships between digital literacy, digital inclusion, public policy, public libraries, and the other societal institutions that foster literacy and inclusion.

FIVE

Libraries as Institutions of Digital Literacy and Inclusion

This chapter examines libraries and the institutions that provide support for digital literacy and inclusion and the variety of services they offer. In the early 2000s, UNESCO partnered with IFLA to strongly recommend that public libraries be government supported through both funding and legislation to the fullest extent possible as a means to promote libraries as a principle intermediary to support information access and use (Gill, 2001). The IFLA/UNESCO alliance also recommends that libraries be organized and managed by members of the local communities they serve; in other words, local development and governance with national interest and support. The 2010 update of the *IFLA Public Library Service Guidelines* specifically calls on public libraries to help bridge the digital divide through provision of public-access ICT, basic computer instruction, and literacy efforts (Koontz & Gubbins, 2010). In a 2012 brief by Beyond Access (an international initiative directed by IFLA, the Bill & Melinda Gates Foundation, the Internet Society, and six other organizations supporting technology for social change), governments are again called upon to "officially recognize public libraries as preferred venues for public access to the Internet, establishing programs and partnerships to offer free Internet services through library branches," and to "include libraries in plans for ICT and broadband expansion, as well as digital inclusion policies" (Beyond Access, 2012, p. 4).

To underscore the idea of public library funding, the International Organization for Standardization (ISO) (2013) emphasizes the need for public libraries to be financed with public funds and offers additional characteristics of a public library, including the need to be open to the public and have basic services free of charge or available for a subsidized fee. These characteristics shape the idea of the public library and how it offers the best means of serving the community's physical, intellectual, and social needs. Nevertheless, the programs, approaches, and concerns about digital access, literacy, and inclusion found in American and other Western public libraries are not shared in all nations. In many countries where writing and literacy do not form an integral part of the native traditions, there has been no historically perceived need for libraries or librarians in the conventional sense. Likewise, additional political, social, and economic factors can have a strong influence on the "library culture" of a given nation or social grouping (Thompson & Adkins, 2012), which means that even if the country has brick-and-mortar libraries, these buildings and the resources housed therein may not be used or perhaps not used in the same way they are in other countries. In many places, public libraries that rely on government support are much less well funded, staffed, and maintained and open fewer hours than libraries with private funding (e.g., private schools and universities, special collections). In these countries, the library culture might be that libraries are exclusively for students and faculty belonging to a private academic community. In other places, the national culture may promote gender or age as requisite criteria for library use, such as male-only/female-only institutions, or a strong focus on promoting literacy skills for minors that makes the public library seem to be a place that caters mainly to the information needs of school-aged children.

As discussed in Chapter 1, the theory of Information Worlds describes the interrelationship of information flow, information behavior, and the social contexts of information between the micro level (small worlds), meso level (intermediaries), and macro level (the lifeworld). The intermediary is particularly important for facilitating the dissemination of information from the macro level to the micro level (small worlds). This chapter discusses the ways that the public library fulfills this roll, including the services and exemplary programs that address access and inclusion needs. As a way of framing the plethora of services, this chapter offers a case study of the services offered by American public libraries in terms of physical, intellectual, and social access. Later chapters discuss approaches used in other countries.

APPROACHES TO DIGITAL LITERACY AND INCLUSION

Countries around the world have reacted very differently to concerns of digital literacy, depending heavily on the existing cultural attitudes toward literacy and libraries as social institutions. Since the advent of the Web in more technologically advanced nations with an established system of libraries, public, school, academic, and government libraries around the world have all struggled with implementing the notions of digital literacy and inclusion. In the United States, libraries quickly embraced the role of digital information provider by means of public access computers and other technologies for accessing the information available through the Internet; however, providing sufficient levels of access has been a challenge, given the continually high levels of demand (Jaeger & Bertot, 2011; Jaeger, Bertot, Thompson, Katz, & DeCoster, 2012). Teaching people to use the technologies has also proven a significant challenge, as it requires an enormous amount of staff time, planning, and technology.

Still, librarians consider the implications of digital literacy and inclusion in the development of new programs and classes offered. School libraries, for example, have developed a range of programs and approaches to incorporating digital literacy into their instructional activities (e.g., Eisenberg & Berkowitz, 1999; Meneses & Momino 2010; Salvador, Rojas, & Susinos, 2010; Schloman & Gedeon, 2007; Subramaniam, Ahn, et al., 2013), as have libraries in institutions of higher education (e.g., Oakleaf & Kaske, 2009; Yakel, 2004). Some libraries have focused on providing digital literacy to specific underserved communities, such as rural patrons or adults (e.g., Boris, 2005; Cathcart, 2008; McLoughlin & Morris, 2004; Real, Bertot, & Jaeger, 2014). Programs have also been developed to promote digital literacy for particular new platforms of access—such as social networking sites—in all types of libraries (e.g., Brandtweiner, Donat, & Kerschbaum, 2012; Click & Petit, 2010; Luo, 2010). For many libraries, efforts to provide digital access, literacy, and inclusion have become the framework for all literacy efforts in the library (Mackey & Jacobsen, 2005, 2011).

The shift in library service to providing and supporting digital access, literacy, and inclusion has raised concerns for the practice of librarianship. For some in the profession, the proper roles of libraries in supporting digital access, literacy, and inclusion remain insufficiently examined questions, including whether libraries should be the institutions with the responsibility of supporting digital literacy, whether digital literacy gaps still even exist, and the ways in which literacy can be defined in a digital age (e.g., DaCosta, 2010; Buschman, 2009; Marcum, 2002; Pawley, 2003; Snavely & Cooper, 1997). Another significant challenge is determining the ways in which to measure digital literacy and assess the impacts libraries have on improving digital literacy and inclusion (Barzilai-Nahon, 2006; McCulley, 2009; Oakleaf, 2008).

While many of the advances in public libraries and librarianship in the United States have grown from similar advances in librarianship elsewhere in the world, there are differences in public library approaches, as is discussed in chapters 6 and 7. Despite these differences, American public librarianship has led the way internationally in many areas of public library practice, professionalism, theory, education, outreach, and advocacy (Lerner, 2009). This is due, in part, to the information-dependent democratic system upon which the country is established (Thompson, 2008). Both the political and religious foundations of the country were and continue to be dependent on an educated populace, and so the basic design of the modern American public library is based on cultural values of education and socialization. The original design of American public libraries was, of course, greatly influenced by early European libraries.

The library of the Western world in the late 19th and early 20th centuries was oriented toward improving the morality of the general public through book selection ("The best reading for the largest number at the least cost," known as the "library faith," as coined by Dewey), providing and encouraging the reading of "good" books in public libraries on the premise that "good" social behavior would naturally follow (Wiegand, 1999). These goals were already present in similar forms in other countries, most notably in the United Kingdom with the early passage of the Public Libraries Act of 1850, which emphasized universal education as a primary purpose of the new institution (Allred, 1972; Williamson, 2000). In the early 1900s, Carnegie libraries built in the United States and Canada were established as "the common man's university," and services to immigrants followed this type of philosophy of socialization, with public libraries targeting children as a means of indoctrinating them to the American experience (Larson, 2001).

However, by 1900, many city libraries had established a wide range of educational and cultural activities as a part of their regular operations, offering everything from tutoring for schoolchildren to classes teaching creative arts and practical skills for adults (Davies, 1974; DuMont, 1977). Simultaneously, libraries provided exhibits, lectures, and meeting spaces for community groups of all types and began to develop services to reach their users across multiple community groups—such as reference services, children's services, and adult education services (DuMont, 1977). Further, libraries were also starting to model practices to improve life in communities. In cities, libraries were often among the first public institutions to adopt modern technologies and approaches for lighting, ventilation, and reducing the spread of disease (Musman, 1993). The collection of diverse resources, representing minority viewpoints and alternative perspectives on current or historical events, was not common in early modern libraries; however, World War I and events leading up to it changed this by increased migration between countries, leading to heightened public awareness of and demand for varying perspectives on world political and social actions (Wiegand, 1989).

By the 1930s, public libraries more firmly began to turn away from their previous roles as agents of social control. Numerous factors affected this reorientation, but a key change was the effect fascist governments were having on public access to information in many parts of the world in the late 1930s, specifically through lethal suppression of expression, closing of libraries, and public book burnings (Gellar, 1984; Robbins,

1996; Stielow, 2001). Many libraries had begun to take on a social service mission in the early 1930s, a change appearing earliest in public libraries in urban settings, where working with largely immigrant patron populations meant that active engagement with multiple community groups became part of libraries' daily activities (Fiske, 1959; Heckart, 1991). This dramatic change in social roles "emerged in an environment in which the concept of the public library's social responsibility was itself changing radically" (Gellar, 1974, p. 1367).

In reaction to these global events and local demographic changes, the ALA passed its Library Bill of Rights in 1939 and began the swing toward the modern ideal of the public library as society's marketplace of ideas (Berninghausen, 1953; Gellar, 1984; Robbins, 1996). The document proclaims that "a responsibility of library service" is that all "reading matter selected should be chosen for values of interest, information, and enlightenment" of the entire community and that "in no case should any book be excluded because of the race or nationality, or the political or religious views of the writer." The Bill of Rights opposed censorship and advocated for the library as a social space open to "all groups in the community regardless of the beliefs and affiliations of their members." A central component of this new stance was the unswerving assertion that voters must have access to a full range of perspectives on all significant political and social issues (Samek, 2001). Public libraries actively participated in voter registration and participation drives to increase voter turnout in the 1952 presidential election, firmly establishing the modern concept of the public library as a reliable "community source for serious, nonpartisan information on a central issue of the day" (Preer, 2008, p. 19).

Although public libraries in many places offered services to diverse groups, the 1979 Public Library Association (PLA) mission statement provided the first mention of outreach, the statement declaring that libraries should embrace the "multicultural heritage of their communities in nontraditional ways." This led to the proliferation of bookmobiles and home library service and additional, innovative services to meet the needs of their diversifying communities. It is upon these foundations that public library roles grew, leading to the current situation in which libraries provide a broad range of services, including mobile services, accessible materials, community meeting spaces, digital and information literacy training, and advocacy for intellectual freedom and other social issues.

In the United States, public libraries often work with government agencies, community groups, and businesses to address patron and community needs, with programs addressing a range of needs (Bertot, Jaeger, & Greene, 2013; Sigler et al., 2012). School libraries often work with public, academic, or special libraries and other information organizations to promote literacy in children and young adults (and even in their parents) through reading programs, after-school programs, portable collections, and representation at community-wide events. The evolution and growth in services offered by libraries both alone and in collaboration with other public organizations has continued with the advancement of digital technology, and the library has become one of the primary institutions of digital literacy and inclusion in American communities. Indeed, the trust that libraries have established with the public makes them an ideal intermediary in the spread of digital technology and information to various small worlds (Jaeger & Burnett, 2005; Jaeger & Fleischmann, 2007). The rest of this chapter discusses the intermediary roles that public libraries in the United States assume with regard to physical, intellectual, and social access to digital tools and information.

LIBRARIES AS INTERMEDIARIES OF PHYSICAL ACCESS

In terms of the physical access that supports digital literacy and inclusion, the most ubiquitous service that the American public library offers is the provision of computers, printers, and other hardware, as well as broadband Internet access. For example, despite the cuts in funding over the past four years, public libraries in the United States have managed to increase the average number of workstations they offer (14.2 in 2010, 16 in 2011, and 16.4 in 2012), increase the percentage of libraries offering broadband (from 76.4 percent in 2009 to 88.5 percent in 2012), and improve the quality of Internet access (connection speeds of greater than 1.5 Mbps increased from 27.5 percent to 69.7 percent between 2008 and 2012) (Bertot, Gorham, Jaeger, & Taylor, 2012; Bertot, McDermott, et al., 2012). Public libraries have also begun to provide access to new technological hardware, such as mobile devices and e-readers (in 2012, 49 percent and 39.1 percent respectively) (Bertot, Gorham, et al., 2012; Bertot, McDermott, et al., 2012).

A diverse population of patrons uses these libraries' digital services, including regular users from each socioeconomic stratum (Zickuhr, Rainie, & Purcell, 2013); however, low-income users often have few choices for physical access besides the public library. For nearly two-thirds of communities in America (62.1 percent in 2012), libraries are the only provider of free public computer and Internet access (Bertot, McDermott, et al., 2012), which means they may be one of the only resources serving Americans earning less than $75,000 per year, who are significantly less likely than their wealthier counterparts to own such devices as desktop and laptop computers, e-book readers, and tablets (Jansen, 2010). Even as smartphone ownership and use rises among lower-income Americans (A. Smith, 2012), the Internet requirements of government information (e.g., complicated forms), filling out employment applications, completing homework assignments, large amounts of reading for any reason, and the interactivity of many websites make smartphones a rather poor alternative to more traditional Internet devices.

As Powell, Byrne, and Dailey (2010) describe, these users "want to be online . . . and most importantly need to be online in order to maintain basic social and economic participation" (p. 164), only they often lack the means to do so outside of a community institution. Without public library services, many of these users would have trouble performing such essential tasks as filing taxes, filling out job applications, and registering their children for school. Additionally, homework increasingly requires a computer, which helps explain why 61 percent of young people (14–24 year olds) who are part of households living below the federal poverty line were users of public library computers and the Internet as of 2009 (Becker et al., 2010, p. 2).

Aside from serving those who cannot afford equipment or devices, the libraries also fill in gaps for those digitally excluded by nature of geography. "With the exception of literacy, no factor has greater influence on the provision of library services than density of population" (Borchardt & Horacek, 1975, p. 3). Rural areas often have slower Internet speeds and gaps in mobile service (Whitacre, Gallardo, & Strover, 2013). While the funding provided by the ARRA of 2009 (discussed in chapter 4) has worked to close this gap in the United States, public libraries still offer many Americans living in rural areas their only source of high-speed Internet; for example, in a 2011 study of 44 rural libraries in Tennessee, information technology access was identified as patrons' most critical information need (Mehra, Black, Singh, & Nolt, 2011).

Libraries also provide accessible technology. Considering the fact that Americans with disabilities are significantly less likely to go online than adults without disabilities (54 percent compared to 81 percent according to 2011 data) and are almost 30 percent less likely to have broadband Internet at home (Zickuhr & Smith, 2012), the services libraries provide to these populations are indispensable to helping this population access essential life information that is increasingly only available online (e.g., government documents, communication tools). The assistive technology that libraries provide, such as screen readers, along with large-print book collections, audio books, and other media formats, allows patrons with disabilities the access to materials they might otherwise be denied.

In the United States, public libraries have begun to dedicate specific divisions to populations with disabilities, such as the District of Columbia Public Library system's adaptive services division, which provides a variety of resources to the deaf community, visually impaired patrons, older adults, and veterans, and hosts events like the "Accessibility Hackathon" that "bring[s] together young adults with disabilities, and companies that develop accessibility solutions, to provide mentorship and create new adaptive technology solutions" (District of Columbia Public Library, 2013). School libraries also are increasingly embracing a universal design for learning, introducing a broader range of media formats into collections and tailoring the library space to better accommodate those with physical disabilities (Blue & Pace, 2011; Subramaniam, Oxley, & Kodama, 2013).

LIBRARIES AS INTERMEDIARIES OF INTELLECTUAL ACCESS

The intellectual skills needed to use technological devices and the Internet are essential to successfully access the physical components of digital life mentioned in the previous section (Jaeger, Bertot, Thompson, Katz, & DeCoster, 2012). Providing assistance with complex information is a role for which public librarians have specific training and skills (Heanue, 2001). Librarians are meeting these needs in many ways, including assisting patrons with language and information literacy, teaching digital skills that can meet both personal and professional needs, helping patrons navigate e-government, and assisting patrons who need help finding employment.

Language literacy, both in terms of English language and basic reading skills, is one of the oldest functions of the public library (Kramp, 1975/ 2010; Reith, 1984). This educational focus continues today with resources in American public libraries for English-language learners (Gorham et al., 2013), programs promoting adult literacy (Kong, 2013), and early language development skill courses for young patrons (Herb & Willoughby- Herb, 2001). These programs help populations who might struggle with digital technology because of a lack of basic literacy skills, including adults who struggle with reading, immigrant and migrant populations, and young people who might have limited exposure to books and other educational materials. Public librarians also help users evaluate information and navigate different sources, especially important in the digital age with the vast array of sources now available. Libraries continue this literacy education by providing assistance, programs, and classes to teach digital skills. As of 2011–2012, 87 percent of American public libraries offer general computer skill classes; 86.5 percent offer general Internet use classes; 75.6 percent offer general online and Web searching classes; 73.3 percent offer general software use; 49.2 percent offer accessing online job-seeking and career-related information classes; and 39.4 percent offer social media classes (Bertot, Gorham, et al., 2012; Bertot, McDermott, et al., 2012).

These literacies are all important to navigating the everyday information that is now online. As mentioned previously, e-government is an area that is now forcing many Americans to complete legally required tasks online, such as paying taxes, filling out forms, and applying for social services. Although the U.S. government believed this digital information would enable a "government-to-citizen" information flow when e-government was first conceived, it quickly became apparent that there is a strong need for intermediaries to help citizens access, navigate, and understand e-government (Taylor, Gorham, Jaeger, & Bertot, 2014; Taylor, Jaeger, McDermott, Kodama, & Bertot, 2012; Taylor, Jaeger, et al., in press). Public libraries quickly became the primary community institution used to address this gap (Jaeger & Bertot, 2009, 2011). In 2011–2012, 96.6 percent of American public libraries provided assistance to patrons applying for or accessing e-government services (Bertot, Gorham, et al., 2012; Bertot, McDermott, et al., 2012) and have implemented programs that offer a wide range of e-government assistance. In Florida, for example, Alachua County has established a shared space with several local government agencies, so while helping patrons with online social service forms and applications, the government agencies requiring these documents are nearby if needed (Blumenstein, 2009; Taylor, Jaeger et al., in press). Many public libraries provide space for outside organizations to use in providing e-government expertise. For example, it is common for libraries to offer space for volunteers serving the Internal Revenue Service Volunteer Income Tax Assistance (VITA) program, which serves Americans making less than $51,000 a year.

Employment and job skills are other essential means of intellectual access. Along with the changes in the types of jobs offered in the new 21st-century economy and the need for new skills (Sigler et al., 2012; Taylor et al., 2012), employers are increasingly moving all job advertisements, descriptions, and applications online. In the United States, public libraries provide physical access to job-related materials in a number of ways: 92.2 percent in 2011–2012 provide access to jobs databases and other job opportunity resources, 77.1 percent provide access to civil service examination materials, and 83.1 percent provide software and other resources to assist patrons create resumes and employment material (Bertot, Gorham, et al., 2012; Bertot, McDermott, et al., 2012). Additionally, 76 percent also provide intellectual access by assisting patrons completing online job applications. Librarians also run programs and divisions that assist patrons with questions about small business (Collins, 2012); teach patrons new, job-related skills (Roy, Bolfing, & Brzozowski, 2010); and help patrons write resumes (Bertot, McDermott et al., 2012). These services not only help patrons with very real intellectual needs but also contribute to growing the new economy by training Americans in new skills they otherwise would lack (Taylor et al., 2012).

LIBRARIES AS INTERMEDIARIES OF SOCIAL ACCESS

In addition to physical and intellectual access, the public library also operates as a place of social inclusion. The physical library space reveals much about the values of a community (Buschman, 2012; Buschman & Leckie, 2007; Durrance & Fisher, 2005; Leckie, 2004; Leckie & Hopkins, 2002). The library operates as a public space, fulfilling most of the characteristics that Oldenburg (1991) identifies as essential to successful third places, including a lack of cost, being accessible to many, having a welcoming environment, and inviting a diversity of people. While budget cuts suggest many policymakers question the necessity of the physical public library in the age of the Internet, libraries continue to serve their communities by offering in-person trainings, maker spaces, and community meeting rooms. Having this type of community-oriented gathering place is especially important for people who might otherwise have limited options for socialization and the social exchange of information. Libraries are serving such groups as immigrants and the homeless, as well as many other disadvantaged groups.

Public library services help connect immigrants and community newcomers to local services, as well as with important legal and governmental processes like permanent residency and naturalization (Gorham et al., 2013; Kennan, Lloyd, Qayyum, & Thompson, 2011; Lloyd, Kennan, Thompson, Qayyum, 2013; U.S. Citizenship and Immigration Services, 2006). They also provide a much-needed space for forming social connections and social capital in a new community (Caidi & Allard, 2005). The types of programs directed toward immigrants, particularly emphasized in urban libraries in North America, Western Europe, and Australia (Lerner, 2009), are good examples of services encompassing multiple types of access. For example, the American Place program at the Hartford Public Library in Hartford, Connecticut, combines literacy classes, community and multicultural resources featured on its website, and citizenship information to create a robust service for immigrants in the area (Poland & Naficy, 2012).

Other programs use technology and digital inclusion to provide social access for very specific local needs. The "Baltimarket" was a recent collaboration among the Baltimore City Enoch Pratt Free Library System, the Baltimore City Health Department, and Santoni's Super Market, which provided Baltimore residents currently living in underserved "food deserts" access to fresh and healthy foods. Through Baltimarket, residents could order groceries online at their local library branch and then collect their food on a designated pickup day (Taylor, Gorham, Jaeger, & Bertot, 2014). Public libraries in San Francisco have social workers to assist recovering drug addicts. The public libraries of the Pima County Public Library of Tucson, Arizona, have public health nurses in the libraries; these nurses provide free basic health care, answer health questions that patrons have, and help them navigate the social services structures (Kim, 2013). In all of these cases, technology and digital inclusion programs are central to creating and providing unique collaborative community services that would not otherwise support the social access to information of members of disadvantaged groups in their communities.

SUSTAINING DIGITAL ACCESS, LITERACY, AND INCLUSION IN LIBRARIES

Libraries are clearly important providers of digital inclusion and literacy in the United States, fostering and sustaining physical, intellectual, and social access for members of their communities. This does not mean, however, that there are not significant challenges to this service provision. As outlined in the preceding chapter, policy decisions strongly affect the types of services libraries can provide. Budget cuts are particularly damaging to services, with many libraries struggling to provide adequate workspaces, assistance, and other materials (ALA, 2012). Budget cuts such as those detailed in chapter 4 clearly have large impacts on the ability of libraries to support digital literacy, even beyond issues of how many hours a week the library will be open.

For example, stemming from persistent staff shortages and a lack of funding, rural libraries in the United States offer fewer formal technology classes and slower Internet connection speeds than their urban and suburban counterparts, despite the critical needs of their patron base (Bertot, McDermott, et al., 2012; Flatley & Wyman, 2009). Funding cuts also fail to take into account the increased roles that libraries now have, such as e-government provision. Governments expect libraries to provide customer service for their products without funding additional staff or training (Bertot, Jaeger, Langa, et al., 2006a, 2006b). Examples of this type of have been seen numerous times in the United States, perhaps most notably with the case of Medicare Part D in Florida, where there was a sudden influx of older adults to the public library attempting to fill out the newly required online applications; librarians had no advance notice about the change so had to scramble to learn the intricacies of the new policy (Jaeger, 2008). Although partnerships between agencies and libraries are a good first step to bridging this information gap, a better understanding on behalf of governments of what services public libraries provide (and what information they need) will be necessary before librarians can adequately prepare for the needs of their patrons.

Public libraries also face the threat of privatization, the bidding out of government responsibilities to private-sector companies to perform librarian functions and provide library services, presumably at lower cost. Some public libraries in the United States, as well as in other countries, that have embraced this philosophy of governance have faced the prospect of being privatized by their local governments as early as the mid-1990s. For example, the Riverside County public library system in California, serving more than 1,000,000 residents, was privatized in 1997, while the same year the residents of Jersey City, New Jersey, protested to prevent the privatization of their library system (Hanley, 1998). The ALA recently published a book called *Privatizing Libraries* (Jerrard, Bolt, & Strege, 2012), which—not surprisingly—begins by stating the strong opposition of the ALA to privatization.

Libraries also must continually work to reach users who do not have experience with library services. Building trust and knowledge of library services among nonusers can be particularly difficult. Librarians themselves have significant work to do in this area, as there are still criticisms of inclusion policies over perceptions that such policies negatively define certain groups and prejudices against certain patrons (Gehner, 2010; Muggleton, 2013).

Although public libraries in the United States have been the main focus of this chapter, institutions in other countries do share some of the same opportunities and challenges. For example, a Dutch study found that many users struggled with operational, formal, information-related, and strategic Internet tasks when given governmental Internet assignments (van Deursen & van Dijk, 2009), echoing the environment of e-government in the United States. However, the U.S. cases also exemplify how different types of infrastructure and cultural contexts affect institutions that provide digital inclusion and digital literacy. The next two chapters focus in detail on the development of policies and programs from around the world related to digital access, literacy, and inclusion, highlighting these differences.

SIX

Models of Digital Inclusion

South Korea, the Netherlands, and Australia

As stated in chapter 2, the discussion of digital inclusion and digital literacy centers on outreach efforts as a means to empower underserved populations through provision of access to digital information, allowing individuals to engage physically, intellectually, and socially in the micro-, meso-, and macro-information world. The following section provides a selection of international case studies that highlight a range of services, collaborations, and policies evident in countries around the world. The purpose of the next two chapters is to provide a snapshot of what is being done in countries outside the United States to promote and support digital inclusion. The case studies identify exemplary practices as well as shortcomings in policies and practices that bear avoidance as future policies and practices are enacted. Understanding services, collaborations, and policies from around the world will benefit practitioners from any country. For example, for practitioners in the United States, understanding digital policy and practices on an international scale will help them to be better equipped to serve international users who arrive in American public libraries. Knowing the infrastructure and expectations for service that this user may bring with him or her from his or her home country will allow greater understanding and common ground for dialogue between the public library staff and the immigrant user.

Factors such as national literacy rates, population density and urbanization, political priorities, economic parities and disparities, social structures, educational support, and national infrastructure all play a part in determining the types of libraries and library services offered in a country. The historical and institutional contexts frame the digital services that libraries and other institutions provide as they work to include diverse populations. Societies without public library services offer other nonlibrary public-access computer resources, mobile devices, and home Internet services and fill many of the gaps to digital information and service in these countries that public libraries fill in countries that have strong national library infrastructures. As the discussion makes clear, however, public libraries remain the ideal place to foster digital inclusion, as they can offer not only physical access to ICTs but also the training and support needed for intellectual access and the local cultural insight needed for social access.

Each case study below begins with a brief overview of the demographics and political structures of the selected country followed by a description of public policies that explicitly focus on digital inclusion efforts, as well as a sample of library-focused efforts aimed at providing physical, intellectual, and social access to digital resources for public use, when identifiable as such. In an attempt to offer as much diversity as possible with a limited number of cases, countries have been selected from Central (Honduras) and South America (Colombia), Europe (the Netherlands), Asia (South Korea), Africa (Ghana), and Oceania (Australia). These examples in no way represent the whole of these regions, just as the overview of United States public library services and related policies discussed throughout this book does not have direct bearing on the services of Canada and Mexico.

In addition, the services provided in one city or with a single outreach program likewise do not provide a complete picture of library services in a given country, state, or community. Instead, the countries and programs selected for the case studies that follow have been chosen because they provide useful examples of approaches that are being implemented around the world that support physical, intellectual, and social access. The case studies are not meant to be comprehensive, but rather these brief country profiles are intended to be used for comparative purposes, providing a view of several different models of service and policy that have been created and are currently employed worldwide. Historical and infrastructural information is included to provide context for a summary of today's services and policies. The selection is largely limited to those for which the authors could find reference material in English or Spanish, which is a limiting factor. For further information, interested readers can consult the original texts cited throughout this book.

Although this book avoids using the labels of *developed* and *developing* nation, examples are provided from countries across the spectrum of economic stability and standards of living using the UN Human Development Index. This index—which charts health (life expectancy at birth), education (both mean years of schooling and expected years of schooling), and living standards (gross national income per capita)—enabled the identification of countries with very high, high, and medium human development ranks. Twenty-four countries are identified as low in human development rank. These countries were explored for possible case studies but too little information was available regarding the digital services and information policies in place to be able to provide a useful description of the services and policies offered there.

These countries appear across the range of the ITU's IDI, as noted in Table 6.1. As discussed in Chapter 4, the IDI measures ICT readiness (i.e., networked infrastructure and physical ICT access), ICT intensity (i.e., level of ICT use and skill), and ICT impact (i.e., outcomes of ICT use). The objective of the IDI is to measure the ICT development of countries over time in relation to other countries, and so the 155 countries evaluated are ranked in relationship to each other. The focus on skills and outcomes of the IDI makes this instrument more useful than a simple count of Internet penetration.

Table 6.1. Case-study country comparison chart

Nation	ITU ICT Dist. Index (IDI) Rank in 2011 (ITU, 2013)	Internet penetration 2012: % of people using Internet (ITU, 2012)	UN e-Gov't Dev. Index (UN, 2012)	UN Int'l Human Dev. Index rank in 2012 (UN, 2013)	GDP per capita 2012 in USD (World Bank, 2013b)	Gov't (CIA, 2013)	Population	Languages (CIA, 2013)	Urban-ization % (CIA, 2013)	Median age (CIA, 2013)
South Korea	1	84.10	1	12 (Very high)	$22,590	Republic	50,004,441 (Statistics Korea, 2012)	Korean, English widely taught in secondary school	83.2	39.7
The Neth.	6	93.00	2	4 (Very high)	$46,054	Constitutional monarchy	16,788,119 (Statistics Netherlands, 2013)	Dutch (official), Frisian (official); English commonly studied	83	41.8
United States	15	81.03	3	3 (Very high)	$49,965	Constitution-based federal republic; strong democratic tradition	316,655,430 (U.S. Census Bureau, 2013)	English 82.1, Spanish 10.7, other 7.2	82	37.2
Australia	21	82.35	12	2 (Very high)	$67,036	Federal parlia-	23,179,419 (Australia	English	89	38.1

						...mentary democracy and Common-wealth realm	...Bureau of Statistics, 2013)			
Colombia	80	48.98	43	91 (High)	$7,752	Republic; executive branch dominates government structure	45,745,783 (CIA, 2013)	Spanish (official)	75	28.6
Honduras	107	18.12	117	120 (Med.)	$2,264	Democratic constitutional republic	8,448,465 (CIA, 2013)	Spanish (official), Amerindian dialects	52	21.6
Ghana	117	17.11	145	135 (Med.)	$1,605	Constitutional democracy	25,199,609 (CIA, 2013)	English (official), 9 addit'l gov't-supported languages	51.9	20.7

Additionally, the countries have been selected with variation in size of population and demographic distribution, cultural history, and primary and official languages to try to be as representative as possible while remaining brief with this small selection of case studies. The countries vary in democratic processes, including one constitutional monarchy (the Netherlands), one constitutional democracy (Ghana), one commonwealth realm (Australia), and three republics with variations in size and economic and political development (South Korea, Colombia, and Honduras).

For purposes of chapter organization, chapter 6 provides an overview of three countries (Australia, the Netherlands, and South Korea) ranked "very high" on the UN Human Development Index. These countries have Internet penetration rates similar to the United States and longer histories of public policy related to digital services but have taken quite different paths to provide physical, intellectual, and social information access. Chapter 7 examines one country with "high" human development (Colombia) and two "medium"-ranked countries (Honduras and Ghana). Additional demographic information is included in Table 6.1. Data from the United States are included in this table for comparative purposes.

SOUTH KOREA

The case studies begin with the Republic of Korea (also known as South Korea) because of this country's first-place ranking on both the ITU measures of digital opportunity and inclusion (International Telecommunications Union, 2012) and the UN's e-governance survey (United Nations, 2013). Korea is Asia's fourth-largest economy (following China, India, and Japan) (World Bank, 2013c) and is a peninsula that shares a land border with the Democratic People's Republic of Korea (North Korea) to the north and is otherwise surrounded by the Yellow Sea, East China Sea, and Sea of Japan to the west, south, and east, respectively. As of 2012, the population of Korea was approximately 50 million (Statistics Korea, 2012), with 83.2 percent of these inhabitants living in urban settings (Central Intelligence Agency, 2013) and nearly one in five Koreans living in the capital city of Seoul (Korea Tourism Organization, 2013). There is good support for education in Korea; the government allots 7.6 percent of South Korea's gross domestic product (GDP) to education, "the second-highest percent of GDP spent on education among [Organisation for Economic Co-operation and Development] countries" (National Center on Education and the Economy, 2012b). Literacy is approximately 98 percent (Central Intelligence Agency, 2013), and Internet penetration country-wide is at 84.1 percent (International Telecommunications Union, 2013).

The Korean language is written in a phonetic script, Hangul, a language that is widely used only in South Korea, North Korea, and a limited area of China that borders North Korea. In fact, only 0.4 percent of all Web content is delivered in Korean (W3Tech, 2013). With 55.5 percent of all website content delivered in English (W3Tech, 2013) and the otherwise strong role English plays in global politics, economics, education, and the global society (Green, Fangqing, Cochrane, Dyson, & Paun, 2012; Phillipson, 1992, 2009; Thompson, 2003), English has become an important language in South Korean society and is included in the core curriculum for primary and secondary schools. The National School Curriculum reads:

> Due to the development of information technology, a move towards a knowledge and information-based society requires all components of society, from individuals to government policies, to be able to understand and communicate knowledge and information. . . . For elementary and secondary school students who must live in the future, the ability to communicate in English is an essential skill that they must learn at school. (National Curriculum Information Center, 2013, p. 41)

It should be understood that English is not taught as a "language of identity" but rather is used as a "language of communication" (House, 2003), a foreign language skill included in the curriculum because of its import for career building in Korea (Park, 2008).

South Korea is included among the "Group of 20" major economies of the world (G20, 2013) but is also a resource-poor country, meaning it cannot support its own population solely using the agriculture and other resources available within its own borders, which creates dependency on industrialization and "outward-oriented policy" (Auty, 2001, p. 841). This industrialization has resulted in South Korea's strength in electronics and telecommunications development and production, automobile and shipbuilding, and chemicals and steel industries (G20, 2013). Samsung and LG, two Korea-based multinational conglomerate electronics corporations, are well known worldwide for their innovative telecommunications technologies, for being "fast followers" of ICT trends, and for developing devices that respond to market demands (Jaruzelski, Loehr, & Holman, 2012, p. 4).

Korea has worked to incorporate information technology into the business of government since the 1960s. In 1967, under then-president Park Chung-Hee, computers were assigned to each ministry in the government by the newly formed Committee on Coordination for Development of Computerized Organization established under the Ministry of Science and Technology. These early computers were used to automate personnel services such as payroll, calculate phone bills, and aid with other computational tasks. The noted efficiency and reduction in errors encouraged government officials to look for more ways to automate and later to computerize—or informationalize—government services using the latest technologies. Every president since Park has maintained this focus on incorporating ICT into Korean government and social services (J. Kim, 2011). Telecommunications is acknowledged as the backbone of Korea's economic development (Ro, 2002), and policymakers have been clearly enthusiastic about advancing informatization in Korea at the federal level.

The National Information Society Agency (NIA) and the Ministry of Information and Communication (MIC) are the two political agencies in South Korea with the authority to create policy for the national information infrastructure, although the newly created (as of January 2013) Ministry of Future Creative Science has been touted as a "super ministry" that may oversee "almost everything in the fields of natural and applied science, research and information technology" (Ministry of Future Creative Science, 2013). As noted in chapter 4, the Korea Agency for Digital Opportunity and Promotion created and marketed digital literacy efforts throughout Korea in the 1990s and early 2000s. This agency has since merged with the NIA.

Digital Inclusion Policies and Initiatives

Korean policy and initiatives are consistent in their focus not only on building the information infrastructure throughout the whole of Korea (physical access) but also to providing digital literacy training (intellectual access) and socializing the Korean people to the digital age (social access). Dozens of policies and initiatives have created an exemplary infrastructure and system of public and private digital services and networks. Some of the key policies and initiatives in South Korea have included:

- National Basic Information System Project (1986): Supported strategic distribution of ICT systems nationwide
- Korea Information Infrastructure Initiative (1995): Laid the fiber-optic network to support a government–industry partnership
- Informatization Promotion Act (1995) and the Master Plan for Informatization Promotion (1996): Provided the legal basis for implementing the informatization agenda and focused on infrastructure for a knowledge society
- Love PC Donation Program (1997): Coordinated, at the national level, donations of secondhand personal computers (PCs) to low-income individuals
- Cyber Korea 21 (1999): Provided support for computers in schools, e-commerce in traditional industries, and an electronic document distribution system for administrative bodies
- The Digital Divide Act (2001): Extended the scope of public interest specifically to include disadvantaged groups in South Korea

- e-Korea Vision 2006 Master Plan (2002): Increased online public services, with a focus on transparency in government and international cooperation; promoted the informatization of industry
- u-Korea Master Plan (2006): Provided a strategy to encourage ubiquitous and universal services in government, industry, technology, and society; infrastructural support for broadband and mobile services
- Smart Korea Master Plan (2010): Focused on information technology convergence and enhancement of innovative ICTs such as smartphones
- Giga Korea Master Plan (2013): Integrates ICT policy in relation to content, platform, network, and device

The National Basic Information System Project (1986) is the first policy that specifically provided support for computers in schools, adding a very early layer of digital literacy training and socialization of ICTs to the 1970s and early 1980s' focus on spreading physical access to technology. Although the basic building blocks for Internet networks were established in South Korea as early as 1982, the Internet was not available to the public in South Korea until 1997 (Chon, Park, Kang, & Lee, 2005). Korean policy shows tremendous foresight in terms of establishing foundations for digital inclusion. Strategic planning has guided South Korea from computerization to digitization and beyond. The plans for CyberKorea, then e-Korea, u-Korea, Smart Korea, and now Giga Korea include increasing levels of citizen participation in government, a focus on bidirectional communication of information, and user-centered services.

Notwithstanding the longevity of Korean attention to physical, intellectual, and social access to digital technology on a national scale, Korea has not been exempt from the effects of digital divides and digital exclusion. The Digital Divide Act (2001, revised in 2006) is very specific in its discussion of underserved groups in the country, specifically describing the disadvantaged as "low income people, people with disabilities, senior people, people living in rural and remote areas, and housewives, etc." (Kang, 2009). Efforts to improve digital inclusion to underserved groups can be seen in policies such as the Government Performance and Results Act of 2006, in which Web accessibility is specifically mandated for e-Government websites, and the Anti-Discrimination against and Remedies for Persons with Disabilities Act of 2007, which establishes information access rights and provides reasonable accommodation legislation for ICT. However, divides still exist, with users in rural settings being found to have lower digital literacy levels and less access to ICTs than individuals in urban settings (Yang, Park, Yoon, & Kim, 2010), and digital inclusion of individuals with disabilities in South Korea is much lower than that of other very high human development countries such as the United States and the United Kingdom (Doh & Stough, 2010). One 2010 article discussing the differences in Internet access and use in South Korea confirms that blue-collar workers and homemakers still have the lowest rates of Internet use in South Korea (Kim & Jeong, 2010). These issues reinforce the argument that digital inclusion is a complex phenomenon that requires serious consideration at micro, meso, and macro levels.

Library Services for Digital Inclusion

Even with high rates of personal connectivity via mobile technologies and wide distribution of home ICT ownership, libraries are still common in Korea. In 2011 USD$493 million was allocated by the Ministry of Culture, Sports and Tourism for the "opening of 66 public libraries and 114 small libraries" (Y. M. Kim, 2011), adding to the 600 public libraries accounted for in the 2008 Library Yearbook and the 3,951 "small libraries," or minimalist libraries placed in shopping malls and other commercial and public venues that provide collections of educational and cultural books, as well as reading classes and cultural programs that have been placed around the country through an initiative sponsored by the government in conjunction with the private sector (Kim, 2006; Lee, 2013; Sohn, 2013). While precise data are not available, according to the IFLA World Report 2010, more than 81 percent of public, academic, school, and special libraries in South Korea provide users with free access to the Internet.

Librarians in South Korea began incorporating information technology into information service in the 1990s. For example, legislation as early as the 1991 Library Promotion Act took such measures as to change school libraries into school media centers and "the roles of teacher-librarians . . . turned into those of media specialists who have professional knowledge and qualifications on instructional media, not to mention printed resources" (Hahm, Lee, Song, & Park, 1998). One recent study that investigated demand for new courses in library science education in South Korea noted that, of the 19 most requested library science courses, students show high demand for

- Information services and Internet resources
- Management of different kinds of libraries, including nonbook material and multimedia management
- Digital libraries
- Automated systems of libraries (Noh, Ahn, & Choi, 2012, p. 363)

As policy related to ubiquitous ICT access and use has advanced in Korean society, it has similarly influenced library services. The central role information technology plays in Korean society and the high level of connectivity the infrastructure provides allows its libraries to advance practices in "ubiquitous librarianship," that is, the ability to deliver information and information services to users anywhere, at any time, using any type of ICT device. As one group of librarians in South Korea has stated:

> The environment is able to satisfy users' needs to open their customized virtual libraries at anytime and from anywhere to get information easily. If we accept the definition that the mission of libraries is to provide information promptly and accurately without limitations of time and location and depending on users' needs, one of the fields in which the ubiquitous technologies must be exploited most intensively should be the library field. (Bae, Jeong, Shim, & Kwak, 2007, p. 211)

The ideal of "the library in my palm" (Bae et al., p. 213), or the ability to access centrally collected digital information resources from wherever one is located using whichever personal digital device one has on hand, has greatly influenced the development of digital library resources in South Korea.

A series of knowledge and information resource management project mentioned earlier, resulted in digital libraries for history, culture, information and telecommunication, science and technology, and current events (Choi, 2003). The projects portals and resources have since been incorporated into the National Library of Korea collection, accessible through Dibrary, inaugurated in 2009 (Dibrary, n.d.). The Dibrary is a digital library collection made up of a range of collections, some of which are accessible in the Dibrary unique physical spaces. The central Dibrary space is located in the national capital city of Seoul and offers "626 computers, 380,000 digitalised books, a digital study room for 252 users, ten million pieces of local academic information, 34 million items of data on local government policy, and 72 million resources from more [than] 700 libraries" (Ng, 2009). Some of the copyrighted e-books and e-journals are also accessible in 800 *small libraries* (Lee, 2013; Sohn, 2013). In the Dibrary central or small libraries, visitors can access digitized copyrighted resources from the National Library of Korea collection with member login, and the Dibrary portal, catalog; and some noncommercial digital resources such as public government documents, electronic newspapers, and old and rare Korean tomes for which the copyright has expired, are accessible to users without library membership (National Library of Korea, 2012). In this manner, the National Library of Korea has incorporated "the library in my palm" technology with library service while still honoring intellectual property laws.

THE NETHERLANDS

The Kingdom of the Netherlands is a constitutional and hereditary monarchy with central executive power resting with the crown and central legislative power jointly shared by the crown and parliament. The nation hosts a population of 16,788,119 (Statistics Netherlands, 2013), and a GDP per capita of USD$46,054 (World Bank, 2013b), with an adult literacy rate measured at higher than 99 percent (Turner, 2012). More than 80 percent of the country's inhabitants are native Dutch, with immigrants coming primarily from other EU countries (5 percent), Indonesia (2.4 percent), Turkey (2.2 percent), Suriname (2 percent), Morocco (2 percent), and the Caribbean (0.8 percent) (Central Intelligence Agency, 2013). There are two official languages, Dutch and Frisian; however English-language education has been prominent in the Netherlands since the 1980s (Dronkers, 1993), and English is a compulsory foreign language requirement in the Dutch primary curriculum (National Center on Education and the Economy, 2012a).

The Netherlands has been liberalizing its communication infrastructure since the 1980s beginning with the privatization of the national telephone industry. In 1994, the government set up an Action Programme, developed through consultation with the private sector, in which it was decreed that by 1998, regulations and incentives should be developed for private investors to be engaged in rapid development in information technology. It was also planned that if the private sector had not engaged by then, the government would consider greater involvement in investment and development of information technology (Mansell, Davies, & Hulsink, 1996). The Dutch Telecommunications Act was passed in 1998, addressing regulations regarding the liberalization of the telecommunication industry (the act was amended in 2012 to address net neutrality, the principle that the Internet should remain free and open) and privacy issues.

The Netherlands ranks in sixth place on the ITU IDI, after South Korea and the four Nordic countries of Sweden, Denmark, Iceland, and Finland. However, the European Commission has created a separate series of indices to chart digital development in the 27 current European Union (EU27) countries and assess factors that affect digital inclusion there. Researchers have created the compound European Digital Development Index (EDDI), made up of three component indices, namely:

1. The Internet Usage Index, which describes autonomy, intensity, and skills related to Internet use
2. The Internet Infrastructure Index, comprising indicators that describe the availability, affordability, and quality of network and Internet connections
3. The Internet Impact Index, assessing the influence of Internet use on the economy, employment, education, health, government, culture, and communication (including entertainment)

When evaluated using the EDDI, the Netherlands is classified as a Group 1 country, meaning the country earned some of the highest marks in provision of Internet use, infrastructure, and impact.

For example, the Internet Usage Index incorporates three indicators: (1) autonomy, a count of the number of individuals who accessed the Internet from home; (2) intensity, a measure of whether individuals accessed the Internet daily or almost every day; and (3) skills, an assessment of the individual's digital skills. The Netherlands ranked first of the EU27 in terms of autonomy, with more than 85 percent of the Dutch accessing the Internet from home in 2009 (EU27 average was 58 percent in 2009); and intensity, increasing from around 40 percent in 2004 to more than 70 percent in 2009 (EU27 average was 24 percent in 2004 and 48 percent in 2009), and users manifest high performance in terms of digital skills (second only to Luxembourg) (Guerrieri & Bentivegna, 2011).

Digital Inclusion Policies and Initiatives

Investment in information technology has been an interest of the Dutch government for many decades. As different policies and advising groups were being established, there was also a concern about the potential divide that could arise between those with access to the new technology and those without. The Rathenau Committee, an advisory group to the Dutch Ministry of Science Policy, warned policymakers in 1979 that "certain consequences of rapid development in information technology . . . might lead to widespread social alienation" (Akkermans & Plomp, 1982, p. 415). Following this reminder, several committees were set up to assess how information technology might be incorporated into future education goals. In 1981, the Minister of Education and Science created the Centre of Education for Information Technology (CEIT), and in 1982, sent a white paper on information technology in education to Parliament, directly addressing the potential sociocultural effects of information technology. The paper warned against creating "a new 'computer literate' elite" and professed a need to pay particular attention to "pupils in special education, girls, and cultural minorities and/or those from socially deprived classes" (Akkermans & Plomp, 1982, p. 417).

The 1990s and 2000s saw continued growth in the government's interest in information technology's impact on society. The government established the Advisory Council for Science and Technology Policy in 1990 and tasked the group with advising the government on issues relating to science and technology policy (Rathenau Instituut, 2013). The country also implemented a policy to help defray the cost of computer ownership; from 1997 to 2004, Dutch residents could purchase personal computers with pretax wages if they used their personal computers for business-related activities, a benefit that could be claimed every three years (O'Brien, 2006). In 2001, a Broadband Expert Group (Nederland Breedbandland) was established to report ways that the Netherlands could become a leading country in ICT and broadband. Again, the impact on different populations was considered:

> Broadband's impact will only really be measurable once the market
> and the Government succeed jointly in translating effectively the op-
> portunities broadband offers into applications for the domains of edu-
> cation, care, public management, security, culture, work, trade and lei-
> sure. These applications must become available not only to the happy
> few in the four major cities, but also for the broad public outside them.
> (Broadband Expert Group, 2002, p. 4)

In the same year, 2001, the government created "digital playgrounds,"
facilities established in disadvantaged areas to provide opportunities for
residents to access the Internet. Cybersoek, a facility in the Amsterdam
district of Zeeburg, was designed to "improve the position of the people
of Zeeburg in the labour market by teaching them how to use computers
and the Internet" and to improve "social cohesion between the local people" (European Urban Knowledge Network, 2004). Another action toward inclusion in the early 21st century was the creation of the Dutch
Web guidelines. In 2004, the Ministry of the Interior and Kingdom Relations tasked the ICT Uitvoeringsorganisatie, or executive ICT oversight
agency, with the development of the standards intended to make the
government "more transparent, more accessible, more effective and more
efficient," while addressing the fact that 95 percent of Dutch government
websites were at least partially inaccessible to certain populations (Logius, n.d.). In 2008, the government passed an agreement that requires
the compliance of all municipalities, provinces, and local governments
with the standards.

These inclusion goals have been continued in the past decade. Currently, the responsibility for digital inclusion is spread among the entire
government, but the following ministries work on most of the related
policies and initiatives:

- The Ministry of Interior and Kingdom Relations: responsible for e-
  Accessibility
- The Ministry of Economic Affairs: responsible for "digital compe-
  tences and the reduction of the administrative burden"
- The Ministry of Health, Welfare, and Sport: responsible for ICT and
  the older population and people with disabilities
- The Ministry of Education, Culture, and Science: responsible for
  ICT education goals
- The Ministry of Interior and Kingdom Relations: responsible for e-
  government (European Commission, 2010, p. 7)

In recent policies and initiatives, the government has focused on persons with disabilities; those lacking digital literacy skills; and older
adults, one of the fastest growing percentages of the Dutch population,
due to both emigration of younger age groups in the early 21st century
and the increase in life expectancy among the general population (Huysmans & Hillebrink, 2008, p. 45)." The 2010 European Commission report,

"eInclusion in the Netherlands," discusses many of these policies and initiatives on inclusion in the past decade; key programs highlighted in the report are summarized below:

- No Barriers: The Ministry of Health, Welfare, and Sport started the No Barriers program in 2000 to assess the accessibility of popular websites (including financial and government sites). Initial analysis was done by consulting "ambassadors" of groups with different disabilities. This work was continued with the endorsement of the "Barrier Free" Quality Mark Foundation, the group that oversees standards related to accessibility, and the usage of a logo designed to be placed on websites that are fully accessible. Accessibility standards are also addressed in e-government initiatives; since 2006, all new government websites must meet Web standards and existing websites had to be updated by 2010. These guidelines apply to local authorities as well as national sites.

- Digital Skills and Awareness: The 2009–2013 program focuses on older adults, youth (particularly in the area of cybersecurity), populations in need of more advanced ICT skills to be able to compete in the changing job market, and civil servants in need of better technological skills, among others (Ingen Housz, 2011). One of the program's projects was Senior Web, a portal designed to coalesce relevant information for the senior population.

- European Union Seventh Framework Programme: The Netherlands participated in this 2007–2013 program that brought together research on growth and employment through a variety of projects. The 2009–2010 ICT Work Programme included nine challenges, one of which ("ICT for Independent Living, Inclusion and Governance") included goals to "foster independent and active living among Europe's ageing population . . . mitigating ICT complexity in order to encourage groups with special needs to uptake and use ICT tools and technologies to their benefit" (European Commission, 2010, p. 17).

- Taskforce for the Disabled and Society: This taskforce is aimed at integrating people with disabilities into society. The taskforce focuses on "ideational and emotional realisation; empowerment; and inclusion" and believes that "every new policy initiative should be designed from ground up taking into account its impact on people with disabilities" (European Commission, 2010, p. 8). To work toward this ideal, the group carries out trainings with local governments and encourages people with disabilities to act as representatives for issues of inclusion.

- Reduction of the Administrative Burden for Citizens: As part of e-government initiatives, the government has aimed to reduce bureaucratic burdens for citizens, particularly for the chronically ill, disabled, and other disadvantaged groups. This program profiles these populations and combines the "laws, regulations and obligations" that they face; "for example, what does the unemployed Johan encounter in his efforts to find work? And with which agencies do the parents of disabled Bart have to deal?" (European Commission, 2010, p. 16). The program incorporates ICT as a means of making contacting agencies easier. Along these same lines, the government required the 25 "most important" forms to be written at an understandable reading level by 2008, a central telephone line for government questions has been developed, and the government is working on a personalized Web portal for government information.

One example of this type of personalized Web service is the e-government site, Regelhulp.nl, which provides assistance to citizens who need help applying for social services. The site allows users to apply for 26 different services (as of 2009) directly through the portal, instead of having to search for services under different sites. The services are typically used by people with disabilities, the chronically ill, and older adults (or those assisting these populations), making ease of application a particularly valuable service (Zandvliet, 2009).

Individual cities have implemented similar programs; one early example is the i-Punt Amsterdam, a service initiated in 2003 through the Virtual Integration Counter project (developed by a partnership between two private Dutch companies and the Dutch Kennisland Foundation). The Virtual Integration Counters are intended to help immigrants, those lacking digital literacy skills, individuals with disabilities, and older adults access government information through easy-to-use multimedia navigation on standalone touch-screen computers and the Internet. By 2009, more than 150 municipalities had implemented some sort of virtual integration application (Codagnone, 2009).

Targeting the intellectual and social aspects of digital inclusion, the Dutch Ministry of Education, Culture, and Science started a media literacy program; as part of this program, the government opened a media literacy center in April 2008 to bring together experts in both the public and private spheres to teach citizens about information and media literacy, ICT skills, and safety issues to consider when using the Internet. In the program's inaugural year, 160 partners took part in the project, and the governing body was made up of groups as diverse as founders of the Digital Skills & Awareness program and the Union of Dutch Public Libraries (Ingen Housz, 2011).

Finally, the government is working on filling the gap between the need for employees working with advanced ICT and the shortage of workers who have these skills. The government established an eSkills Task Force to assess the gap and make recommendations to address the situation; as part of these recommendations, the government has focused more on public awareness of the lack of ICT skilled workers, encouraging more citizens to pursue technology-focused education, and creating eSkills standards and training goals (Ministerie van Economische Zaken, Landbouw en Innovatie, 2011).

Even given the very high level of Internet ownership and use in the country, there are factors that negatively influence digital inclusion. Income can also play a part in whether households have a computer at home; data from 2009 show that those in the higher income quartiles are more likely to have a computer than those making less (though it should be noted that the difference between the two groups is smaller than in other European countries) (Montagnier & Wirthmann, 2011). According to a 2011 study by van Deursen and van Dijk (2013), while Internet penetration in the Netherlands may be exemplary, the differences in Internet use between marginalized and privileged groups strongly reflect other social inequalities. For example, they found that although Dutch people with disabilities and those with lower levels of education access the Internet more than their peers in their free time, this use is characterized by gaming and social media use rather than information seeking or civic involvement, making Internet use similar to television or telephone use rather than use as an information tool or a resource for community participation (van Deursen & van Dijk, 2013). In an earlier study, van Deursen and van Dijk (2009) also found that spending more time online did improve motor-technical skills for computer use but had no benefit in terms of digital literacy skills.

One government report cites research that states that close to one in ten people in the Netherlands struggles with digital activities (Ingen Housz, 2011) and data show that the ability of Dutch residents to perform higher-level Internet skills is far from universal (van Deursen & van Dijk, 2009). The government also has found that workers spend 8–10 percent of their workdays dealing with problems arising from working with technology (ECDL Foundation, 2012). Taking these potential obstacles into consideration, the government will need to continue to assess the needs of marginalized groups' physical, intellectual, and social access to digital information.

Library Services for Digital Inclusion

From 1998 onward, the public library system in the Netherlands has been in a state of reconstructing. Government assessments in the late 20th century found a "lack of cohesion in the library sector," which led to the establishment of a steering committee to lead restructuring from 2001 to 2007, an effort that created "'basic libraries' with separate front and back offices, and the transformation of provincial central libraries into provincial service organizations" (Huysmans & Hillebrink, 2008, p. 9). This service orientation was affirmed in the 2005 Steering Committee report, "Guideline for Basic Libraries," which outlined the five core functions of the public library:

- Provision of knowledge and information: the library as a storehouse of knowledge and information;
- Education: the library as a centre for development and education;
- Culture: the library as an encyclopedia of art and culture;
- Reading and literature: the library as a source of inspiration for reading and literature; and
- Meeting and debate: the library as a podium for meeting and debate. (Huysmans & Hillebrink, 2008, p. 43)

Public libraries work to meet these goals through a variety of projects. For example, they allow space for "Digital Internship," a program in which participation is required for secondary school students. The students teach Internet basics to those who lack digital skills using "Klik & Tik," an online training program developed as part of the aforementioned Digital Skills and Awareness program. "Klik & Tik" is also used to explain Web safety in "Internet Keeps You Going," a program designed to help older adults who are not online gradually become accustomed to using the Internet by introducing them to relevant subjects (Gdansk Roadmap for Digital Inclusion, 2011).

Another project, developed by the Dutch Public Library Association, is a website (www.meertalen.nl) designed for educators or caregivers who need help teaching children who do not speak Dutch as their primary language. The site includes information such as teaching materials and reading programs designed for this population, multilingual primary resources, lists of other institutions that support education of bilingual and language learners, and links to other resources (Libraries for All—ESME Project, 2009). Several Dutch public libraries are using their spaces in interesting ways. For example, the Amsterdam Central Public Library has 700 computers and the public library in Rotterdam features

a theatre; a restaurant with a full bar; a ticket-purchasing outlet for many other events in the city; an information center for individuals new to Rotterdam; a partnership with an independent music store . . . ; and live feeds from hair dressers in Rotterdam that tie into their youth area's current theme on 'hair and identity.'" (Birdsong, 2010)

These services acknowledge inclusion goals of physical access and social spheres while continuing to meet intellectual needs as well.

Despite these valuable programs and spaces, in many ways, the Dutch public library system is going through similar contextual changes as that in the United States. The availability of information on the Internet and the growth of digital documents (books, reports, etc.) have led to questions about the library's role in society. Although the emphasis on service in the guidelines helps characterize what libraries offer, there is increased need for advocacy on their importance. Indeed a 2012 Online Computer Library Center, Inc. (OCLC) survey of Dutch libraries shows that public library staff members are focused on: (1) the visibility of the library's collection; (2) forming community partnerships; and (3) demonstrating library value to local government (OCLC, 2012). The need to demonstrate value makes sense in the context of the changing information society. Indeed, the threats to eliminate funding to more than a third of Dutch public libraries are good reminders of the urgency of these goals. One project developed to help usher in a new age of librarianship is the new library training program, LibrarySchool, taught through the Netherlands Open University and sponsored by various corporations. Major Dutch public libraries also act as partners. The one-year certificate program emphasizes innovation and focuses on four main themes in the distance education courses:

- The library and culture
- The library and technology
- The library and society
- The library and organization

From this one-year program, students can continue to higher degrees (Putnam, 2012).

The public library has a strong historical basis in the country, and it will be essential for the government to recognize its potential contributions to digital inclusion goals. In addition, the library must continue to evolve to meet the changing needs of users, particularly considering the falling rates of membership and library borrowing among almost all ages and populations (Huysmans & Hillebrink, 2008). It is predicted that by 2017 the most popular Dutch library use will be for databases and electronic materials (OCLC, 2012); while this is a worthy enterprise, libraries should continue to target the growing populations in the Netherlands who may need digital assistance, such as older adults and immigrants. The fact that Dutch teenagers of Turkish and Moroccan origin use the library at higher frequency than their indigenous peers is a prime example of services beyond digital resources (such as space to study and access to computers) that are central aspects of community support (Huysmans & Hillebrink, 2008).

The future of digital inclusion in the Netherlands looks to be strong, considering the proliferation of Internet users and the almost ubiquitous availability of computers and other technological hardware. That said, it will be important for the country to continue to consider groups that could be left behind and for the country to assess the need for advanced ICT skills so that the 21st-century economy does not disproportionally favor some populations over others.

AUSTRALIA

The Commonwealth of Australia is the sixth largest country in the world in terms of area, approximately the same size in land mass as the continental United States. In fact, there are several important commonalities between Australia and the United States that makes it a useful comparison for analysis. Both of these countries have a notable range of ethnic and racial minorities, and including indigenous populations that were dislocated by British colonizers more than 200 years ago and at the same time maintain populations where the majority is of white European descent (Central Intelligence Agency, 2013). While neither Australia nor the United States has an official language, English is by far the most common language and the language of government of both countries. Literacy is nearly universal, 99 percent in both Australia and the United States (Central Intelligence Agency, 2013). Australia ranks second only to Norway on the 2012 UN Human Development Index, and the United States is ranked third (United Nations, 2013). According to ITU data (2013), in 2012, 82.5 percent of Australian people were using the Internet, slightly more than the 81.03 percent of Americans.

Notwithstanding these similarities, there are key differences between the United States and Australia. Although similar in land size, Australia is known for its vast deserts, low population density, and coastal population dispersion. Australia's population is around 7 percent that of the United States, more than 85 percent of Australian inhabitants live within 50 miles of the coast, and 77 percent of the population lives in the eastern states of New South Wales, Victoria, and Queensland (Australian Bureau of Statistics, 2013). Although Australia is a very high-income country—gross domestic product per capita in 2012 was US$67,036, compared with America's US$49,965 (World Bank, 2013b)—Australia faces unique issues related to equitable distribution of goods and services to rural and remote areas of the country.

Digital Inclusion Policies and Initiatives

One of the first Australian national policies that clearly focused on digital inclusion was the 1997 policy Networking the Nation, by which funds from the privatization of the country's telecommunications network (Telstra) were used to increase physical access to the Internet in regional, rural, and remote areas across the country, eventually (by 2002) providing 100 percent access to the Internet by way of dial-up connections (Notley & Foth, 2008). Then-prime minister John Howard released the Investing for Growth policy in 1997, promoting the use of digital technology to support both economic and social objectives on a macro level. Investing for Growth resulted in initiatives and policies to:

1. Provide strong leadership and a commitment to develop a national strategy for the information economy
2. Support and encourage private-sector-led development of the information economy
3. Encourage Australia's governments, businesses, and communities to use online and Internet technologies, including a commitment to place all appropriate Commonwealth government services online by the end of 2001
4. Foster the development of the information industries to capitalize on the employment, growth, and export opportunities offered by the information sector. (Australian Government: The Treasury, 1997, n.p.)

By 1999, the Commonwealth government had created a federal agency now known as the Department of Broadband, Communications and the Digital Economy (originally named the Department of Communications, Information Technology and the Arts). The Department of Broadband, Communications and the Digital Economy oversees Australian engagement with the digital economy; regulates telecommunication efforts, including radio, television, telephony, mobile services, and Australia Post; and manages cybersafety and security (Australian Government, 2013). The Department of Broadband, Communications and the Digital Economy has oversight of the currently in progress National Broadband Network (NBN) initiative, by which federal monies are providing broadband infrastructure (fiber, fixed wire, or satellite) to bring broadband Internet service to all Australian premises—homes, schools, workplaces, and so forth—by 2021. With this initiative, the NBN provides the infrastructure and then private service providers complete the "last mile" connections and end-user service (NBN, 2013).

Not all Australian policy related to digital inclusion is focused solely on physical access, however. Australia's Strategic Framework for the Information Economy 2004–2006, for example, demonstrates government-level understanding of digital inclusion as more than simply an issue of physical access to ICT with wording such as:

> It is not enough to create and disseminate information and knowledge. It is also necessary to have people and societies that know how to use them. For this reason, an effective education and skills development system to develop human capital which recognises the increasing importance of cross-disciplinary skills is an essential building block of an information economy. (Department of Communications, Information Technology and the Arts, 2004, p. 21)

This acknowledgment of the need for intellectual as well as physical access to digital resources is also reflected in the ITU rankings that put Australia 21st globally in the 2011 IDI, meaning that, relative to the other 153 countries evaluated, Australia shows very good progress in providing not only the networked infrastructure and physical access to information technology (ICT readiness) but also shows good information technology use and skill (ICT intensity), and their information technology-related economic and social outcomes are measurable (ICT impact) (International Telecommunication Union, 2012).

One example of what might be a step in the direction of encouraging both intellectual and social access for digital inclusion can be seen in the 2007 Australian government election commitment by the Labor Party (originally made by Kevin Rudd and then carried out by Julia Gillard) of more than US$2 billion to provide funding for four years, from mid-2009 through June 2013, to "generate an immediate, large-scale boost to enhance the integration of information and communication technology (ICT) into teaching and learning in Australian schools" (Dandolopartners Pty, 2013, p. 4) to ensure student and teacher access to and use of digital resources in the classroom. The so-called Digital Education Revolution initiative achieved a one-to-one computer-to-student ratio for grades 9 through 12 in all secondary public, Catholic, and independent schools in every state and territory across the country. Funding was provided for the laptops as well as for support for maintenance, and, importantly, secondary teachers were trained in how to enhance the educational experience through the use of ICTs inside and outside the classroom.

The true test of positive change in social access will be what happens next, as the Digital Education Revolution funding ended June 30, 2013 (Commonwealth of Australia, 2009). Early evaluations of the Digital Education Revolution initiative indicate that the outcomes have been both positive and profound, "generating a catalytic positive impact across Australian schools" (Dandolopartners Pty, 2013, p. 5). While it is possible that this "catalytic positive impact" is largely due to the extra time and money spent to improve infrastructures and teacher training in lower income areas, it is also possible that, to some extent, this could be seen as a step toward social change in Australian secondary education.

Early evaluations report that embedding ICT in educational practice led to substantial shifts in pedagogical approaches, the impacts being "most profound in low [socioeconomic status] schools" (Dandolopartners Pty, 2013, p. 5). Now that the funding has expired, the schools in the Australian state of New South Wales have announced that are trying to implement "Bring Your Own Device" policies, wherein students are invited to bring in their own (or their family's) laptop, tablet, smartphone, or whatever other digital device they can use daily. Issues related to this method include problems for students who have no digital devices or who share devices with other family members and so do not have the access needed to bring the technology to the classroom every day. Another problem is that the Digital Education Revolution laptops were uniform, all the same operating system, and all maintained by information technology staff in the school. Myriad ICTs brought into the classroom introduce a range of operating systems, hardware, software, and other technology needs that the teacher will have neither the training to troubleshoot nor the time to work on during the class time. This could pass the responsibility for technology troubleshooting on to the student, which could potentially interrupt rather than enhance the educational experience.

Another significant issue related to the Digital Education Revolution is that the initiative in no way included the school or public libraries in this program. In fact, there is no mention of library support at all beyond the provision of access to an educational database or "online library" made available to teachers in one state (Victoria) during the course of Digital Educational Revolution (Dandolopartners Pty, 2013). Perhaps this oversight is due to the brevity of the window of available funding; principals overseeing the program's funding for their schools might have been forced to remain myopically technology-focused in order to use the funding quickly, without building support teams or utilizing the range of resources already available in the infrastructure. Without more in-depth evaluation and critical analysis of the initiative, it is difficult to say, and perhaps further funding will be forthcoming from the federal level should the program evaluations demonstrate marked improvement in student learning. This is an area for future research.

Outreach to underserved populations is included in the Australian policies mentioned above, including attention to service to indigenous communities, individuals with disabilities, the elderly, and those in regional, rural, and remote locations. Pledges for the 2002 Telecommunications Action Plan for Remote Indigenous Communities and the 2006 Backing Indigenous Ability totaled more than USD$89 million (Department of Communications, Information Technology and the Arts, 2006). Services for the elderly have been created with Broadband for Seniors, wherein nearly USD$14 million was spent to create 2,000 Internet kiosks and serve 160,000 seniors. In addition the NBN rollout has been targeted to first serve underserved locales and users, as seen with the Digital Communities Initiative and the Digital Local Government programs, by which more than USD$35 million was spent on "Digital Hubs" in 40 underserved communities chosen to be first in the rollout of the NBN (Perlgut, 2011). These Digital Hubs provided both digital technology and "the training and assistance to explain the benefits of participating online and to drive greater digital literacy skills" (Department of Broadband, Communications and the Digital Economy, 2009).

The the Australian state of Victoria, Melbourne nonprofit organization called Infoxchange has undertaken the largest pilot digital inclusion efforts in Australia. A 2008 evaluation report undertaken by the management firm A. T. Kearney concludes that from 2002 to 2008 Infoxchange provided more than USD$5.4 million in benefits for digital inclusion initiative projects, including programs that provided training in information technology skills for education and employment outcomes, offered discounted Internet access, and helped participants with involvement in online government, financial, and health services and networks (A. T. Kearney, 2008).

Finally, in national reports, libraries are recognized as institutions necessary for digital inclusion efforts; for example, the Department of Broadband, Communications and the Digital Economy 2009 report "Australia's Digital Economy: Future Directions" specifically names public libraries as vital institutions for the provision of public-access Internet connections and ICT as well as digital literacy training, support, and outreach. Likewise, the Australian Communications and Media Authority's (2009) "Audit of Australian Digital Media Literacy Programs" specifically mentions local government support of public libraries as a means to improve local digital media literacy efforts.

Library Services for Digital Inclusion

Public libraries hold a prominent place in Australian culture, with half of Australians holding memberships. Public library funding amounted to approximately USD$38 per head of population in 2011 (Regional Access and Public Libraries, 2013), with 84 percent of public library expenses coming from local government (McEntyre & Associates Pty, 2013). Each of Australia's six states and two territories has oversight of its own public library services, and each state and territory has its own state or territory library policies and directs and funds services in different ways. For example, the island state of Tasmania has created a state system called LINC Tasmania which provides library services as well as adult literacy and community learning support, archive and heritage services, and online database access. LINC Tasmania operates under the Tasmanian Libraries Act (1984) and the Tasmanian Archives Act (1983) and receives 100 percent of its funding from the Tasmanian state government.

On the other end of the spectrum, public libraries in the state with the greatest population, New South Wales, are funded 92 percent by local government and only 8 percent by the state government (McEntyre & Associates Pty, 2013). The State Library of New South Wales provides digital collections and other resources and services to citizens through the state library website (http://www.sl.nsw.gov.au/) as well as interlibrary loans of resources to support outreach services for underserved populations such as indigenous and multicultural information services, and adaptive technology for users with disabilities (State Library New South Wales, 2013). Policy governing public services is found in the NSW Libraries Act 1939 and the NSW Local Government Act 1993.

At the local level, public library services across Australia support digital inclusion with programming, outreach, and specialized services for disadvantaged groups. For example, in regional New South Wales, Wagga Wagga City Library has regular "Technology Tuesday" events that include topics such as Introduction to iPads, Facebook 101 for Parents, Embracing E-Reader, and Introduction to Text Messaging for Seniors classes (Wagga Wagga City Library, 2013). In the state of Queensland, the Brisbane City Library has created Learning Lounges, which offers space, up-to-date technology (hardware and software), and ICT troubleshooting support for small group and small business education-based initiatives (Brisbane City Council, 2013).

In 2006 the State Library of Victoria launched a website, Inside a Dog (http://www.insideadog.com.au/), specifically targeted at including adolescent boys, a group often underrepresented in literacy programs (McShane, 2011). The site pairs literacy with digital literacy and inclusion, providing training in and a forum for blogging, book reviewing, and other literacy and literary activities. The site is also supported by the Victoria Department of Education and Early Childhood Development, and what is particularly interesting about the initiative is that it does not manifest itself as a marketing tool to entice youth to come to the library or engage in school reading but rather appears to exist simply as an online forum for social inclusion with a literary theme. The site has more than 12,000 registered members, creating a forum for digital inclusion for school-aged children.

A final example is found in the Northern Territory, where the population density is the lowest in Australia at 0.2 people per square kilometer (Australia Bureau of Statistics, 2013), and wherein more than 30 percent of the populace identify as Indigenous, and 22 of the 33 public libraries are "situated in isolated and remote Indigenous communities" (Northern Territory Government, 2013). The Northern Territory Library has created a public Libraries and Knowledge Centres program to develop the local community through libraries, to connect people to information, and to preserve Northern Territory documentary and cultural heritage (Northern Territory Government, 2006). The Libraries and Knowledge Centres not only invite Indigenous communities to partake of the information services offered therein but also have created a digital "Our Story" database wherein locals are asked to contribute local and traditional knowledge to the library collection by way of storytelling. The Libraries and Knowledge Centres program has received international recognition, including receiving the 2007 Bill & Melinda Gates Foundation Access to Learning Award.

SEVEN

Moving toward Digital Inclusion

Colombia, Honduras, and Ghana

Moving from the case studies in the previous chapter, which focused on countries ranked "very high" on the UN Human Development Index and that have relatively strong government support for digital literacy and digital inclusion, this chapter focuses on countries that are still moving toward digital inclusion as a priority in public policy. While the previous chapter examined different social and policy paths to ensuring access, this chapter illuminates the ongoing processes of articulating access goals and the means to accomplish them. The countries discussed in this chapter include one country with "high" human development (Colombia) and two "medium"-ranked countries (Honduras and Ghana) on the UN Human Development Index. As with the preceding case studies, the role of the public library in digital literacy and digital inclusion efforts varies by nation, but the public library remains a key component to various conceptions of achieving physical, intellectual, and social access.

COLOMBIA

The Republic of Colombia is located in the northwest of South America bordered by the Pacific and Caribbean oceans and Panama to the northwest, and Ecuador, Peru, Brazil, and Venezuela to the south, southeast, and east. Colombia is the third-most populated country in Latin America, with just over 47 million inhabitants (DANE, 2013), three-quarters of whom live in urban areas (Central Intelligence Agency, 2013), mainly in the Andean region and along the Caribbean coast. Colombia was a Spanish colony until independence was won in 1819, and Spanish remains the main language used in Colombia (and the fifth-most common language in which online materials are delivered worldwide), with an additional 67 non-Spanish languages also used in communities throughout the country. While the majority of Colombians consider themselves to be either white or mestizo (a mix of European and indigenous decent), 10.4 percent of the population self-identify as Afro-Colombian and 3.4 percent as solely indigenous (LaRosa & Mejía, 2012).

At the national level, Colombia is an upper-middle-income country with a gross domestic product per capita in 2012 of US$7,752 (World Bank, 2013b, 2013c) and a "high" rank on the UN Human Development Index (United Nations, 2012), but is simultaneously a country wherein nearly one-third of the population (32.7 percent) lives in poverty and 10 percent live in extreme poverty (DANE, 2012). Government resources and services are distributed inequitably across Colombia, with electricity, water, sewerage, and other public services seldom reaching high-poverty areas and communities (Manrique et al., 2003). Although there have been substantial improvements in infrastructure in the past decade, as of 2011, one-quarter of rural Colombians still did not have access to an improved water source (World Bank, 2013a). As is the case in many other countries, a disproportionate number of individuals living in these high-poverty areas are of indigenous heritage (Manrique et al., 2003). Indigenous groups in Colombia have been fairly active in pursuing a place on the national agenda and have made some progress—for example, two of the 102 Senate seats are exclusively reserved for senators who specifically represent indigenous communities (Constitution of Colombia, 1991, Article 171); however, indigenous communities are nevertheless underrepresented in political, economic, and social realms.

Violent and petty crimes are significant concerns in Colombia. According to the United Nations Office on Drugs and Crime's (2011) Global Study on Homicide, much of the violent crime in Colombia is related to the drug trade, as most of the illegal coca-based drugs trafficked in the United States are farmed in Colombia; however, in the past decade, strict policing efforts in Colombia targeting organized crime and drug trafficking has more than halved the homicide rate there. While studies have not yet explored whether digital inclusion affects rates of violent crime, there are studies that indicate that increased levels of social inclusion decrease crime, particularly juvenile crime (Coalter, 2005; Farmer, 2005; Smith, 2006). More research is needed on this topic, but if digital inclusion includes socializing factors, increases in digital inclusion could conceivably help with programs to help prevent youth from becoming involved in criminal activities.

Nearly half (48.98 percent) of Colombians are using the Internet (International Telecommunication Union, 2013), 90 percent of Colombians have mobile telephones (Barón & Valdés, 2012), and in 2009, "70 percent of Colombians report[ed] having easy access to public libraries"

(Center for Information & Society, 2009, p. 1). Literacy is relatively high in Colombia, with 93.6 percent of individuals over age 15 able to read and write (Central Intelligence Agency, 2013). Newspapers, magazines, radio, television, and the Internet are available for Colombians to access on a daily basis, although, because the news media is largely owned by "wealthy families, national conglomerates, and major political parties," many "journalists practice self-censorship for fear of corrupt officials, criminals, and members of illegal armed groups" (Hudson, 2010, p. xl). These mass media are generally more accessible in the urban areas but are not absent from rural areas altogether.

Digital Inclusion Policies and Initiatives

Similar to most other countries, the first national policies and programs directly related to digital inclusion in Colombia focused on the physical distribution of ICT. For example, the National Policy for Science and Technology 1994–1998, the National Development Plan 1998–2002, the National Connectivity Agenda 2000, and the 2002 Telecommunications Policy Guidelines primarily worked to provide telephone and Internet services throughout Colombia. Government initiatives such as the creation of Compartel, a government program providing telephone and Internet service to rural and low-income areas, and the Computers for Education program, bringing computers to the classroom, both resulted from the National Development Plan 1998–2002 and greatly contributed to the building of the Colombian digital infrastructure. The subsequent National Development Plan 2006–2010 and the 2007 Colombia's Vision for 2019 also provide good focus on the distribution of ICT throughout the country, but with no obvious consideration of the training needed for digital literacy and inclusion. The more recent National ICT Plan 2008–2019 includes broad discussion of the need for digital literacy training and specifically creates programs that provide ICT infrastructures for education, health, justice, business, community, e-government, and research and development (Ministerio de Comunicaciones, 2008). Government-funded (i.e., Compartel) community telecenters have been created as part of these development efforts (Barón-Porras & Gómez, 2012).

Finally, the 2010 Library Act includes a great deal of language not only supporting the preservation and communication of information through libraries and literacy but also promoting community support for "lifelong learning and the development of an information culture based on knowledge and skills related to new technology" (Ley 1379, Article 60.4). The act lists basic library services as including both Internet access and "the promotion of reading and digital literacy" (Ley 1379, Article 20.1). The Library Act puts the responsibility for these efforts on the Ministry of Culture, in coordination with the Ministry of National Education and the Ministry of ICT, creating a powerful committee to support digital inclusion. Additional efforts supporting the physical, intellectual, and social aspects of digital inclusion are directly linked with library services, and that support is discussed in the following section.

Library Services for Digital Inclusion

A 2007–2009 research endeavor by a research team led by Ricardo Gomez of the University of Washington Information & Society Center resulted in a series of publications that provide a snapshot of public access computing in 25 countries worldwide; Colombia was one of the countries examined. Writing specifically of Colombia, the researchers note that rather than strive for universal service (that is, personal ICT and Internet access in all homes, businesses, schools, and government offices as well as other public and private locales), governmental and non-governmental organizations have instead turned to universal access (or public venues for accessing ICT and digital services) as the priority for ICT access and use:

> This situation has developed because people have found ICTs an essential tool for individual and social development. Public libraries, telecenters, and cybercafés, constitute the best training and ICT access opportunity for marginalized and vulnerable populations that still make up a high percentage of all Colombians. (Barón & Valdés, 2013, p. 169)

This suggests that the value added regarding training and assistance available in public venues makes public-access computing centers a preferred venue for digital access.

According to the University of Washington study, Colombia has approximately 18,300 public-access venues in the forms of public libraries, nonprofit telecenters, and for-profit cybercafés. The distribution of resources among these three institutions is quite skewed. The study team reports that only about 16 percent of the 1,563 public libraries in Colombia offer public Internet service "with plans to dramatically extend this to all public libraries by 2015" (Baron & Gomez, 2012, p. 3). On the other hand, 2,730 community telecenters, and 14,166 cybercafés in the country provide Internet access for a reasonable fee. The Colombian research participants responded that even when they were asked to pay for access to public computer and Internet services, the costs were affordable and so the cost did not prevent them from using fee-based public resources; in fact, only 4.1 percent of public-access computer use was in public locales that were cost-free. Cybercafés are by far the most prolific public-access centers in Colombia and are, perhaps not surprisingly, much more frequently used (47.2 percent of use). Additional access points included are home (43.8 percent of use) or someone else's home (16.3 percent of use), schools (26.6 percent of use), and the workplace (24.6 percent of use) (Gomez, 2012a).

While for-profit cybercafés seem to be at the forefront in the provision of ICT and Internet physical resources, the nonprofit and government sectors are making headway in the promotion of intellectual and social access to ICT at the community level. Fundalectura, a nonprofit literacy organization in Colombia, has teamed with the mayor of Bogotá and public libraries, with the support of the Ministry of Culture, Recreation, and Sport, to create BiblioRed—a citywide library network providing books and ICT access in public parks, the marketplace, mass-transit system stops, and other where-the-public-already-is locales (Fundalectura, 2013)—and was awarded a Bill & Melinda Gates Foundation 2002 Access to Learning Award (Bill & Melinda Gates Foundation, 2012). The Colombian Ministry of ICT has an additional initiative for distribution of digital services: live digital kiosks. As of June 2013, 1,144 live digital kiosks had been placed in rural school buildings in towns with populations of more than 100 inhabitants wherein public Internet services had not previously been available, with a goal of more than doubling that number in the next few years (Ministerio de Tecnologías de la Información y Comunicaciones, 2013).

HONDURAS

The Republic of Honduras is bordered by the Caribbean Sea to the north and the Pacific Ocean (Golfo de Fonseca) to the southwest and shares land borders with El Salvador, Guatemala, and Nicaragua. As of July 2013, the population of Honduras was estimated to be 8,448,465, with the population divided nearly evenly between urban and rural areas. Nearly a million inhabitants reside in the nation's capital, Tegucigalpa, and another million in San Pedro Sula, the industrial capital, but 48 percent of the populace remains in rural areas. The official language of Honduras is Spanish, with a distribution of indigenous languages, including an English dialect among the Garifuna minority, in some Caribbean coastal cities (Central Intelligence Agency, 2013).

In terms of national infrastructure, Honduras gained global attention in 1998 when Hurricane Mitch ravaged the country, including the capital city. Flooding destroyed roads and structures, landslides erased entire neighborhoods from the landscape, and winds toppled telecommunication infrastructures. International aid programs quickly responded to the disaster, working to rebuild roads, schools, hospitals, and other structures. In 2009, this work was still in progress when, in June of that year, Honduran president Manuel Zelaya was forcibly ousted from his executive position for attempting to amend the constitution to allow himself to extend his time to more than the constitutionally delineated single four-year term as president. The political unrest resulted in the immediate withdrawal of much of the international support that was then in place. In November 2009, Porfirio Lobo Sosa was elected to replace Zelaya and worked throughout his time in office to reestablish international support for Honduras. Both governmental and nongovernmental international organizations are interested in strengthening democracy, protecting human rights, and promoting the rule of law in Honduras (Arias & Camacho, 2011).

In terms of the UN Human Development Index, Honduras is ranked as supporting "medium human development," ranking 120th out of 187 countries, and it has shown consistent progress in a positive direction since the start of the rankings in 1980, with approximately 1.0 percent increase per annum (United Nations, 2013). Still, the World Bank (2013e) reports that 61.2 percent of the population lives in poverty, and the United Nations International Fund for Agricultural Development (2011) reports that 36 percent of Hondurans "live under extreme poverty conditions"; in rural areas, the figure rises to 50 percent (p. 1). The homicide rate in Honduras is the highest in the world (82.1 homicides per 100,000 people), and homicides have more than doubled since 2005 (United Nations Office on Drugs and Crime, 2011).

In addition, Honduras was recently given the second-to-lowest ranking in a measure of social inclusion in the Western hemisphere—an index that reflects "the emerging consensus that social inclusion comprises an institutional, social, political, and attitudinal environment that goes beyond economics and the reduction of poverty and inequality" (*Americas Quarterly*, 2013, p. 47). The Social Inclusion Index focuses on social factors such as the perceived opportunities available to individuals, regardless of race, gender, and other social and economic factors, "necessary for an individual to enjoy a safe, productive life as a fully integrated member of society" (p. 47). Returning to the idea of digital inclusion reflecting social inclusion and social inclusion having a positive impact in reducing crime, it seems political attention to digital inclusion issues potentially could be of benefit to the country's social progress.

Digital Inclusion Policies and Initiatives

The aforementioned University of Washington study of public-access ICT distribution and use in 25 countries worldwide included Honduras as a focus case. The researchers report, "Honduras suffers a remarkably high level of poverty, high unemployment, and a near-total absence of public policies, projects, and programs to address the basic needs of the population. . . . When the basic needs of the population are not satisfied, information and ICTs cannot play a significant role in the development of the country" (Arias & Camacho, 2012, pp. 215, 218). The researchers provide a list of problems identified, also including limited government funding, higher relative costs of public access to ICTs because of the less-developed national telecommunication infrastructure (i.e., "high connectivity costs because the link can only be made as a satellite connection," p. 218), and a variety of social factors that influence choice of public ICT venues such as political interests (i.e., venues being closed down because the owners or operators appeared to have political views opposing those of the prevailing party) and lack of social awareness of and training in the use of ICT for satisfying information needs (Arias & Camacho, 2012).

The Honduran Council of Science, Technology, and Innovation is the primary government organization dedicated to promoting and stimulating ICT development and use in country, and the Ministry of Education has made some attempt to create training programs to help educators use technology in the classroom. Because of scarce resources in the schools, this has led to teachers creating homework assignments whereby the students are asked to use technology outside of the classroom to complete assignments. This creates strong demand in public libraries and other venues for public-access ICTs. The researchers recommend that if the government cannot supply the resources and training needed, members of society, nonprofits, and other nongovernmental entities in the country will need to take responsibility (Gomez, 2012b, p. 89).

Library Services for Digital Inclusion

Two government ministries—the Ministry of Municipal Governments and the Ministry of Culture, Tourism, and Information—share responsibilities for public libraries by providing materials and resources including facilities and staff training. Although there has been no formal degree-granting library science higher education program to date (Thompson & Adkins, 2012), basic training in library skills is offered to school librarians through the school library program of the Ministry of Education (Arias & Camacho, 2011; García de Paso Gómez, 1998), and the Universidad Pedagógica Nacional Francisco Morazán.

As noted above, the Honduran public library infrastructure is primarily geared to provision of literacy training and support for school-aged children. This has created a situation in which the library is not seen as directly beneficial to older youth or adults (Arias & Camacho, 2011), and so Hondurans may not feel that they have a "library culture" for adult use (Thompson & Adkins, 2012). This has been altered, in part, through the efforts of one large-scale nonprofit effort to promote libraries in Honduras. From 2000 to 2008, a U.S.-based philanthropic organization, the Frances and Henry Riecken Foundation, has funded a total of 53 libraries in Honduras (Arias & Camacho, 2011). The primary audience for Riecken programming and collection development is to meet the needs of children ages 0–13, but young adults and adults are invited to use library spaces and resources as well. These libraries, outfitted with books and shelves, study tables and chairs, and computer terminals with Internet access have been designed to follow the U.S. tradition of open stacks and book clubs, "programs and outreach initiatives to encourage a love of reading, as well as critical thinking and leadership skills" (Erickson, 2013).

The foundation hires educators from the community to be the Riecken librarians (Arias & Camacho, 2011) and, as there was no degree-granting formal library science education available in Honduras or neighboring countries during the foundation period of these centers, the Riecken Foundation has offered basic training in information technology maintenance and library service to their library workers, and supported employees attending library science training workshops offered in the region (Thompson & Adkins, 2012). In Honduras, because "libraries are most often used by children and students in response to school imposed requirements" (Arias & Camacho, 2012, p. 219), these libraries begin with 1,000 books that are selected specifically to be *non-academic* in an attempt to change beliefs that libraries are meant purely for academic purposes (Arias & Camacho, 2011).

These libraries thus provide not only free public access to ICTs but also the social environment wherein users are welcome to ask for help and gain the necessary training for improved digital access. "Through the Riecken libraries, people in widespread regions and communities can use the technology to connect, while a member of the Foundation has the role of moderating and fostering sharing among participating users" (Arias & Camacho, 2012, p. 221). The libraries are open to all, with a particular focus on outreach to underserved members of the community.

Because the Riecken libraries were fully funded with foundation dollars, when the foundation lost funding during the global financial crisis of the early 2000s, all of the Riecken libraries were temporarily closed because of lack of financial support. The foundation has slowly regained footing, however, and each of the 53 libraries in Honduras has reopened but is now relying on local government support for salaries and utilities (Riecken, 2013). The Riecken Foundation website now petitions for Internet donations (the website is in English and so the targeted donors are not necessarily local to Honduras) and has reorganized to become supported more by community and volunteer financial support, while still posting full records of income received and spent in efforts to promote and exemplify transparency in community programming.

> Once accustomed to receiving their salaries, operating expenses, programming, and book funds from a single wealthy American donor, Riecken libraries that were not supported by local residents could have easily closed. Instead, every one of the [53] libraries [has reopened and] is still operating, and they are now working to strengthen themselves and their budgets through advocacy, networking, and training. (Erickson, 2013)

The Riecken Community Libraries endeavor was acknowledged in 2012 with an American Library Association Presidential Citation for Innovative International Library Projects because of the focus on helping residents address community problems and on forming partnerships that provide the infrastructure for a range of development projects.

GHANA

The Republic of Ghana, with an estimated July 2013 population of 25,199,609, has a largely rural and young population, with nearly half (48.1 percent) of the population living in rural or regional areas and more than half (56 percent) under age 25 (Central Intelligence Agency, 2013). A former British colony, English is the nation's official language, and several local languages are also spoken. The three most commonly used dialects are derived from Niger–Congo language family (Central Intelligence Agency, 2013; Government of Ghana, 2013). Ghana possesses one of the more literate communities in Africa with almost three-quarters of the population over 11 years of age able to read and write in either English or at least one of the traditional languages (Ghana Statistical Service, 2012). However, levels of literacy vary across the nation depending upon gender or physical location. Females and residents of rural communities are most at risk of having literacy needs neglected due to traditional views of duty, access restrictions, and problems related to mobility (Sossou, 2006).

Ghana is a multiparty democracy with the National Democratic Congress currently in power (Government of Ghana, 2013). Ghana is given a rank of medium (in 135th place out of 154 countries) on the UN Human Development Index and is still a long way from possessing both the resources and infrastructure needed to rival richer nations. It is, however, one of the more progressive countries in Africa. In 2007, only 3.85 percent of Ghanaians were online; in 2012, the count was 17.11 percent of individuals using the Internet. This is an almost 12 percent increase in just five years (International Telecommunication Union, 2012). While Ghana still ranks as one of the "least connected countries" in the ITU (2012) report "Measuring the Information Society" (ranked at 117th of 192 countries), Ghana is also noted in the report as a country that is leapfrogging the traditional wired broadband infrastructure, having become in 2011 "the country with the highest mobile-broadband penetration in Africa" (International Telecommunication Union, 2012, p. 27). Even with this substantial increase, however, barriers such as the high cost of personal computers and Internet access limit exposure for many Ghanaians outside of Internet cafés and shared access (Ngugi et al., 2007). These are areas of interest for the government and have been addressed in policies and initiatives developed in the past decade.

Digital Inclusion Policies and Initiatives

In the late 1990s and early 2000s, the Ghanaian government held two national communications policy conferences on ICT development. From the discussions and planning around these conferences, the Ghanaian government's ICT Policy and Plan Development Committee developed the ICT for Accelerated Development policy, which was formally adopted in 2004 (Ngugi et al., 2007). The ICT for Accelerated Development policy focuses on a number of issues related to digital inclusion, including access issues (e.g., building infrastructure) and goals, such as:

- ICT as a social-enabler (education, health, poverty reduction, income distribution)
- ICT as an enabler of rapid socioeconomic development
- ICT as a tool for bridging the gender inequality gap in social, economic, and political development (Republic of Ghana, 2003)

As part of the ICT for Accelerated Development policy, the Ghana Investment Fund for Electronic Communications was established as a means of implementing the Ministry of Communications' projects "to facilitate the provision of ICT, Internet connectivity and infrastructure to underserved and unserved areas of the country and thereby increase direct participation in development and decision-making processes at local and national levels" (Ghana Investment Fund for Electronic Communications, 2013a). The fund was further supported by the 2008 Electronic Communications Act, which provides licensing guidelines, infrastructural plans, and funds to support universal service. Projects that have been carried out under the Ministry of Communications' Universal Access to Electronic Communications Programme target ICTs in educational institutions, rural populations, and issues related to health, among others. Two specific projects that are prime examples of how inclusion has been considered are the Library Connectivity Project (discussed later in this chapter) and the Disability Employment Project, which was instituted in conjunction with the Ghanaian National Council on Persons with Disability. The project helped fund Easy Business Centers for Persons with Disability, which are "kiosks where persons with disabilities . . . sell telecom accessories such as phone recharge cards, USB data modems, SIM [mobile phone] cards and also carry out SIM registration" (Ghana Investment Fund for Electronic Communications, 2013b).

One interesting quality of many of these projects is the lack of information available post-implementation. In the case of the Disability Employment Project, it is likely the program has been suspended, since the latest news on the National Council on Persons with Disability is that the government has failed to fill the positions of the office members whose terms expired in early 2012 (Ghana News Agency, 2013a). This lack of continuity appears to be a common occurrence for outreach projects, although some ICT for Accelerated Development projects have been more successful, particularly when paired with nonprofits and local businesses. For example, the Ghana Information Network for Knowledge Sharing was launched in 2003 by the International Institute of Communication and Development (a Dutch non-profit foundation) as a way for community leaders who are working on ICT for Accelerated Development initiatives to come together to discuss their projects. The group is focused on such issues as ICT and health, education, and gender, and also places emphasis on working with leaders in rural areas to make sure their communities have a voice (Ghana Information Network for Knowledge Sharing, 2013). In addition, other international organizations have assisted the effort. In 2006, the World Bank pledged $40 million to help the Ghanaian government implement sections of ICT for Accelerated Development, particularly "(i) Creating the Enabling Environment necessary for the growth of the sector (ii) Supporting local ICT businesses and IT (Information Technology) Enabled Services . . . and (iii) Promoting e-Government applications and Government communications" (World Bank, 2006). The project, eGhana, has been approved for continued funding through 2014 (World Bank, 2012).

In 2006, the Ghana Ministry of Education and Sports prepared a draft of a policy for ICT in education with the goals of expanding equitable access to education, using ICTs to enhance teaching and learning, and developing educational practices that allow for individual differences and learning styles, among others. While this seems to reflect some understanding of the need for intellectual and social access to ICTs, a report to stakeholders based on a survey of schools in Ghana found that "though Ghana's national curricula for the various subjects contain policy statements about the use of ICT in teaching and learning, the limitations imposed by inadequate number of computers in institutions, poorly trained educators and lack of Internet connectivity pose a major challenge to the implementation of the policy to integrate ICT into teaching and learning" (Mereku et al., 2009, p. 13), demonstrating that all three levels of access—physical, intellectual, and social—are needed for digital inclusion.

One program working to address the shortfall in physical access to personal computers is the Better Ghana ICT Project, supported by the Ministry of Environment, Science, and Technology, along with the Ministry of Education, the Ministry of Communication, and the Ghana Education Trust Fund, which gives free, Ghana-assembled laptops to students. Similar projects have been developed in conjunction with the private sector, such as a program initiated with Intel and Microsoft to bring specially designed computers to local markets for what was described by news briefs as a "digital inclusion programme" (Korantemaa, 2006). Though many of these nonprofit programs are not specifically designed for educational purposes, they do address the lack of general computer availability in the country.

The Ghana–India Kofi Annan Centre of Excellence in ICT is Ghana's first Advanced Information Technology Institute, offering advanced ICT education and development in African countries, working within the interests of the Economic Community of West African States. Since 2004 the institute has

> trained over 300 ICT instructors from more than 250 schools nationwide in computer programming using Q-BASIC and Ruby. This has generated tremendous interest in computer programming among [secondary] students with many of them continuing to pursue professional careers in computer science and related areas as well as computer science at the tertiary level. (Advanced Information Technology Institute, 2013)

Although computer programming skills are not necessary for digital inclusion on an individual level, the training provided to these instructors can potentially help build the social interest in and acceptance of ICT and digital delivery of information in Ghana.

Issues of transparency can also limit interest in digital inclusion on a social level. The issue of transparency in government is currently being addressed at the national level. In June 2013, Ghana's cabinet approved the Right to Information Bill, a bill initiated in 2010 that would "give Ghanaians the right to ask any public sector organisation for all the recorded information they have on any subject" (GhanaWeb, 2013). The bill is currently making its way through Ghana's legislative process. There are criticisms to the proposed bill, however, with some Ghanaians suggesting that the exceptions, such as costs associated with information requests and a lack of independent enforcement body, would render the bill ineffective (Ghana Business News, 2013). Another open data project in progress is the Open Data Initiative, started in 2012 by Ghana's National Information Technology Agency in collaboration with the Web Foundation. The initiative, which ended in December 2013, includes the development of an "Open Data strategy" for the Ghanaian government, the development of an Open Data community and platform, and evaluation (World Wide Web Foundation, 2013). Although the efforts are very useful in establishing the beginnings of a digital infrastructure and collections of resources for Ghanaians, it is partnerships between nongovernmental organizations and public libraries that provide the greatest contributions to intellectual and social information access in Ghana.

Library Services for Digital Inclusion

Ghana is noted in history as being "the first black African country to create a nationwide public library system" (Cornelius, 1993, p. 323). The Ghana Library Board, also known as the Government Library Authority, is a statutory body created by the Public Library Act of 1950 (Elbert, Fuegi, & Lipeikaite, 2012, p. 152). They have been responsible for the creation of 10 regional libraries and 53 branch libraries during their time overseeing the running of the nation's public libraries. The Ghana Library Board has worked with Western countries such as the United States and Canada to establish libraries and improve services to the public (Ghana Library Association, 2009; "Information Professionals in Ghana Benefit from United States Library Week Workshop," 2009). In addition, many Library Board projects are supported by the nonprofit Electronic Information for Libraries (EIFL), an international group that supports projects related to increasing access to digital information. Examples of projects that Electronic Information for Libraries has supported include the Mobile Library Service, run in conjunction with the Volta Regional Library to provide computers to schools in the Ho Municipality (Electronic Information for Libraries, 2013b); a maternal health initiative run in a regional library (Electronic Information for Libraries, 2013a); and a leadership training center for young people (Electronic Information for Libraries, 2011a).

In 2012, the Mobile Library Service began providing weekly computer classes in conjunction with area teachers and librarians through the use of a mobile van equipped with netbook computers. In a 2013 impact assessment, Electronic Information for Libraries found that the service:

- Built ICT competencies of more than 200 students, increasing their potential to pass their exams
- Attracted additional support from the local technology agency, Ghana Investment Fund for Electric Communication, which donated five desktop computers, a router, two canopies for outdoor lessons, desks, and chairs to the service
- Won recognition across the municipality, receiving requests to expand the service to include more schools
- Increased visibility of the library: Mobile library user numbers increased by 38 percent, from 553 in 2012 to 762 in 2013 (Electronic Information for Libraries, 2013b)

In addition, in a survey with the participating students, "63 percent said they had learn[ed] basic computer skills; 38 percent said they had improved existing skills; [and] . . . 91 percent said they did not have access to computers or the Internet before the service" (Electronic Information for Libraries, 2013b).

The public library offers space, free of charge, to the Ghanian non-governmental organization Savana Signatures and its partner, the Ghana Information Network for Knowledge Sharing, to offer a regular ICT for Development forum the last Thursday of every month (Electronic Information for Libraries, 2012b). The monthly ICT for Development forum brings together community stakeholders, government officials, and non-governmental organization representatives to discuss the value of ICT, including such topics as "visiting the Ghanaian city of Tamale on Google maps, "tweeting Tamale", and Web2.0 for teachers. The forum was moved from Institute for Local Government Studies to the Northern Regional Library in Tamale because the organizers "saw the library as an important stakeholder in development . . . in the heart of the community" (Electronic Information for Libraries, 2012b).

The Technology for Maternal Health project was also started at the Northern Regional Library with support from Savana Signatures and Electronic Information for Libraries. The project's goal was to increase awareness of maternal health issues and to use ICT to assist expectant mothers find health information. In the project's first year, the library:

- Trained 15 health workers to use computers, to conduct online health research, and to access the preloaded material
- Sent weekly text messages to 82 expectant mothers' mobile phones, and reached 12 nonliterate women through their husbands' phone
- Launched a maternal health education campaign over radio, including two radio phone-in programs on northern Ghana's most listened-to station, Radio Savannah
- Organized three health information events, for health workers, expectant mothers, and the community, attracting 180 people, and reaching nonliterate women and women with limited English-language skills. (Electronic Information for Libraries, 2013a)

Savana Signatures secured funding to expand the program to four more districts and the library will continue to offer ICT access in the Maternal Health Corner, an area of the library devoted to five free computers preloaded with maternal health information.

Young people have also been targeted in EIFL projects. The Internet Access and Training Programme, also run out of the Northern Regional Library, was targeted to help train youth in ICT skills. Approximately 190 participants completed the training, held at a training center in the library that had been set up with 25 computers. The 2011 project was notable also for the high involvement of young women—125 participants were female (Electronic Information for Libraries, 2011a).

TechAide, a Ghana-based international nonprofit, has also worked with the Library Board, including support with the Mobile Library Service. In addition, it is currently working under an initiative called Public Libraries Initiative for Development, and have signed a five-year agreement with the Ghana Library Authority with the intention of helping libraries "to utilize technology to deliver and manage library services; assist libraries to develop innovative services; improve infrastructure of libraries; train librarians to develop and submit wining proposals" (Ghana News Agency, 2013b). The group also has plans to work with the Ghana Investment Fund for Electric Communication and the National Information Technology Agency on the initiative.

The government itself has also recognized the need for institutionalized funding for ICTs in libraries. The Library Connectivity Project, an initiative funded by Ghana Investment Fund for Electric Communication from 2010 to 2012, aimed at equipping all 63 public libraries under the Ghana Library Board with ICT equipment. The plan was to "equip ten (10) Regional Digital Library and Information Centers and ten (10) Mobile Digital-Cottages in the country with computers, accessories and Internet connectivity in 2010 and roll out 53 more District Digital Library and Information Centers in subsequent years" (Ghana Investment Fund for Electronic Communications, 2013a). In 2011, Ghana Investment Fund for Electric Communication and the Library Board began another initiative, the Mobile Library Internet Connectivity Initiative or "E-Library" to bridge the gap between rural and urban populations' access to ICTs by taking computers and the Internet to rural areas with a library van service (Ghana News Agency, 2010). Unfortunately there seems to be no public assessment of these programs, so it is unclear whether the initiatives were successful.

Outside of the "official" libraries run by the Library Board, there are also several community libraries that are run outside of the public library system. One notable example of this is the network of children's libraries supported by the Osu Children's Library Fund (based in Canada). Seven of the fund's libraries are located in the greater Accra region, but the fund also supports a library at the School for the Blind in Akropong and a school library in Ho. Although the libraries focus more on books and traditional literacy skills, the principles of these libraries support such digital inclusion goals as building community (by partnering with local community leaders), supplying physical infrastructure, and teaching reading skills (Osu Children's Library Fund, 2013). Ghana also has an active library association, established in 1962, that brings together librarians from all types of Ghanaian libraries to hold events and provide support.

While these projects and the increased attention for ICT in libraries are encouraging, there are still challenges to building this infrastructure. Despite improvements, libraries are still woefully underequipped to deal with their communities' ICT equipment needs. A 2010–2011 EIFL survey found that "only 10 percent of users are using computers or the Internet in public libraries in Ghana [and] just under 60 percent of libraries have computers, but these are mainly for the operations of the library and not

for users. Only 24 percent of libraries surveyed have computers for users" (Electronic Information for Libraries, 2011b). In addition, 37 percent
of librarians feel they do not have the skills to be able to offer ICT training
and services (Electronic Information for Libraries, 2011b). In addition, at
least one library (in Sunyani, the Brong Ahafo regional capital) has re-
sorted to charging patrons to enter the library in order to keep the facility
open. According to the regional director for the Ghana Library Authority,
in 2011 and 2012, the government had only paid for two months of funding and "six months into 2013, nothing has been paid to them to survive
on" (Alarti-Amoako, 2013). In addition, as yet the national library in Ghana has not come to fruition, meaning that many of the tasks usually
carried out by these institutions have instead been taken on by academic
libraries (Elbert, Fuegi, & Lipeikaite, 2012, p. 152) because academic libraries in Ghana hold the largest collection of resources aimed at supporting the education and research of individuals and the community
(Alemna, 1997, p. 36). Finally, little collaboration seems to occur with
other African nations. This is unfortunate given the varying success of
programs throughout the continent and the impact sharing and collaboration between nations can have (de Jager & Nassimbeni, 2009).

Even with these challenges, however, Ghanaians seem to have a
strong connection to their library system. The 2010–2011 Electronic Information for Libraries survey (EIFL, 2011b) found that library users visit
frequently (40 percent visit weekly and 29 percent visit daily). Also, most
nonusers know about the library (75 percent) and more than a third say
they will likely become users soon (37 percent). The government has an
opportunity to build on the library successes to this point and to continue
this progress by providing additional funding and support; in fact, 20
percent of nonusers say they would use the library if there were more
online resources and 17 percent would if there were more available computers. There is tremendous potential for the library to participate in
digital inclusion projects, but the government must make sustainable in-
vestments in public library infrastructure and staff. In 2012, Electronic
Information for Libraries began addressing advocacy needs by forming
Africa Awareness Raising Groups, which include "library leaders, librarians, media and communication specialists, government officials and representatives of non-governmental organizations" who "will raise awareness about public libraries and engage in advocacy" (Electronic Information for Libraries, 2012a). These nonprofit groups can only do so much,
however, and a long-term investment by establishing a stable national
library or extending the reach and investment in the Library Board is
necessary to sustaining libraries' contributions to digital inclusion.

EIGHT

Recommendations for Practice, Advocacy, and Research

The preceding chapters have detailed a range of practices, policies, and politics from the United States and around the world related to digital literacy and digital inclusion, each basing at least part of its strategy on a central role for the libraries in the country. Embedded within the preceding chapters is the tension among the policies, politics, and approaches to meeting the challenges of building digitally inclusive communities. Solutions range from strong government intervention to market-based solutions to hybrid approaches involving cross-sector partnerships. Regardless of approach, there is widespread belief that promoting digital inclusion is essential for social and economic advancement.

This chapter focuses on drawing these threads together into recommendations to improve the development of professional practices and the implementation of policy instruments that promote digital literacy and digital inclusion. The primary goal of these recommendations for policy, practice, and advocacy is to support libraries and other institutions that foster the access, assistance, and education needed to ensure that all members of society have opportunities to achieve digital literacy and digital inclusion. Central to the recommendations is the idea of libraries, schools, nonprofits, and local government agencies collaborating on coordinated policies, coherent budget priorities, and integrated practices to provide digital literacy and digital inclusion to meet unique local community needs and prepare members of the public with the necessary 21st-century information skills.

DIGITAL INCLUSION AND HUMAN RIGHTS

In 2008, when the World Wide Web was only 15 years old, billions of people with Web access could visit tens of billions of Web pages, more than 100 million of which were blogs (Golbeck, 2008). Google has made most of the Web searchable, while retail giants like Amazon sell virtually everything purchasable. More recent innovations in social media services, such as Facebook, YouTube, Flickr, and Twitter, have created new levels of social interaction online. In 2010, when all of these tools were merely a few years old, Facebook had more than 500 million users and Twitter had 200 million users posting 650 million messages a day, truly astounding numbers in a world of 6 billion people. In 2007, there were approximately 1 billion devices with wi-fi chipsets in existence; now, more than 1 billion are produced every year (Mackenzie, 2010).

The promise of the Internet and its related technologies has been predicted to affect every corner of life, and many of these promises have already come to fruition to some extent. In an age where a message can crisscross the globe in a matter of seconds and all news is instant, it almost beggars belief that the ability of the telegraph to share news across continents over a period of days was an undisputed wonder of its time (Hanson, 2008). Until roughly 150 years ago, the rate of technological change related to information was fairly placid. Writing appeared thousands of years ago, while the printing press and movable type began the process of democratizing literacy about 500 years ago. For thousands upon thousands of years, the means of communicating information were very limited. People could speak face to face, and written materials could be conveyed on foot, on horseback, or by boat. Direct long-distance communication was limited to smoke signals and flags, neither of which could cover actual long distances.

Within the scope of human history, the modern period of the development of information technologies is breathtaking in its speed. A technology that now seems quaint or commonplace was utterly revolutionary not that many decades ago. Consider two developments that were groundbreaking in the mid-1800s. Mechanization of printing, cutting, and folding of papers led to dramatic increases in distribution and readership of printed materials—particularly newspapers—and in levels of literacy (Hanson, 2008). Soon after, the telegraph increased the power of the press by allowing them to report on events soon after they occurred and spread these reports around the world. "The telegraph was the first technology to inform the public as well as leaders about events as they were still occurring. There was less time to make decisions. The press gained influence. Public opinion could be more easily aroused" (Hanson, 2008, p. 20). The increased speed of the spread of news forced governments to react to events at a much faster pace, and the telegraph in turn gave empires the technology to more tightly control their colonies. Mechanized printing is completely taken for granted now, the telegraph has been consigned to the dustbin of history, and newspapers may soon be as well. Yet these technologies—along with telephone, the radio, and the television—were enormous advances a very short time ago in the overall course of human history and now have been absorbed and seem perfectly normal and unremarkable.

These technologies were all still fairly new when the United Nations issued the Universal Declaration of Human Rights in 1948. Since its passage, however, the idea of human rights has been evolving and adapting to social, cultural, and technological change. Though the computer, the Internet, and mobile devices were developed long after the Universal Declaration of Human Rights was originally drafted, many of the principles articulated in the Universal Declaration related directly to information, communication, and technology; many more rely on information, communication, and technology to support the principles. As examples, freedom of speech, press, assembly, and expression are far more practicable when involving a literate populace with access to ICTs. The human rights to education and development are possible without access to ICTs, but they are much more effective with ICTs.

Article 19 of the Universal Declaration most explicitly deals with issues of information, enshrining rights to "freedom of opinion and express" and to "seek, receive and impart information and ideas through any media," as well as the freedom from "interference" in seeking and exchanging information and ideas. Based on this article and many other parts of the Universal Declaration, the ability to access and use the Internet for purposes of education and expression has been identified as a human right in many quarters. Not long after use of the World Wide Web became commonplace, scholars of law, information, technology, and education began making arguments for universal Internet access being a necessary part of human rights (e.g., Brophy & Halpin, 1999; Lievrouw & Farb, 2003; Mart, 2003; McIver, Birdsall, & Rasmussen, 2003; Willingham, 2008). As Internet-enabled technologies have become more mobile and omnipresent—and vital to education, employment, civic engagement, communication, and entertainment—these arguments have matured into assertions that the abilities both to access and to successfully use the Internet are human rights (e.g., Jaeger, 2013; Jaeger, Gorham, Bertot, & Sarin, 2014; Lyons, 2011; Sturges & Gastinger, 2010). Even the Internet Society declared the ability to use the Internet a human right in 2011.

The ALA, the IFLA, and other library professional organizations have adopted Article 19 and the principles of information access as a human right into their bylaws and policies. In the past 15 years, arguments have been made for the central role of educational and cultural heritage institutions—including public libraries, public schools, academic libraries, archives, and museums—in ensuring human rights related to the Internet in an age so dependent on information and technology (e.g., Duffy, 2001;

Hoffman, 2001; McCook & Phenix, 2006; Phenix & McCook, 2005; Stinnett, 2009; Suarez, 2007). Not surprisingly, most attention has focused on public libraries because of their presence, commitment to serving all members of the community, and embrace of the roles of providing Internet access and education. Some even believe that the Universal Declaration "will be the lodestar that guides public library service in the twenty-first century" (McCook, 2011, p. 339).

PUBLIC LIBRARIES, PARTNERSHIPS, AND NEW WAYS TO MEET COMMUNITY NEEDS

The Internet and related technologies have not only created new responsibilities for public libraries in ensuring digital literacy and digital inclusion in communities, but they have also created new ways for public libraries to meet community needs. One of the most compelling recent developments in meeting community needs is the cultivation of partnerships with other local government and nonprofit entities to meet unique community needs that cannot otherwise be fulfilled. Many of these initiatives are directly tied to digital literacy and digital inclusion efforts of the libraries. In these initiatives, libraries are not only supporting human rights related to information, they are also promoting access to food, health care, and other basic rights.

All over the country, public libraries have developed programs, often as collaborative community partnerships, that meet community needs of all shapes and sizes that would likely be otherwise ignored (Taylor, Gorham, Jaeger, & Bertot, 2014). In 2012, 30.9 percent (up from 24.7 percent reported in 2010–2011 and 20.5 percent reported in 2009–2010) of reporting libraries indicate that they partnered with government agencies, nonprofit organizations, and others to provide e-government services (Bertot, McDermott, et al., 2012). Some examples of these partnerships have been mentioned earlier in the text, but they are worth revisiting here:

- The Queens Borough Public Library in New York runs the New Americans Project to provide better services to immigrants through English as a Second Language (ESL) classes, cultural arts programs, coping skills programs, and collection development in a variety of other languages (Carnesi & Fiol, 2000; Winkel, 2007). Due to the linguistic diversity of its staff, Queens Borough Public Library is able to provide programming in a wide variety of languages and on a wide range of topics, often in conjunction with one of the many community organizations that are part of its extensive network of partners, such as the Mayor's Office of Immigrant Affairs. In addition to reaching out to immigrants through programming, Queens Borough Public Library has also compiled a number of citizenship and immigration resources on its website, including referral lists for both citizenship and English as a Second Language classes offered by various community organizations (e.g., the Turkish Cultural Center, Catholic Charities), as well as the New York City Department of Education. Also available through the Queens Borough Public Library is a Community Resources database of agencies offering low-cost or free social and human services, searchable by services offered, locations, target groups, languages, and ethnic groups. Detailed guidance prepared by the Office of Immigrant Affairs is published on Queens Borough Public Library's website, thereby ensuring that immigrants are receiving accurate information from the actual providers of the government services. In addition to encouraging applicants to use the library's computers to complete the application, Queens Borough Public Library has also set up designated times at different branches during which immigrants can receive assistance with scanning photographs to be submitted with their applications.

- In Alachua County, Florida, Alachua County Library District, working with the local office of the state's Department of Children and Families, the Partnership for Strong Families, and Casey Family Programs, opened up a new facility ("The Library Partnership"), a 4,500-square-foot space devoted to the library and housing approximately 40 nonprofit organizations and local government agencies that provide social services focused on child welfare, greatly facilitating the ability to work with all of the interrelated agencies to get needed support as quickly as possible.
- The Hartford Public Library in Connecticut created the American Place, a program with the principal goals of helping an increasingly diverse group of immigrants secure citizenship and achieve language literacy (Naficy, 2009). By forming innovative partnerships that utilize local resources, and securing grant funding, Hartford Public Library has taken steps to create a community-wide approach that involves the U.S. Citizenship and Immigration Service, the local school district, and community nonprofit agencies to reach the target populations.
- The Pima County Public Library of Tucson, Arizona, has public health nurses from the county health department stationed in the library branches. These nurses provide free basic health care, answer health questions that patrons have, and help them navigate the social services structures (Kim, 2013).
- The Austin Public Library in Texas created the New Immigrants Program, which features eight branches with study centers that offer computer and Internet access, English conversation programs, and English as a Second Language classes (Miranda-Murillo, 2006). Since the inception of the program, Austin Public Library has part-

nered with both Austin Community College and the Austin Independent School District to offer English as a Second Language classes. The New Immigrants Program also maintains an online presence through a website that provides Internet-based tools to help immigrants with their English-language skills, as well as links to U.S. Citizenship and Immigration Service information and international news.

- Public libraries in San Francisco have social workers with offices in the libraries to assist homeless patrons and recovering drug addicts.

- The innovative roles in responding to major hurricanes in the early 2000s have evolved into standard roles for public libraries to help their communities through more commonplace disasters, like recovery from tornadoes and wildfires, by providing access to necessary forms for assistance and coordinating relief and aid efforts with local, state, and national government agencies and nonprofit organizations (Jaeger, Langa, McClure, & Bertot, 2006; Bishop & Veil, 2013).

- In recent years, the Baltimore-based (Maryland) Enoch Pratt public libraries worked with the Baltimore City Health Department to ensure the availability of fresh groceries to those living in food deserts by providing opportunities for patrons to order their groceries through library computers and have the food delivered the next day to the library. What differentiated this online grocery order system (Baltimarket) from those run by major grocery chains were the accommodations made for those who are on the wrong side of the digital divide. The availability of computers, as well as people to provide one-to-one assistance in using the system, at the program sites made the program more accessible to those who are unable to or uncomfortable with using an online ordering system at home. In 2013, the program was suspended due to funding cuts, demonstrating the tension between community needs and government support discussed in further detail below.

These are but a small sampling that demonstrates the amazing range and diversity of these partnerships in meeting unique community needs.

The growth of partnerships was born, at least in part, out of necessity: The public is increasingly relying upon the libraries in their communities to deliver these additional services at a time when these very institutions are contending with budgetary constraints. Partnerships are one means for public libraries to meet the heightened demand for their services without a corresponding increase in staff and resources. However, notwithstanding criticism that public libraries are becoming increasingly irrelevant, what each of these partnerships demonstrates is that their role in communities across the country is not diminishing, merely evolving.

Their value now lies less with the printed information that is available within the four walls of the library and more with the myriad services that they provide in an effort to connect members of the public with information that is central to their day-to-day lives. As Watson (2010) observed, "for libraries . . . the vision and purpose must switch from resource provision to being about people and making a real contribution to the learning landscape" (p. 45).

In virtually all of these examples—ordering fresh food, applying for social services, establishing residency, learning a new language—the ability to access and use Internet technology is an essential component. In finding ways to meet important community needs that are not information centered, libraries are still taking on the responsibilities of teaching those using the services to access and use the Internet. Public libraries are evolving into community institutions that—individually and through partnerships—meet a wide range of community needs, but digital literacy and digital inclusion remain at the center of all of initiatives. If concerns of human rights are now the guiding force for public libraries, these rights are linked by digital literacy and inclusion. It is imperative, then, that public policies, library advocacy, and library practices align to support the digital literacy and digital inclusion roles of public libraries.

Such collaborative community partnerships also offer a key way forward for libraries in meeting local digital literacy and digital inclusion needs. Expanding these partnerships, particularly to include local government agencies, will allow libraries to further develop existing services and provide new services, even if more traditional forms of support for libraries continue to decrease. Partnerships with local government also offer terrific means to demonstrate to the local government the contributions of the library and the importance of sufficient funding of the library to support the digital literacy and digital inclusion of the community.

POLICIES TO SUPPORT LITERACY AND INCLUSION IN PUBLIC LIBRARIES

As this book has hopefully made clear, public libraries around the world are relied upon more than any other cultural institution to overcome the digital divide, teach digital literacy, and foster digital inclusion. As discussed in chapter 4, the federal policies in the United States acknowledge this reality, relying specifically on public libraries in a number of ways to promote digital literacy and digital inclusion. Yet public libraries are predominantly excluded from the funding made available for digital literacy and digital inclusion, as well as from the decision-making processes related to policy in this area.

Further exacerbating this disjunction between federal policy and public library practice in terms of digital literacy and digital inclusion, public
library budgets have been heavily reduced during the economic downturn of the past several years, even though the use of libraries has skyrocketed (Sigler et al., 2012). Although governments at all levels are relying on public libraries to ensure digital inclusion, the same governments
are reducing the funding of the libraries that are being relied upon. This
situation places public libraries in the untenable situation of greater service demands, higher service expectations, and fewer resources by which
to meet these demands and expectations.

If this situation is to be addressed, the solution can only be found in
reconciling the incompatibility between funding cuts at the state and
local levels, as well as limited support at the national level, with the
increased view at the federal level that libraries are part of the solution to
large-scale technological problems. As with many other current areas of
information policy, this situation evidences a clear lack of harmonization
between major policy goals (Shuler, Jaeger, & Bertot, 2010). Simply put,
public libraries cannot be simultaneously promoted as the solution to
digital divide issues by the FCC, the IMLS, DigitalLiteracy.gov, and other
government agencies and also face the significant reduction of the small
amount of federal funding they receive by losing funding from the E-rate
program to other policy goals.

No other cultural institutions are prepared to serve the public in the
digital literacy and digital inclusion capacities that public libraries do, for
a lack of sufficient public access technology and for a lack of the ability to
provide education and training related to the Internet. As such, the
change has to be in policy rather than practice, unless the federal government opts to abandon policy focused on promoting digital literacy and
digital inclusion.

Several core changes could help to harmonize the policy and the practice of digital literacy and digital inclusion. The first is extremely straightforward: When demanding more of libraries to fulfill these digital literacy and digital inclusion functions, do not reduce library funding. The
FCC proposal to take away E-rate funds from libraries, while state and
local governments are also drastically cutting library budgets, will not
serve to increase digital literacy and digital inclusion. Libraries have been
placed in the social role of ensuring digital literacy and digital inclusion
and their support from all levels of government needs to increase to a
level that such services, training, and resources can be adequately provided. Surprisingly, many national and regional governments have simultaneously acknowledged the need to address issues related to digital
inclusion and reduced funding for such efforts (Huang & Russell, 2006).

Second, governments at all levels should consider geography, infrastructure, and history when making demands on libraries. A library system that has received specialized government grants (such as the Broad-

band Technology Opportunities Program [BTOP] funding discussed in chapter 4)—by itself or as part of a group of community institutions—is going to have a much greater chance of meeting the physical access needs of its patrons than one constrained by a less-robust local telecommunication infrastructure and local and state policies that hinder better connections. A potential solution is improved coordination among local, state, and national governments on policy decisions relating to issues such as telecommunication support and equality of grant funding. Unfortunately, such political coordination is unlikely to occur in the current political climate in the United States, in which the prevailing political and economic ideologies among politicians have resulted in years of policies that have hindered the ability of libraries to meet the needs of the communities (Jaeger, Gorham, Bertot, & Sarin, 2014).

Third, policymaking related to the digital divide, digital literacy, and digital inclusion needs to bring public libraries into the discussions, designs, and decisions. A place in the policymaking process for libraries would have quickly illuminated the problems with relying on libraries while cutting their funding. For instance, input from the social institutions that work to foster digital literacy and digital inclusion into the development of DigitalLiteracy.gov would likely have resulted in a website far better equipped to promote digital literacy and digital inclusion. In that event, libraries would have been better positioned to interject the needs of those with limited digital literacy and the goals that they need to achieve with technology into the policymaking process, a perspective that is often completely neglected. "Curiously, even policy or intervention-focused discussions pay far more attention to the conditions that encourage or hinder use than to the kinds of uses to which the Internet might, or should, be put" (Livingstone & Helsper, 2007, p. 682).

Too often, however, the government approach in the United States and many other countries is to assume that making technology available is sufficient, and that people will immediately understand how to use, be comfortable using, and know what to do with that new technology. Such assumptions are quite misguided. "Technology does not in itself solve social and economic discrepancies within societies, and can often exacerbate them" (Cullen, 2003, p. 248). Public libraries are the institution that makes technology-based and Internet-enabled government initiatives available and accessible to all members of the public; their roles must be acknowledged and their participation in policymaking facilitated for public libraries to ensure digital literacy and inclusion.

Though there are attempts to create and/or foster partnerships between libraries and government agencies that could benefit communities greatly, they may not come with the funding, governance, or other structures necessary to ensure success. One example is the partnership between the IMLS and the U.S. Department of Labor (IMLS, n.d.). Though announced in June 2010 with the intent of bringing together the Department of Labor's employment services and one-stop career centers and libraries as community-based institutions, there is little evidence of a broad national collaboration. For example, the resources provided on the IMLS website are more than a year old, and when one heads to the CareerOneStop site (http://www.careeronestop.org/) one cannot find materials directed at libraries that want to partner and/or engage the Department of Labor's resources. Indeed, the resources are directed at the public seeking employment and/or training and do not seemingly consider that those in need of assistance may not have access to, or be facile with, Internet-enabled technologies to take advantage of the provided resources and information.

In addition to policy changes, libraries need to take more initiative in terms of advocacy. Libraries have accepted—and, in most cases, embraced—these responsibilities without the needed support from governments. The failure of public libraries to clearly articulate what they contribute and to advocate for sufficient support has long been a detriment to the success of libraries (Jaeger, Gorham, Sarin, & Bertot, 2013). "Public librarians have, for the most part, kept quiet. . . . We certainly do not assert our position as the very public heart and soul of the information age" (Kent, 1996, p. 212).

As libraries take on more and more responsibilities tied to digital literacy and digital inclusion, this attitude must change for libraries to survive. The innovative partnerships noted above have received little attention in the media, for example. Engaging the politics related to digital inclusion is particularly important as there are still people, including some in positions of power, who do not believe digital literacy and digital inclusion are pressing issues. There are even some people who believe digital inequality is not even a problem, arguing instead that people only do not participate online by choice (Block, 2004). This attitude was endorsed by Michael Powell, who in 2003 as the then-chair of the FCC, compared the digital divide to a "Mercedes divide."

More commonly, many of the people who live in technological richness can easily forget that many people lack such richness. Near the end of 2013, two venues that cater to digitally savvy readers—*Salon* and the *BetaBeat*—each published an article detailing ways in which digital inequalities still exist, with one article focusing on the lack of access to technology and the other on the lack of digital literacy (Holiday, 2013; Sankin, 2013). While it is commendable that these issues received attention in technology-oriented media venues, it is also quite revealing that the readers of these venues need to be informed that these large social problems have not magically disappeared.

Public libraries must make a stronger, more public case for the support they need to further encourage digital literacy and digital inclusion and to sustain related services. A fear of direct engagement with the political process has long plagued public libraries, a result of the belief held by many in the profession that librarians must be neutral and apolitical. The flaw in the belief in neutrality is that it ignores that a "government structure such as the public library can never be neutral" to the extent that it "benefits some groups more than others" (Shavitt, 1986, p. 3). The same groups do not always benefit from government policies, however, and that the benefits of these policies are not uniformly distributed among all members of the populations belies any assertions of neutrality (Durrani & Smallwood, 2006). While neutrality has many critics who have raised valid refutations of the notion (e.g., Alfino & Pierce, 2001; Budd, 2006; Burton, 2009; Cornelius, 2004; Durrani & Smallwood, 2006; Floridi, 2002; Good, 2006/2007; Graham, 2001), the fear of political engagement continues to drive many of the actions of public libraries and public library organizations.

This neutrality stance, unfortunately, frequently places libraries in the position of having major political and policy decisions happen to them, their voice basically unheard and ignored (Jaeger & Bertot, 2011; Jaeger, Bertot, & Gorham, 2013). "It is often the case that the librarian's role as advocate is often undermined not merely by society but by librarians themselves" (McMenemy, 2007, p. 178). For example, the self-imposed voicelessness of libraries in the political process has made it much easier for governments to shift significant e-government and emergency response duties to public libraries in the past few years (Jaeger & Bertot, 2011). One legal scholar recently labeled libraries as possessing "compelling answers" to current major policy problems pertaining to privacy and intellectual freedom, while bemoaning the disinclination of libraries to engage these issues in the political arena (Richards, 2013).

Without changes in policy in this area, public library roles in promoting digital literacy and digital inclusion are not sustainable. For each member of a population who is disadvantaged in terms of digital literacy and digital inclusion, and for society as a whole, such an outcome would have dismal consequences. Without the public library as a capable intermediary, the gaps between the digital haves and the digital have-nots will quickly escalate as digital inclusion becomes more and more central to participation in education, employment, government, and many other areas.

DIGITAL LITERACY AND INCLUSION IN LIBRARY PRACTICE AND ADVOCACY

Many different conceptions of and approaches to digital literacy and digital inclusion from around the world have been presented throughout the preceding chapters of this book. Many ideas for practices, programs, and services can be gleaned from the endeavors of the United States and around the world that are documented and discussed. While every library serves a unique community with individualized needs, some key ideas in approaching practices related to digital literacy and digital inclusion can help to frame the local approach developed in each library.

An important starting point is focusing on the reasons that members of the community seek help at the library for digital literacy. The lack of access is the primary reason for nonusage of the Internet across all age groups, while the lack of skills is a greater barrier for adults than for youth (Livingstone & Helsper, 2007). Such a lack of access and skills can be rooted in issues of geography, education, economics, culture, age, disability, and many other issues, each of which presents challenges in achieving digital inclusion (Jaeger, Subramaniam, Jones, & Bertot, 2011). Programs and services to promote digital literacy and digital inclusion need to start from the basis of awareness of and sensitivity to the reasons for lack of digital literacy and the barriers to achieving it.

In promoting digital literacy and digital inclusion, it is also central to create programs and services that are not one-size-fits-all. Family and personal attitudes and background heavily shape attitudes toward and interactions with technology (Meneses & Momino, 2010). Literacies are social, diverse, numerous, and not necessarily related or overlapping, which means that achieving digital literacy will be a very personal journey (Roberts, 1993, 1995). "Literacy is an activity, a way of thinking, not a set of skills" (Langer, 1987, p. 426). As digital literacy builds on other literacies—reading, writing, and other skills are applied to the new context—barriers and challenges with other types of literacy may be present before digital literacy can be considered.

The setting of the digital literacy instruction is also worth considering, as the ways in which it makes participants feel will influence their ability to learn. Digital skills are most easily learned in informal settings. As initial interactions with and highest levels of technology usage are most likely outside of formal learning environments, creating environments that are welcoming rather than stern or intimidating will promote learning and reduce anxiety (Meneses & Momino, 2010).

Tying digital literacy to key skills that people need and goals they wish to fulfill will also help demonstrate the importance of achieving digital literacy. If digital literacy programs and services are linked to tasks that members of the community want and need to accomplish, such as submitting their taxes online or registering their children for school, digital literacy programs will have more context. "The great divide in literacy is not between those who can read and write and those who have not yet learned how. It is between those who have discovered what kinds of literacy society values and how to demonstrate their competencies in ways that earn recognition" (Meek, 1991, p. 9). Consider the Baltimarket program described above, as it taught digital literacy by allowing people to order fresh food and develop healthier dietary habits.

Building partnerships to support digital literacy and digital inclusion efforts will allow for more ambitious services and programs that have greater reach than the library might have on its own. Digital literacy and digital inclusion are community issues, and such partnerships also help to convey the message about library contributions to the community. Working in conjunction with other libraries in the system, state, or region will help to develop shared standards and practices that can link efforts in different places and that create coherent larger-scale digital inclusion efforts (Chang et al., 2004; Kelly, Phipps, Sloan, Petrie, & Hamilton, 2005). Partnerships with other libraries also will generate enhanced opportunities for teaching alliances, team teaching, and co-planning and development of services and programs, all of which are central to efforts to promote digital literacy in school settings (Mackey & Jacobsen, 2005; O'Brien & Schraber, 2008).

The lessons from the case studies can also be very useful for librarians in considering the policies to collectively advocate for at the national level. South Korea, the Netherlands, and Australia have all taken a more centralized and organized approach to promoting digital literacy and digital inclusion at the national level through policies that have supported the creation of specific literacy and inclusion goals and national agencies to promote literacy and inclusion. Each of those nations has a much smaller and much more homogeneous population than the United States, which means fewer people to include and fewer different cultural, linguistic, and other differences to negotiate in providing literacy and inclusion. However, the greater national commitment and coordination in approaches to access, literacy, and inclusion provide many important models that can be applied to policy in countries like the United States.

The development of such policies depends on a more active engagement of policy and political processes by librarians to advocate for support in their roles as ensurers of digital literacy and digital inclusion (Jaeger, Gorham, Bertot, & Sarin, 2014). These policy and political dimensions are an essential part of the larger picture of ensuring that digital literacy and digital inclusion are available to all. Access, literacy, and inclusion must be provided in modern societies, and no institution has better demonstrated the ability to provide such access, literacy, and inclusion than public libraries. To be successful, however, libraries need these activities to be supported by sensible policy decisions and through adequate funding.

INFORMATION WORLDS AND FUTURE RESEARCH

In many places in the text of this book, the discussion notes a lack of or limited amount of relevant data that would be extremely helpful to understanding some aspect of digital literacy and digital inclusion. As in the contexts of policymaking and advocacy, issues of digital literacy and digital inclusion merit far greater attention than they currently receive in research. While these issues have implications for many fields, their sizeable implications for the library profession—coupled with the uniquely appropriate skills of scholars of information—suggest that increased research about digital literacy and digital inclusion are a priority for scholars of library and information science.

Much of the needed research is in the area of evaluation and assessment, such as measuring the effectiveness of literacy and inclusion programs, identifying best practices from programs, and determining the most useful ways to improve existing efforts. Similarly, a greater focus on policy analysis of the roles of digital literacy and digital inclusion as issues in advocacy, policy, and politics would help to illuminate the best means to advocate for digital literacy and digital inclusion support and policies from governments, as well as the most effective programs for which to advocate. Finally, we also need to simply know more about who is using the digital literacy and digital inclusion programs in libraries, the ways in which these patrons are benefiting, and the ways to create programs to draw and help other underserved and disadvantaged groups not currently being served.

With so many important research gaps in such an important area of study, increased scholarly attention will be of great utility not only for the field of library and information science and to library professionals but also for the government as it tries to promote literacy and inclusion and for society as a whole as it tries to include those currently on the wrong side of digital literacy. The greater the levels of literacy and inclusion in a society, the lower the number of resources that need to be devoted to helping bridge gaps and the greater productivity across all of the members of the community.

The theory of Information Worlds facilitates the examination of the interrelated aspects of information access (physical, intellectual, and social) occurring through the different levels of social interactions (micro, meso, and macro) among individuals, social groups, and larger influences. While it is a complex mechanism for conceptual analysis, the problems being examined are functions of extremely complex sociopolitical systems that shape the needs for literacy and inclusion, as well as the abilities of libraries to meet these needs. It also has the benefit of being a theoretical structure about information, and issues of access, literacy, and inclusion are inherently problems of information.

A greater commitment to research in this area will also likely identify further research methods, concepts, and theoretical structures that will be beneficial in the study of digital literacy and digital inclusion, the ways to promote them, the best programs for providing them, and the best policy means to support them. All of these abilities to move the research forward require more attention in research. Scholars of library and information science and library professionals can use the research gaps identified in this book—along with many others that their own work and experiences have identified—as starting points. Of similar importance, though, is engaging other fields in these problems through collaboration. The insights from other fields, particularly those like government, public policy, and education, will be extremely valuable in crafting broad understandings and ambitious approaches to addressing large-scale societal challenges of literacy and inclusion.

MOVING FORWARD

In the contemporary world, digital literacy and digital inclusion are issues of social justice and human rights. Without literacy and inclusion online, an individual is cut off from the broadest available tool for education, information, and communication. Opportunities for participation in the workforce, school, civic engagement, entertainment, and many other facets of society are similarly curtailed or unavailable. These issues are of significant importance to societies, governments, and the libraries that are frequently tasked with ensuring the provision of education and access necessary for literacy and inclusion.

This book is designed to facilitate the broad discussion of the relationships between policies about literacy and inclusion and the efforts of libraries to ensure literacy and inclusion. It is a conversation of great importance to library professionals and students, teachers and scholars of information, policymakers, and politicians. The implications of such a conversation are considerable for individuals, communities, libraries, and the cultural institutions that serve as pivotal access agents to participation in the dynamic digital society, as well as the schools, corporations, and governments of a society.

The ideas presented in this book are meant to fuel this conversation in a number of ways. First, by tracing the development and evolution of the concepts of information poverty, access, literacy, and inclusion, the book provides the historical context that has shaped the contemporary situation. Second, by analyzing the existing research and the research gaps, this book points to areas of focus and need for research going forward. Third, by examining policies and practices across nations, the book begins the process of detailing best practices in providing digital literacy and digital inclusion by libraries and by governments. Fourth, the theory of Information Worlds is explored as a scaffold on which to better understand issues of literacy and inclusion. All aspects of this conversation spin around the central intersection of public policy and public libraries—the former relies on the latter to ensure literacy and inclusion, while the latter relies on the former for support in policy and funding. Yet this dialogue is still insufficient in professional, public, and scholarly discourse.

A key step in promoting this dialogue is for librarians to more strongly express the breadth and depth of their literacy and inclusion activities to politicians, policymakers, and members of the public. Libraries have to advocate for themselves in a strong and coordinated voice with messages that use language and data that make sense to the people making decisions about policies (Bertot, Jaeger, & Sarin, 2012; Jaeger, Bertot, & Gorham, 2013; Jaeger, Gorham, Sarin, & Bertot, 2013; Jaeger, Gorham, Bertot, & Sarin, 2014). Most people, even those who regularly use the library, do not know the full range of its services and contributions to communities (Zickuhr, Rainie, & Purcell, 2013). Public libraries will be more likely to make an impact by simultaneously communicating the value and contributions of the library through marketing (e.g., selling to the community) and advocating for policies that positively impact libraries (e.g., lobbying in the policy process) (Nelson, 2006).

These messages need to come from more voices than simply the library directors and administrators. Empowering all members of the library staff to advocate is vital, as is encouraging coordinated advocacy by trustees, friends of the library, patrons, library partners, community members, community leaders, educators, and retired library staff (Imhoff, 2006; Jaeger, Gorham, Sarin, & Bertot, 2013). These advocacy campaigns can include support of high-level community members, organized committees, speaker bureaus for community events, polling, public relations, focusing on the groups most likely to be supportive and engaged, guest editorials in local media, statements of support from local politicians, information tables in libraries, advertisements, and endorsements from colleges and universities, homeowner and condominium associations, celebrities, unions, and Chambers of Commerce (Imhoff, 2006). Using social media and other new technologies to engage the discussion will also be of great value to library advocacy efforts (Zabriskie, 2013).

Engaging policy and advocating for support in these areas may not be the most comfortable activity for librarians, but it is very necessary. The combination of the long-term commitment by public libraries to social inclusion and social justice with libraries' rapid adoption of Internet access and provision of Internet training made them the best situated organization in the United States and many other societies to provide access, literacy, and inclusion. Their success at promoting and supporting digital literacy and digital inclusion now makes them the de facto social guarantor of literacy and inclusion. With the public and the government expecting libraries to fulfill these roles, they must in turn educate the public and the government about the supports that libraries need to continue to guarantee access, literacy, and inclusion. For all of the benefits that individuals, communities, and governments receive from library activities related to literacy and inclusion, they still need to be made aware of the library activities and ensuing benefits.

As libraries move forward in working to expand and improve digital literacy and digital inclusion activities, identify and exchange best practices, and articulate needs in terms of policy and funding support, they will be shaping their own future. Many nonusers of libraries—including many politicians and members of the media—have openly suggested that libraries are completely irrelevant in a world where there is Google (e.g., Davlantes, 2010; Elmore, 2008; LaRue, 2011; Rosenblum, 2013). There is increasing pressure for public libraries to have available all types of information, based on the misconception that public libraries can be like a search engine (Waller, 2009). Most of the private sector and nonprofit entities that filled similar community spaces and community learning roles as public libraries—bookstores, music stores, video stores, orchestras, and other community-based arts organizations—have been greatly reduced or have completely disappeared in the past decade as the Internet has overwhelmed their activities (DePillis, 2013). Recent articles in *Forbes* magazine even declared that a master's degree in LIS is the worst type of master's degree based on career earning potential on the presumption that the Internet is making libraries irrelevant (J. Smith, 2012, 2013).

Yet digital literacy and digital inclusion are human rights issues, and the unique knowledge and skills of librarians are a central part of promoting and protecting these rights. Public libraries have built a well-deserved reputation on being able to provide trusted information sources and guidance using those sources, while a search engine, in presenting all information it can find without any sense of evaluation other than the number of hits a page receives, is the antithesis of the approach and skills of public libraries. Search engines also cannot teach people how to use the Internet or provide access to the Internet for those with no other means to reach it. In the world of the Internet, digital literacy and digital inclusion activities are not only of vital importance to the individuals and communities served by libraries; access, literacy, and inclusion are necessary functions that are only provided by the public library in most communities.

Digital literacy and digital inclusion are also emblematic of the social justice mission of libraries, as libraries perpetually evolve to meet the information needs of their patrons and communities. And the commitment to meeting ever-evolving community needs indicates that public libraries will continue to be essential community institutions in spite of future technological changes or obstacles created by political ideologies. Greater support in politics, policy, and funding would obviously help libraries to meet these vital community needs, but the importance of digital literacy and digital inclusion in library activities appears likely to keep growing. It is imperative that libraries continue to improve their digital literacy and digital inclusion activities, educate the public about the services they provide, and advocate for support for these activities. These activities will be central both to the present and to the future of libraries.

References

Advanced Information Technology Institute (2013). *Projects and research.* Available: http://www.aiti-kace.com.gh/?q=-projects-and-research-.

Akkermans, J., & Plomp, T. (1982). Information technology in Dutch education: Will there be a national policy? *European Journal of Education, 17*(4), 411–420.

Alarti-Amoako, F. T. (2013). Cash and carry at public library. *Modern Ghana*, June 7. Available: http://www.modernghana.com/news/467576/1/cash-and-carry-at-public-library.html.

Alemna, A. A. (1997). A review of library provision in Ghana. *Library Review, 46*(1), 34–44.

Alfino, M., & Pierce, L. (2001). The social nature of information. *Library Trends, 49*, 471–485.

Allred, J. R. (1972). The purpose of the public library: the historical view. *Library History, 2*(5), 185–204.

American Library Association (2010). *Libraries Connect Communities: Public Library Funding & Technology Access Study 2009–2010.* Chicago, IL: American Library Association. Available: http://www.ala.org/plinternetfunding/

American Library Association (2012). *The 2012 state of America's libraries.* Available: http://www.ala.org/news/sites/ala.org.news/files/content/StateofAmericasLibraries-Report2012Finalwithcover.pdf.

American Library Association (2013a). Digital literacy, libraries and public policy. *Office for Information Technology (OITP) Policy's Digital Literacy Task Force.* Available: http://www.districtdispatch.org/wp-content/uploads/2013/01/2012_OITP_digilitreport_1_22_13.pdf.

American Library Association (2013b). *Advocacy, legislation, and issues.* Available: http://www.ala.org/advocacy/home.

Americas Quarterly (2013). The social inclusion index 2013. *Americas Quarterly*, Summer. Available: http://americasquarterly.org/charticles/Social_Inclusion_Index_2013/SI_INDEX_FINAL_7-29-13.pdf.

Arias, M., & Camacho, K. (2011). *Las bibliotecas públicas: Una mirada a los sistemas de bibliotecas en centroamérica.* Costa Rica. Available: Cooperativa Sulá Batsú. http://sulabatsu.com/wp-content/uploads/2011-bibliotecas-centroamerica.pdf.

Arias, M., & Camacho, K. (2012). Public access ICT in Honduras. In R. Gomez (Ed.), *Libraries, Telecentres, Cybercafes and Public Access to ICT: International Comparisons* (pp. 115–227). Hershey, PA: Information Science Reference.

Aschmann, A. (2002). Providing intellectual access to cooperative extension materials. *Quarterly Bulletin of the International Association of Agricultural Information Specialists, 47*(3/4), 89–92.

Australia Bureau of Statistics (2013). *Population: 12 September 2013.* Available: http://www.abs.gov.au/ausstats/abs@.nsf/0/1647509ef7e25faaca2568a900154b63?opendocument.

Australian Communications and Media Authority (2009). *Audit of Australian digital media literacy programs.* Available: http://www.acma.gov.au/webwr/_assets/main/lib310665/audit_of_aust_digital_media_literacy_programs.pdf.

Australian Government (2013). *Department of Broadband, Communications and the Digital Economy.* Available: http://www.dbcde.gov.au/

Australian Government: Department of Communications, Information Technology and the Arts (1997). *Networking the Nation*: the commonwealth government's regional telecommunications infrastructure fund.

Australian Government: The Treasury (1997). *Investing for Growth*. http://archive.treasury.gov.au/documents/185/PDF/Full.pdf.

Auty, R. M. (2001). The political economy of resource-driven growth. *European Economic Review, 45*(4–6), 839–846.

Bae, K. J., Jeong, Y. S., Shim, W. S., & Kwak, S. J. (2007). The ubiquitous library for the blind and physically handicapped: A case study of the LG Sangnam Library, Korea. *IFLA Journal, 33*(3), 210–219. Available: http://www.gzlib.gov.cn/shipin/qtkj/mxyd.pdf.

Barber, B. R. (1997). The new telecommunications technology: Endless frontier or the end of democracy? *Constellations, 4*, 208–228.

Barón, L. F., & Gomez, R. (2012). Perceptions of connectedness: Public access computing and social inclusion in Colombia. *Hawaii International Conference on Systems Sciences, Maui, HI, January 2012*. Available: http://ieeexplore.ieee.org/stamp/stamp.jsp?tp=&arnumber=6149096.

Barón, L. F., & Valdés, M. (2012). Public access ICT in Colombia. In R. Gomez (Ed.), *Libraries, telecentres, cybercafes and public access to ICT: International comparisons* (pp. 169–183). Hershey, PA: Information Science Reference.

Barón-Porras, L. F., & Gomez, R. (2012). Same but different: Comparing public access computing venues in Colombia. *Information Technologies & International Development, 8*(4), 43–57.

Barzilai-Nahon, K. (2006). Gaps and bits: Conceptualizing measurements for digital divide/s. *Information Society, 22*, 269–278.

Battistella, E. (2010). What a library closure taught me. *Library Journal*. Available: http://www.libraryjournal.com.

Bawden, D. (2001). Information and digital literacies: A review of concepts. *Journal of Documentation, 57*(2), 218–259.

Bawden, D. (2008). Origins and concepts of digital literacy. In C. Lankshear and M. Knobel (Eds.), *Digital literacies: Concepts, policies and practices* (pp. 17–32). New York: Peter Lang.

Becker, S., Crandall, M. D., Fisher, K. E., Kinney, B., Landry, C., & Rocha, A. (2010). *Opportunity for all: How the America public benefits from Internet access at U.S. libraries*. Washington, DC: Institute for Museum and Library Services. Available: http://impact.ischool.washington.edu/documents/OPP4ALL_FinalReport.pdf.

Bednarek, M. (1993). Intellectual access to pictorial information. *Australian Library Journal, 42*, 33–46.

Bell, D. (1960). *The end of ideology: On the exhaustion of political ideas in the fifties*. Glencoe, IL: Free Press.

Bennett, S., Maton, K., & Kervin, L. (2012). The "digital natives" debate: A critical review of the evidence. *British Journal of Educational Technology, 39*(5), 775–786.

Berman, S. (March 1998). On my mind—Libraries, class, and the poor people's policy. *American Libraries, 29*, 38.

Berninghausen, D. K. (1953). The history of the ALA intellectual freedom committee. *Wilson Library Bulletin, 27*(10), 813–817.

Bertot, J. C. (2003). The multiple dimensions of the digital divide: More than technology "haves" and "have-nots." *Government Information Quarterly, 20*, 185–191.

Bertot, J. C. (2009). Public access technologies in public libraries: Impacts and implications. *Information Technology & Libraries, 28*(2), 84–95.

Bertot, J. C., Gorham, U., Jaeger, P. T., & Taylor, N. G. (2012). Public libraries and the internet 2012: Key findings, recent trends, and future challenges. *Public Library Quarterly, 31*, 303–325.

Bertot, J. C., & Jaeger, P. T. (2006). User-centered e-government: Challenges and benefits for government websites. *Government Information Quarterly, 23*(2), 163–168.

Bertot, J. C., & Jaeger, P. T. (2012). Implementing and managing public library networks, connectivity, and partnerships to promote e-government access and education. In S. Aikins (Ed.), *Managing e-government projects: Concepts, issues and best practices* (pp. 183–199). Hershey, PA: IGI Global.

Bertot, J. C., Jaeger, P. T., Gorham, U., Taylor, N. G., & Lincoln, R. (2013). Delivering e-government services and transforming communities through innovative partnerships: Public libraries, government agencies, and community organizations. *Information Polity, 19*(2), 127–138.

Bertot, J. C., Jaeger, P. T., & Greene, N. N. (2013). Transformative e-government and public service: Public libraries in times of economic hardship. In V. Weerakkody & C. G. Reddick (Eds.), *Public sector transformation through e-government: Experiences from Europe and North America* (pp. 35–46). New York: Routledge.

Bertot, J. C., Jaeger, P. T., & Grimes, J. M. (2010). Using ICTs to create a culture of transparency: E-government and social media as openness and anti-corruption tools for societies. *Government Information Quarterly, 27*, 264–271.

Bertot, J. C., Jaeger, P. T., & Grimes, J. M. (2012). Promoting transparency and accountably through ICTs, social media, and collaborative e-government. *Transforming Government: People, Process and Policy, 6*, 78–91.

Bertot, J. C., Jaeger, P. T., & Hansen, D. (2012). The impact of polices on government social media usage: Issues, challenges, and recommendations. *Government Information Quarterly, 29*, 30–40.

Bertot, J. C., Jaeger, P. T., Langa, L. A., & McClure, C. R. (2006a). Public access computing and Internet access in public libraries: The role of public libraries in e-government and emergency situations. *First Monday, 11*(9). Available: http://www.firstmonday.org/issues/issue11_9/bertot/index.html.

Bertot, J. C., Jaeger, P. T., Langa, L. A., & McClure, C. R. (2006b). Drafted: I want you to deliver e-government. *Library Journal, 131*(13), 34–39.

Bertot, J. C., Jaeger, P. T., McClure, C. R., Wright, C. B., & Jensen, E. (2009). Public libraries and the Internet 2008–2009: Issues, implications, and challenges. *First Monday, 14*(11). Available: http://firstmonday.org/htbin/cgiwrap/bin/ojs/index.php/fm/article/viewArticle/2700/2351.

Bertot, J. C., Jaeger, P. T., Munson, S., & Glaisyer, T. (2010). Engaging the public in open government: The policy and government application of social media technology for government transparency. *IEEE Computer, 43*(11), 53–59.

Bertot, J. C., Jaeger, P. T., & Sarin, L. C. (2012). Forbes folly: The lessons of being labeled the worst master's degree. *American Libraries, 43*(9/10), 30–33.

Bertot, J. C., & McClure, C. R. (1999). Public library Internet connectivity: Status and policy implications. *Library and Information Science Research, 21*, 281–298.

Bertot, J. C., McClure, C. R., & Jaeger, P. T. (2008). The impacts of free public Internet access on public library patrons and communities. *Library Quarterly, 78*, 285–301.

Bertot, J. C., McDermott, A., Lincoln, R., Real, B., & Peterson, K. (2012). *2011–2012 Public Library Funding and Technology Access Survey: Survey Findings and Results.* College Park, MD: Information Policy and Access Center. Available: http://plinternetsurvey.org/sites/default/files/publications/2012_plftas.pdf.

Bethea, A. D. (2011). Has Charlotte survived? *Library Journal, 136*(9), 28–32.

Beyond Access (2012). *Providing Internet access through public libraries: An investment in digital inclusion and twenty-first century skills* [Issue brief], November. Available: http://www.ifla.org/files/assets/clm/WSIS/libraries_public_access.pdf.

Bill & Melinda Gates Foundation (2012). *2002 Access to Learning Award: BiblioRed.* Available: http://www.gatesfoundation.org/atla/Pages/2002-biblored-colombia.aspx.

Birdsong, L. (2010, March). The innovative Dutch: Libraries, universities, and research institutes in the Netherlands. *Information Today, 18*(2). Available: http://www.infotoday.com/searcher/mar10/Birdsong.shtml.

Bishop, B. W., & Veil, S. R. (2013). Public libraries as post-crisis information hubs. *Public Library Quarterly, 32*, 33–45.

Block, W. (2004). The "digital divide" is not a problem in need of rectifying. *Journal of Business Ethics, 53*, 393–406.

Blue, E. V., & Pace, D. (2011). UD and UDL: Paving the way toward inclusion and independence in the school library. *Knowledge Quest, 39*(3), 49–55.

Blumenstein, L. (2009). In Gainesville, FL, "The Library Partnership" merges branch, social services. *Library Journal*, July 22. Available: http://www.libraryjournal.com/.

Booz Allen Hamilton (2002). *International e-economy benchmarking: The world's most effective policies for e-government*. Washington, DC: Author.

Borchardt, D. H., & Horacek, J. I. (1975). *Librarianship in Australia, New Zealand, and Oceania: A brief survey*. Potts Point, NSW: Pergamon Press.

Borgman, C. (2007). *Scholarship in the digital age*. Cambridge, MA: MIT Press.

Boris, L. (2005). The digital divide and its impact on the rural community. *Rural Libraries, 25*(2), 7–35.

Boyd, P., & Berejka, M. (2009). *Consolidated comments of Microsoft Corporation before the Department of Commerce, National Telecommunications and Information Administration, Department of Agriculture, Rural Utilities Service, and the Federal Communications Commission in the matter of American Recovery and Reinvestment Act of 2009 broadband initiatives, the commission's consultative role in the broadband provisions of the Recovery Act*. Redmond, WA: Microsoft Corporation. Available: http://www.ntia.doc.gov/broadbandgrants/comments/78A.pdf.

Brandtweiner, R., Donat, E., & Kerschbaum, J. (2012). How to become a sophisticated user: A two-dimensional approach to e-literacy. *New Media & Society, 12*(5), 813–833.

Branscomb, L. M. (1979). Information: The ultimate frontier. *Science, 203*(4376), 143–147.

Brisbane City Council (2013). *Computer and Internet facilities*. Available: http://www.brisbane.qld.gov.au/facilities-recreation/libraries/library-facilities-and-services/computer-and-internet-facilities/index.htm.

Broadband Commission for Digital Development (2012, September). *The state of broadband 2012: Achieving digital inclusion for all*. Available: http://www.broadbandcommission.org/Documents/bb-annualreport2012.pdf.

Broadband Commission for Digital Development (n.d.). Overview. Available: http://www.broadbandcommission.org/about/overview.aspx.

Broadband Expert Group (2002, May 30). Nederland Breedbandland: Recommendations to the Cabinet from the national Broadband Expert Group for achieving a national lead in the field of broadband infrastructures and applications [Unofficial translation prepared for use as room document for the OECD broadband workshop in Seoul, 4–5 June 2002]. The Hague: The Netherlands. Available: http://www.oecd.org/internet/ieconomy/1936570.pdf.

Brophy, P., & Halpin, E. F. (1999). Through the Net to freedom: Information, the Internet, and human rights. *Journal of Information Science, 25*, 351–354.

Bryne, A. (2006). Zones of silence: A framework beyond the digital divide. *First Monday, 11*(5).

Buckley, F. J. (1987). Knowledge–access issues. *The Information Society, 5*(1), 45–50.

Budd, J. M. (2006). Politics and public library collections. *Progressive Librarian, 28*, 78–86.

Bureau of Labor Statistics (2012). Occupational outlook handbook: Librarians. Available: http://www.bls.gov/ooh/education-training-and-library/librarians.htm.

Burnett, G., Besant, M., & Chatman, E. A. (2001). Small worlds: Normative behavior in virtual communities and feminist bookselling. *Journal of the American Society for Information Science and Technology, 52*, 536–547.

Burnett, G., & Jaeger, P. T. (2012). Information worlds: Social context and information behavior. In A. Spink & J. Heinstrom (Eds.), *New research in information behaviour* (pp. 161–180). London: Emerald.

Burnett, G., Jaeger, P. T., & Thompson, K. M. (2008). Normative behavior and information: The social aspects of information access. *Library & Information Science Research, 30*(1), 56–66.

Burton, J. (2009). Theory and politics in public librarianship. *Progressive Librarian, 32*, 21–28.

Buschman, J. E. (2009). Information literacy, "new" literacies, and literacy. *Library Quarterly, 79*, 95–118.

Buschman, J. E. (2012). *Libraries, classrooms, and the interests of democracy: Marking the limits of neoliberalism.* Lanham, MD: Scarecrow.

Buschman, J. E., & Leckie, G. J. (Eds.) (2007). *The library as place: History, community, and culture.* Westport, CT: Libraries Unlimited.

Caidi, N., & Allard, D. (2005). Social inclusion of newcomers to Canada: An information problem? *Library & Information Science Research, 27*, 302–324.

Campbell, A. (1960). Surge and decline: A study of electoral change. *Public Opinion Quarterly, 24*(3), 397–418.

CapGemini (2008). *Technology futures and digital inclusion.* Department for Communities and Local Government, October. London: Crown Copyright.

Carlton, J. (2009). Folks are flocking to the library, a cozy place to look for a job: Books, computers and wi-fi are free, but staffs are stressed by crowds, cutbacks. *Washington Post*, January 19, A1.

Carnesi, M. S., & Fiol, M. A. (2000). Queens Library's New Americans Program: 23 years of services to immigrants. In Salvador Guerena (Ed.), *Library services to Latinos: An anthology* (pp. 133–142). Jefferson, NC: McFarland.

Cary, K., & Ogburn, J. L. (2000). Developing a consortial approach to cataloging and intellectual access. *Library Collections, Acquisitions, & Technical Services, 24*, 45–51.

Cathcart, R. (2008). Librarian or social worker: Time to look at blurring the line? *Reference Librarian, 49*(1), 87–91.

Center for Digital Inclusion (n.d.). *CDI in the community.* Available: http://www.cdi.org.br/projeto_post/cdi-comunidade-2/?lang=en.

Center for Information & Society (2009). *Colombia: Public access landscape study su mmary.* Washington: University of Washington.

Center on Budget and Policy Priorities (2012). *States continue to feel recession's impact.* Washington, DC: Author. Available: http://www.cbpp.org/cms/index.cfm?fa=view&id=711.

Central Intelligence Agency (2013). *The world factbook.* Available: https://www.cia.gov/library/publications/the-world-factbook/.

Chang, B. L., Bakken, S., Brown, S. S., Houston, T. K., Kreps, G. L., Kukafka, R., Safran, C., & Stavri, Z. (2004). Bridging the digital divide: Reaching vulnerable populations. *Journal of American Medical Informatics Association, 11*, 448–457.

Chatman, E. A. (1987). Opinion leadership, poverty, and information sharing. *RQ, 26*, 341–353.

Chatman, E. A. (1990). Alienation theory: Application of a conceptual framework to a study of information among janitors. *RQ, 29*, 355–368.

Chatman, E. A. (1991). Channels to a larger world: Older women staying in contact with the great society. *Library & Information Science Research, 13*, 281–300.

Chatman, E. A. (1996). The impoverished life-world of outsiders. *Journal of the American Society for Information Science, 47*, 193–206.

Chatman, E. A. (1999). A theory of life in the round. *Journal of the American Society for Information Science, 50*, 207–217.

Chatman, E. A. (2000). Framing social life in theory and research. *New Review of Information Behaviour Research, 1*, 3–17.

Chen, H., & Rasmussen, E. M. (1999). Intellectual access to images. *Library Trends, 48*(2), 291–302.

Chen, S. (2010). The new hungry: College-educated, middle-class cope with food insecurity. *CNN.com.* Available: http://www.cnn.com.

Childers, T., & Post, J. (1975). *The information poor in America.* Metuchen, NJ: Scarecrow Press.

Chinn, M. D., & Fairlie, R. W. (2007). The determinants of the global digital divide: A cross-country analysis of computer and Internet penetration. *Oxford Economic Papers, 59,* 16–44.

Choi, W. (2003). The development of digital libraries in South Korea. *Libri, 53,* 130-141.

Chon, K., Park, H., Kang, K., & Lee, Y. (2005). *A brief history of the Internet in Korea.* [White paper]. Manoa, HI: East West Center. Available: http://net.its.hawaii.edu/history/Korean_Internet_History.pdf.

Clark, L., & Vissner, M. (2011). Digital literacy takes center stage. *Library Technology Report.* ALA Office for Research and Statistics, 38–42.

Clear, F., & Dennis, C. (2009). E-government, disability, & inclusion. In L. Budd & L. Harris (Eds.), *E-governance: Managing or governing?* (pp. 213–236). New York: Routledge.

Click, A., & Petit, J. (2010). Social networking and Web 2.0 in information literacy. *International Information & Library Review, 42,* 137–142.

Coalter, F. (2005). Sport, social inclusion, and crime reduction. In G. E. J. Faulkner & A. H. Taylor (Eds.). *Exercise, health and mental health: Emerging relationships* (pp. 191–208). New York: Routledge.

Codagnone, C. (Ed.) (2009, March). *Vienna study on inclusive innovation for growth and cohesion: Modelling and demonstrating the impact of eInclusion.* Available: http://ec.europa.eu/information_society/activities/einclusion/library/studies/docs/eco_compendium.pdf.

Coleman, J. S. (1972). The children have outgrown the schools. *Psychology Today, 5,* 72–75, 82.

Collins, B. (2012). How public libraries are a boon to small business. *American Libraries,* August 13. Available: http://americanlibrariesmagazine.org/features/08132012/how-public-libraries-are-boon-small-business.

Collis, B. (1996). *Tele-learning in a digital world: The future of distance learning.* London: International Thompson.

Comaromi, J. P. (1990). Summation of classification as an enhancement of intellectual access to information in an online environment. *Cataloging & Classification Quarterly, 11*(1), 99–102.

Commonwealth of Australia (2009). *National partnership agreement on the digital education revolution.* Available: http://www.federalfinancialrelations.gov.au/content/npa/education/digital_education_revolution/national_partnership.pdf.

Companie, B. M. (1986). Information gaps: Myth or reality? *Telecommunications Policy, 10*(3).

Constantino, R. (2005). Print environments between high and low socioeconomic status (SES) communities. *Teacher Librarian, 32*(3), 22–25.

Constitution of Colombia (1991).

Cornelius, D. (1993). Ghana. In R. Wedgeworth (Ed.), *World encyclopedia of library and information services* (3rd. ed., 322–324). Chicago: American Library Association.

Cornelius, I. (2004). Information and its philosophy. *Library Trends, 52,* 377–386.

Cullen, R. (2003). The digital divide: A global and national call to action. *Electronic Library, 21*(3), 247–257.

Culnan, M. J. (1983). Environmental scanning: The effects of task complexity and source accessibility on information gathering behavior. *Decision Sciences, 14*(2), 194–206.

Culnan, M. J. (1984). The dimensions of accessibility to online information: Implications for implanting office information systems. *ACM Transactions on Office Information Systems, 2*(2), 141–150.

Culnan, M. J. (1985). The dimensions of perceived accessibility to information: Implications for the delivery of information systems and services. *Journal of the American Society for Information Science, 36*(5), 302–308.

DaCosta, J. W. (2010). Is there an information literacy skills gap to be bridged? *College & Research Libraries, 71*(3), 203–222.

Dandolopartners Pty Ltd. (2013). DER mid-program review: Assessing progress of the DER and potential future directions. Available: http://deewr.gov.au/digital-education-revolution-program-review.

DANE (2012). Pobreza en Colombia. *Departamento Administrativo Nacional de Estadística*. Bogotá, Colombia.

DANE (2013). Contador de población. Available: http://www.dane.gov.co/reloj/reloj_animado.php.

Dasgupta, S., Lall, S., & Wheeler, D. (2007). Policy reform, economic growth, and the digital divide. *Oxford Development Studies, 33,* 229–243.

Davies, D. W. (1974). *Public libraries as culture and social centers: The origin of the concept.* Metuchen, NJ: Scarecrow.

Davis, D. M. (2009). Challenges to sustaining library technology. *Public Libraries, 48*(4), 12–17.

Davis, D. M. (2011). Public library funding: An overview and discussion. In J. C. Bertot, P. T. Jaeger, & C. R. McClure (Eds.), *Public libraries and the Internet: Roles, perspectives, and implications* (pp. 193–214). Westport, CT: Libraries Unlimited.

Davlantes, A. (2010). Are libraries necessary, or a waste of tax money? *Fox News Chicago,* June 28. Available: http://www.myfoxchicago.com/story/17835324/are-libraries-necessary-or-a-waste-of-tax-money.

De Cindio, F., Gentile, O., Grew, P., & Redolfi, D. (2003). Community networks: Rules of behavior and social structure. *Information Society, 19,* 395–406.

de Jager, K., & Nassimbeni, M. (2009). Information literacy in practice: Engaging public library workers in rural South Africa. *IFLA Journal, 33*(4), 313.

Deines-Jones, C. (1996). Access to library Internet services for patrons with disabilities: Pragmatic considerations for developers. *Library Hi Tech, 14*(1), 57–64.

Dempsey, B. (2009). Library referenda 2008: Libraries build the case for voter support. *Library Journal,* March 15. Available: http://www.libraryjournal.com.

Dempsey, B. (2010). Library referenda 2009: Voters step up. *Library Journal,* March 15. Available: http://www.libraryjournal.com.

Department of Broadband, Communications and the Digital Economy (2009). *Australia's digital economy: Future directions.* Canberra: Author. Available: http://www.archive.dbcde.gov.au/__data/assets/pdf_file/0006/117681/DIGITAL_ECONOMY_FUTURE_DIRECTIONS_FINAL_REPORT.pdf.

Department of Communications, Information Technology and the Arts (2004). *Australia's strategic framework for the information economy 2004–2006.* Canberra: Author. Available: http://www.archive.dcita.gov.au/2007/11/australias_strategic_framework.

Department of Communications, Information Technology and the Arts (2006). *Backing indigenous ability: Delivering a comprehensive telecommunications package in indigenous communities* [Discussion paper]. Canberra: Author. Available: http://www.archive.dcita.gov.au/__data/assets/pdf_file/0007/37996/BIA_discussion_paper_approved.pdf.

DePillis, L. (2013). Barnes & Noble can succeed, but not by competing with Amazon. *Washington Post,* July 14. Available: http://www.washingtonpost.com.

Dervin, B. L., & Greenberg, B. S. (1972). The communication environment of the urban poor. *CUP Report No. 15.* East Lansing: Michigan State University, Department of Communication.

Dhillon, J. S. (1980). *Information consumption by low income families to reduce rural poverty in Florida.* Tallahassee: Community Development and Research Program, Florida Agricultural and Mechanical University.

Dibrary (n.d.). Available: http://www.dlibrary.go.kr/.

DigitalLiteracy.gov (n.d.). Available: http://www.digitalliteracy.gov/about.

Dilevko, J., & Dali, K. (2003). Electronic databases for readers' advisory services and intellectual access to translated fiction not originally written in English. *Library Resources & Technical Services, 47*(3), 80–95.

District of Columbia Public Library (DCPL) (2013). *Accessibility hackathon 2.* Available: http://dclibrary.org/node/32540.

Dobransky, K., & Hargittai, E. (2006). The disability divide in Internet access and use. *Information Communication & Society, 9,* 313–334.

Doh, S., & Stough, R. (2010). Analysis of the impact of the perceived usefulness of ICT on the digital divide between disabled and non-disabled people in South Korea. *International Review of Public Administration, 14*(3), 53–70.

Dronkers, J. (1993). The causes of growth of English education in the Netherlands: Class or internationalisation? *European Journal of Education, 28*(3), 295–307.

DTZ Pieda Consulting & TNS Social Research (2004). Digital communities: Final report. *Scottish Executive.* Available: http://www.scotland.gov.uk/Resource/Doc/17002/0024843.pdf.

Dubey, Y. P. (1985). *Information poverty: A third-world perspective.* ERIC document ED 314051.

Duffy, T. M. (2001). Museums of "human suffering" and the struggle for human rights. *Museum International, 53*(1), 10–16.

DuMont, R. R. (1977). *Reform and reaction: The big city public library in American life.* Westport, CT: Greenwood.

Duran, D. F. (1978). Information status and the mass media: The case of the urban poor. *Collection Building, 1,* 49–60.

Durrance, J. C., & Fisher, K. E. (2005). *How libraries and librarians help: Assessing outcomes in your library.* Chicago: ALA Editions.

Durrani, S., & Smallwood, E. (2006). The professional is political: Redefining the social role of public libraries. *Progressive Librarian, 27,* 3–22.

Eberhart, G. (2013). The prescription for finding healthcare information. *American Libraries.* Available: http://www.americanlibrariesmagazine.org/blog/prescription-finding-healthcare-information.

ECDL Foundation (2012). *NL/EU: Workers' lack of ICT skills can contribute to a productivity loss of up to € 19.3 billion per annum.* Available: http://www.epractice.eu/en/news/5343331.

Economist (2013, July 26). Whatever happened to municipal wi-fi? *Babbage science and technology blog.* Available: http://www.economist.com/blogs/babbage/2013/07/wireless-networks.

Eisenberg, M., & Berkowitz, B. (1999). *Big6 information skills.* Available: http://nb.wsd.wednet.edu/big6/big6_resources.htm.

Elbert, M., Fuegi. D., & Lipeikaite, U. (2012). Public libraries in Africa—Agents for development and innovation? Current perceptions of local stakeholders. *International Federation of Library Associations Journal, 38,* 148–165.

Electronic Communications Act (2008). Act 775. Available: http://www.nca.org.gh/downloads/regdocs/NCA_Electronic_Communications_Act_775.pdf.

Electronic Information for Libraries (2011a). *Internet access and training programme.* Available: http://www.eifl.net/ghana-library-board-ghana.

Electronic Information for Libraries (2011b). *Perceptions of public libraries: Ghana.* Available: http://www.eifl.net/perception-study.

Electronic Information for Libraries (2012a). *EIFL-PLIP training inspires library champions.* Available: http://www.eifl.net/news/eifl-plip-training-inspires-library-champions.

Electronic Information for Libraries (2012b). *Ghana public library hosts ICT4D lecture series.* Available: http://www.eifl.net/news/ghana-public-library-hosts-ict4d-lecture-seri.

Electronic Information for Libraries (2013a). *Library SMS service contributes to maternal health.* Available: http://www.eifl.net/ghana-library-board-northern-regional-library.

Electronic Information for Libraries (2013b). *Mobile library lessons improve children's ICT skills.* Available: http://www.eifl.net/ghana-library-board-mobile-library-service.

Elmore, G. (2008). Pull the plug on the library. *Gainesville Sun*, March 3. Available: http://www.gainesvillesun.com.

Ennis, P. H., & Fryden, F. N. (1960). The library in the community use studies revisited. *Library Quarterly, 30*, 253–265.

Erickson, C. A. (2013). In Central America, community-minded libraries become community funded: Report on Guatemala and Honduras libraries. *American Libraries* (January/February). Available: http://www.americanlibrariesmagazine.org/article/central-america-community-minded-libraries-become-community-funded.

Eshet-Alkali, Y. (2004). Digital literacy: A conceptual framework for survival skills in the digital era. *Journal of Educational Multimedia and Hypermedia* (1391), 93–106. Available: http://www.openu.ac.il/Personal_sites/download/Digital-literacy2004-JEMH.pdf.

Eshet-Alkali, Y., & Amichai-Hamburger, Y. (2004). Experiments in digital literacy. *CyberPsychology and Behavior, 7*(4), 421–429.

European Commission (2010, July). *eInclusion in the Netherlands.* Available: http://www.epractice.eu/files/eInclusion percent20in percent20NL- percent20July percent202010 percent20-2.0_1.pdf.

European Commission (2013). Pillar VI: Enhancing digital literacy, skills, and inclusion. *Digital Agenda for Europe.* Available: http://ec.europa.eu/digital-agenda/en/our-goals/pillar-vi-enhancing-digital-literacy-skills-and-inclusion.

European Commission Press Room (2006, December 6). *Internet for all: EU ministers commit to an inclusive and barrier-free information society* [Press release]. Available: http://europa.eu/rapid/press-release_IP-06-769_en.htm.

European Urban Knowledge Network (2004, December 31). *Digital playground Cybersoek – Amsterdam, the Netherlands.* Available: http://www.eukn.org/E_library/Social_Inclusion_Integration/Quality_of_Life/Skills_Improvement/Digital_Skills/Digital_playground_Cybersoek_Amsterdam_the_Netherlands.

Fairlie, R. W. (2005). *Are we really a nation online? Ethnic and racial disparities in access to technology and their consequences.* Santa Cruz: University of California.

Farmer, L. S. J. (2005). *Digital inclusion, teens, and your library.* Westport, CT: Libraries Unlimited.

Faulkner, W., & Lie, M. (2007). Gender in the information society: Strategies for inclusion. *Gender, Technology, & Development, 11*, 157–177.

Federal Communications Commission (2010). *The national broadband plan: Connecting America.* Washington, DC: Author. Available: http://www.broadband.gov/.

Ferlander, S., & Timms, D. (2006). Bridging the digital divide: A local net and an IT café in Sweden. *Information, Communication, & Society, 9*, 137–159.

Ferro, E., Helbig, N. C., & Gil-Garcia, J. R. (2011). The role of IT literacy in defining digital divide policy needs. *Government Information Quarterly, 28*, 3–10.

Fink, C., & Kenny, C. J. (2003). W(h)ither the digital divide? *Info, 5*, 15–24.

First, P. F., & Hart, Y. Y. (2002). Access to cyberspace: The new issue in educational justice. *Journal of Law and Education, 31*, 385–411.

Fisher, K., & Naumer, C. M. (2005). Information grounds: Theoretical basis and empirical findings on information flow in social settings. In A. Spink & C. Cole (Eds.), *New directions in human information behavior* (pp. 93–111). New York: Springer.

Fiske, M. (1959). *Book selection and censorship: A study of school and public libraries in California.* Berkeley: University of California Press.

Flatley, R., & Wyman, A. (2009). Changes in rural libraries and librarianship: A comparative survey. *Public Library Quarterly, 28*(1), 24–39.

Floridi, L. (2002). On defining library and information science as applied philosophy of information. *Social Epistemology, 16*, 37–49.

Fox, S. (2004). *Older Americans and the Internet.* Washington, DC: Pew Research Center.

Fox, S., & Livingston, G. (2007). *Latinos online: Hispanics with lower levels of education and English proficiency remain largely disconnected from the Internet.* Washington, DC: Pew Research Center. Available: http://www.pewinternet.org.

Fox, S., & Madden, M. (2005). *Generations online*. Washington, DC: Pew Research Center. Available: http://www.pewinternet.org.

Fundalectura (2013). Available: www.fundalectura.org/.

G20 (2013). *About G20 Member Countries*. Available: https://www.g20.org/about_G20.

Gabel, D. (2007). Broadband and universal service. *Telecommunications Policy*, 31(6/7), 327–346.

Gannett Center for Media Studies (1987). *The cost of technology: Information prosperity and information poverty*. New York: Columbia University.

García de Paso Gómez, E. (1998). ¿Y después del Mitch? Un recorrido de las bibliotecas públicas de Centroamérica. *Boletín de la ANABAD*, 48(3–4).

Gdansk Roadmap for Digital Inclusion (2011). Available: http://innodig.eu/download/Gdansk_Roadmap_Reworked_text_7.10.11.pdf.

Gehner, J. (2010). Libraries, low-income people, and social exclusion. *Public Library Quarterly*, 29(1), 39–47.

Gellar, E. (1974). Intellectual freedom: Eternal principle or unanticipated consequence? *Library Journal*, 99, 1364–1367.

Gellar, E. (1984). *Forbidden books in American public libraries, 1876–1939: A study in cultural change*. Westport, CT: Greenwood.

Ghana Business News (2013). Campaigners oppose right to Information Bill. *Ghana Business News*, July 26. Available: http://www.ghanabusinessnews.com/2013/07/26/campaigners-oppose-right-to-information-bill/.

Ghana Information Network for Knowledge Sharing (2013). *GINKS: Promoting ICT as a tool for development*. Available: http://www.ginks.org/home.aspx.

Ghana Investment Fund for Electronic Communications (2013a). *GIFEC—Making electronic communication accessible to the nation*. Available: http://gifec.gov.gh/index.php?option=com_content&view=article&id=177 percent3Agifec-making-electronic-communication-accessible-to-the-nation&Itemid=175.

Ghana Investment Fund for Electronic Communications (2013b). *The Disability Employment Project*. Available: http://gifec.gov.gh/index.php?option=com_content&view=article&id=138:uuniversal-access-to-electronic-communications-programme&catid=38:projects&Itemid=248.

Ghana Library Association (2009). Homepage. Available: http://www.gla-net.org/.

Ghana News Agency (2010). Ghana launches mobile library Internet connectivity initiative. *Ghana Business News*, December 25. Available: http://www.ghanabusinessnews.com/2010/12/25/ghana-.

Ghana News Agency (2013a). Gov't urged to revive Board of National Council on Persons with Disability. *Ghana Business News*, June 5. Available: http://www.ghanabusinessnews.com/2013/06/05/govt-urged-to-revive-board-of-national-council-on-persons-with-disability/.

Ghana News Agency (2013b). TechAide to support public libraries in Ghana under PLIFOD initiative. *Ghana Business News*, July. Available: http://techaide.net/blog/2013/07/15/techaide-to-support-public-libraries-in-ghana-under-plifod-initiative/.

Ghana Statistical Service (2012). *2010 population and housing census: Summary report of final results*. Available: http://www.statsghana.gov.gh/docfiles/2010phc/Census2010_Summary_report_of_final_results.pdf.

GhanaWeb (2013, June 7). *Cabinet approves right to information bill*. Available: http://www.ghanaweb.com/GhanaHomePage/NewsArchive/artikel.php?ID=276279.

Gibbs, N. (2009). Thrift nation. *Time*, April 27, p. 24.

Gibson, A. N., Bertot, J. C., & McClure, C. R. (2009). Emerging roles of public libraries as e-government providers. Paper presented at the 42nd *Hawaii International Conference on Systems Sciences*.

Gil-Garcia, J. R., Helbig, N. C., & Ferro, E. (2006). Is it only about Internet access? An empirical test of a multi-dimensional digital divide. *Lecture Notes in Computer Science*, 4084, 139–149.

Gill, P. (Ed.) (2001). *The public library service: The IFLA/UNESCO guidelines for development*. Munchen: K. G. Saur.

Gilliland, A. J. (1988). Introduction: Automating intellectual access to archives. *Library Trends, 38*, 495–499.

Gilroy, A. A., & Kruger, L. G. (2002). *Broadband Internet access: Background and issues.* Congressional Research Service. Available: https://opencrs.com/document/IB10045/2002-11-01/.

Gilster, P. (1997). *Digital literacy.* New York: John Wiley.

Golbeck, J. (2008). Introduction to computing with social trust. In J. Golbeck (Ed.), *Computing with social trust* (pp. 1–5). London: Springer.

Goldberg, B. (2009). Board president denounces closing of Colton libraries. *American Libraries*, November 17. Available: http://www.americanlibrariesmagazine.org.

Goldfarb, A., & Prince, J. (2008). Internet adoption and usage patterns are different: Implications for the digital divide. *Information Economics and Policy, 20*, 2–15.

Gomez, R. (2012a). Users' perceptions of the impact of public access computing in Colombia: Libraries, telecenters, and cybercafés. *Information Technologies and Community Development, 8*(3), 19–33.

Gomez, R. (2012b). Success factors for public access computing: Beyond anecdotes of success. In R. Gomez, *Libraries, telecentres, cybercafes and public access to ICT: International comparisons* (pp. 82–94). Hershey, PA: Information Science Reference.

Good, J. (2006/2007). The hottest place in hell: The crisis of neutrality in contemporary librarianship. *Progressive Librarian, 28*, 25–29.

Goodfellow, R. (2011). Literacy, literacies, and the digital in higher education. *Teaching in Higher Education, 16*(1), 131–144.

Gorham, U., Bertot, J. C., Jaeger, P. T., & Taylor, N. G. (2013). E-government success in public libraries: Library and government agency partnerships delivering services to new immigrants. In J. Ramon Gil-Garcia (Ed.), *E-government success factors and measures: Concepts, theories, experiences, and practical recommendations* (pp. 41–59). Hershey, PA: IGI Global.

Government of Ghana: Official Portal (2013). *Homepage.* Available: http://www.ghana.gov.gh/.

Graham, P. T. (2001). Public librarians and the civil rights movement. *Library Quarterly, 71*, 1–27.

Granovetter, M. S. (1973). The strength of weak ties. *American Journal of Sociology, 78*, 1360–1380.

Granovetter, M. S. (1983). The strength of weak ties: A network theory revisited. *Sociological Theory, 1*, 201–233.

Green, A., Fangqing, W., Cochrane, P., Dyson, J., & Paun, C. (July 8, 2012). English spreads as teaching language in universities worldwide. *University World News: Global, 229.* Available: http://www.universityworldnews.com/article.php?story=20120621131543827.

Greenberg, B. S., & Dervin, B. L. (1970a). Mass communication among the urban poor. *Public Opinion Quarterly, 34*, 224–235.

Greenberg, B. S., & Dervin, B. L. (1970b). *Use of the mass media by the urban poor: Findings of three research projects, with an annotated bibliography.* New York: Praeger.

Grubesic, T. H. (2008). The spatial distribution of broadband providers in the United States: 1999–2004. *Telecommunications Policy, 32*(3/4), 212–233.

Guerrieri P., & Bentivegna, S. (Eds.) (2011). *The economic impact of digital technologies: Measuring inclusion and diffusion in Europe.* Cheltenham, UK: Edward Elgar.

Gunkel, D. (2003). Second thoughts: Towards a critique of the digital divide. *New Media and Society, 5*(4), 499–522.

Gurstein, M. (2003). Effective use: A community informatics strategy beyond the digital divide. *First Monday, 8*(12). Available: http://www.firstmonday.org.

Hahm, M., Lee, B., Song, K., & Park, H. (1998). Media skills of school librarians to teach the new subject information and media in schools and the implications to all librarians: Instruction as a positive reference service. *64th IFLA General Conference, Amsterdam, August 16–21, 1998.* Available: http://archive.ifla.org/IV/ifla64/092-78e.htm.

Hanley, R. (1998). Jersey City librarians protest plan for private contractor. *New York Times*, June 29, pp. B1, B6.

Hanson, E. C. (2008). *The information revolution and world politics*. Lanham, MD: Rowman & Littlefield.

Harrington, M. (1962). *The other America: Poverty in the United States*. New York: Macmillan.

Hatch, J. (2004). Employment in the public sector: Two recessions' impact on jobs. *Monthly Labor Report*, October, 38–47.

Hazemi, R., Hailes, S., & Wilbur, S. (1998). *The digital university: Reinventing the academy*. Springer Verlag: London.

Heanue, A. (2001). In support of democracy: The library role in public access to government information. In N. Kranich (Ed.), *Libraries and democracy: The cornerstones of liberty* (pp. 121–128). Chicago, IL: American Library Association.

Heckart, R. J. (1991). The library as marketplace of ideas. *College and Research Libraries, 52*, 491–505.

Helling, J. (2012). *Public libraries and their national policies: International case studies*. Oxford: Chandos.

Helsper, E. J. (2012). A corresponding fields model for the links between social and digital exclusion. *Communication Theory, 22*, 403–426.

Hendry, J. D. (2000). Social inclusion and the information poor. *Library Review, 49*(7), 331–336.

Herb, S., & Willoughby-Herb, S. (2001). Preschool education through public libraries [computer file]. *School Library Media Research, 4*.

Herdman, M. M. (1943). The public library in the Depression. *Library Quarterly, 13*, 310–334.

Hill, C. (2009). Inside, outside, and online. *American Libraries, 40*(3), 39.

Hill, N. M. (2009). Three views. *Public Libraries, 48*(4), 8–11.

Hoffert, B. (2009). It's the economy. *Library Journal, 134*(3), 34–36.

Hoffman, D. L., & Novak, T. P. (1998). Bridging the racial divide on the Internet. *Science, 280*, 390–391.

Hoffman, M. (2001). Developing the electronic collection: The University of Minnesota Human Rights Library. *Legal Reference Services Quarterly, 19*, 143–155.

Holiday, R. (2013). The new digital divide: Privilege, misinformation and outright b.s. in modern media. Available: http://betabeat.com/2013/11/the-new-digital-divide-privilege-misinformation-and-outright-b-s-in-modern-media/.

Horrigan, J. B. (2008). *Home broadband adoption 2008: Adoption stalls for low-income Americans even as many broadband users opt for premium services that give them more speed*. Washington, DC: Pew Research Center. Available: http://www.pewinternet.org/~/media//Files/Reports/2008/PIP_Broadband_2008.pdf.

Horrigan, J. B. (2009). *Obama's online opportunities II: If you build it, will they log on?* Washington, DC: Pew Research Center. Available: http://www.pewinternet.org/~/media//Files/Reports/2009/PIP_Broadband percent20Barriers.pdf.

Horrigan, J. B., & Rainie, L. (2002a). *Getting serious online*. Washington, DC: Pew Research Center. Available: http://www.pewinternet.org/.

Horrigan, J. B., & Rainie, L. (2002b). *Counting on the Internet*. Washington, DC: Pew Research Center. Available: http://www.pewinternet.org/.

House, J. (2003). English as a lingua franca: A threat to multilingualism? *Journal of Sociolinguistics, 7*(4), 556–578.

Hudson, R. (Ed.). (2010). *Colombia: A country study*. Washington, DC: Library of Congress. Available: http://lcweb2.loc.gov/frd/cs/pdf/CS_Colombia.pdf.

Huang, J., & Russell, S. (2006). The digital divide and academic achievement. *Electronic Library, 24*, 160–173.

Huysmans, F., & Hillebrink, C. (2008). The future of the Dutch public library: Ten years on. *The Netherlands Institute for Social Research*. The Hague: The Netherlands.

ICT Digital Leadership Council (2010). *Digital literacy pathways in California*. Available: http://www.ictliteracy.info/rf.pdf/Digital percent20LiteracyMaster_July_2010.pdf.

IFLA (2010). *IFLA world report 2010*. Available: http://ifla-world-report.org/.

Ifrah, G. (2001). *The universal history of computing: From the abacus to the quantum computer*. New York: John Wiley.

Imhoff, K. R. T. (2006). Creating advocates for public libraries. *Public Library Quarterly*, 25(1/2), 155–170.

Information professionals in Ghana benefit from United States library week workshop (2009). *African Journal of Library, Archives and Information Science, 19*(2), 183.

Ingen Housz, F. J. (2011). Dutch policy on media literacy and digital skills: Brief outline for EURODIG. *IRIS plus*. Available: http://www.guarder.net/kleinwaechter/images/eurodig/2009/Dutch policy on_ media literacy and digital skills-versie Freek (2).pdf.

Institute of Museum and Library Services (n.d.). *Public libraries and the workforce*. Available: http://www.imls.gov/about/workforce.aspx.

Institute of Museum and Library Services (2011). *Building digitally inclusive communities*. Available: http://www.imls.gov/resources/resources.shtm.

Institute of Museum and Library Services, University of Washington, & International City/ County Management Association (2012, January). *Building digital communities: A framework for action*. Washington, DC: Institute of Museum and Library Services.

International Fund for Agricultural Development (2011). *Enabling poor rural people to overcome poverty in Honduras*. Rome, Italy: Author. Available: http://www.ifad.org/operations/projects/regions/pl/factsheet/honduras_e.pdf.

International Telecommunication Union (n.d.). Digital inclusion for people with special needs. *Digital Inclusion*. Available: http://www.itu.int/en/ITU-D/Digital-Inclusion/Pages/default.aspx.

International Telecommunication Union (2012). Percentage of individuals using the Internet. *ICT-Eye: Key ICT Data and Statistics*. Available: http://www.itu.int/net4/itu-d/icteye/.

International Telecommunication Union (2013). *Measuring the information society 2012*. Available: http://www.itu.int/ITU-D/ict/publications/idi/.

Internet Society (2011). *Internet Society Board of Trustees views the Internet as an enabler of human rights*. Available: http://www.internetsociety.org.

Intner, S. S. (1991). Intellectual access to patron-use software. *Library Trends, 40*(1), 42–62.

Jacobi, P. (2006). Public and private responses to social exclusion among youth in Sao Paulo. *ANNALS of the American Academy of Political Social Science, 606*, 215–230.

Jaeger, P. T. (2008). Building e-government into the library and information science curriculum: The future of government information and services. *Journal of Education for Library and Information Science, 49*, 167–179.

Jaeger, P. T. (2012). *Disability and the Internet: Confronting a digital divide*. Boulder, CO: Lynne Rienner.

Jaeger, P. T. (2013). Internet justice: Reconceptualizing the legal rights of persons with disabilities to promote equal access in the age of rapid technological change. *Review of Disability Studies, 9*(1), 39–59.

Jaeger, P. T., & Bertot, J. C. (2009). E-government education in public libraries: New service roles and expanding social responsibilities. *Journal of Education for Library and Information Science, 50*, 39–49.

Jaeger, P. T., & Bertot, J. C. (2010). Transparency and technological change: Ensuring equal and sustained public access to government information. *Government Information Quarterly, 27*, 371–376.

Jaeger, P. T., & Bertot, J. C. (2011). Responsibility rolls down: Public libraries and the social and policy obligations of ensuring access to e-government and government information. *Public Library Quarterly, 30*(2), 91–116.

Jaeger, P. T., Bertot, J. C., & Gorham, U. (2013). Wake up the nation: Public libraries, policy-making, and political discourse. *Library Quarterly, 83*, 61–72.

Jaeger, P. T., Bertot, J. C., Kavanaugh, A., Viselli, T., & Nassar, D. (2012). Online community networks, e-government, and community-sourcing actions. *Proceedings of the 13th Annual International Digital Government Research Conference, June 4–7, 2012* (pp. 255–257). College Park, MD: ACM.

Jaeger, P. T., Bertot, J. C., Kodama, C. M., Katz, S. M., & DeCoster, E. J. (2011). Describing and measuring the value of public libraries: The growth of the Internet and the evolution of library value. *First Monday, 11*(7). Available: http://www.uic.edu/htbin/cgiwrap/bin/ojs/index.php/fm/article/viewArticle/3765/3074.

Jaeger, P. T., Bertot, J. C., McClure, C. R., & Rodriguez, M. (2007). Public libraries and internet access across the United States: A comparison by state 2004–2006. *Information Technology and Libraries, 26*(2), 4–14.

Jaeger, P. T., Bertot, J. C., & Subramaniam, M. (2013). Preparing future librarians to effectively serve their communities. *Library Quarterly, 83*, 243–248.

Jaeger, P. T., Bertot, J. C., Thompson, K. M., Katz, S. M., & DeCoster, E. J. (2012). Digital divides, digital literacy, digital inclusion, and public libraries: The intersection of public policy and public access. *Public Library Quarterly, 31*(1), 1–20.

Jaeger, P. T., & Bowman, C. A. (2005). *Understanding disability: Inclusion, access, diversity, & civil rights.* Westport, CT: Praeger.

Jaeger, P. T., & Burnett, G. (2005). Information access and exchange among small worlds in a democratic society: The role of policy in shaping information behavior in the post-9/11 United States. *Library Quarterly, 75*(4), 464–495.

Jaeger, P. T., & Burnett, G. (2010). *Information worlds: Social context, technology, and information behavior in the age of the Internet.* New York: Routledge.

Jaeger, P. T., & Fleischmann, K. R. (2007). Public libraries, values, trust, and e-government. *Information Technology and Libraries, 26*(4), 34–43.

Jaeger, P. T., Gorham, U., Bertot, J. C., & Sarin, L. C. 2014. *Public libraries, public policies, and political processes: Serving and transforming Communities in times of economic and political constraint.* Lanham, MD: Rowman & Littlefield.

Jaeger, P. T., Gorham, U., Sarin, L. C., & Bertot, J. C. (2013). Democracy, neutrality, and value demonstration in the age of austerity. *Library Quarterly, 83*, 368–382.

Jaeger, P. T., Langa, L. A., McClure, C. R., & Bertot, J. C. (2006). The 2004 and 2005 Gulf Coast hurricanes: Evolving roles and lessons learned for public libraries in disaster preparedness and community services. *Public Library Quarterly, 25*(3/4), 199–214.

Jaeger, P. T., McClure, C. R., & Bertot, J. C. (2005). The E-rate program and libraries and library consortia, 2000–2004: Trends and issues. *Information Technology and Libraries, 24*(2), 57–67.

Jaeger, P. T., Subramaniam, M., Jones, C. B., & Bertot, J. C. (2011). Diversity and LIS education: Inclusion and the age of information. *Journal of Education for Library and Information Science, 52*, 166–183.

Jaeger, P. T., & Thompson, K. M. (2003). E-government around the world: Lessons, challenges, and new directions. *Government Information Quarterly, 20*(4), 389–394.

Jaeger, P. T., & Thompson, K. M. (2004). Social information behavior and the democratic process: Information poverty, normative behavior, and electronic government in the United States. *Library & Information Science Research, 26*(1), 94–107.

Jaeger, P. T., & Yan, Z. (2009). One law with two outcomes: Comparing the implementation of the Children's Internet Protection Act in public libraries and public schools. *Information Technology and Libraries, 28*(1), 8–16.

James, S. E. (1985). The relationship between local economic conditions and the use of public libraries. *Library Quarterly, 55*, 255–272.

James, S. E. (1986). Economic hard times and public library use: A close look at the librarian's axiom. *Public Library Quarterly, 7*(3–4), 61–70.

Jansen, J. (2010). *Use of the Internet in higher-income households.* Washington, DC: Pew Research Center. Available: http://pewinternet.org/~/media//Files/Reports/2010/PIP-Better-off-households-final.pdf.

Jaruzelski, B., Loehr, J., & Holman, R. (2012). *The global innovation 1000: Making ideas work.* Washington, DC: Booz. Available: http://www.booz.com/media/uploads/BoozCo_The-2012-Global-Innovation-1000-Study.pdf.

Jerrard, J., Bolt, N., & Strege, K. (2012). *Privatizing libraries*. Chicago: American Library Association.

Johnson, L. B. (1964a). Proposal for a nationwide war on the sources of poverty. *Modern history sourcebook*. Available: http://www.fordham.edu/halsall/mod/1964johnson-warpoverty.html.

Johnson, L. B. (1964b). Great Society speech. *Public Papers of the Presidents of the United States: Lyndon B. Johnson, Book I (1963–1964)*. Available: http://coursesa.matrix.msu.edu/~hst306/documents/great.html.

Jue, D. K., Koontz, C. M., Magpantay, J. A., Lance, K. C., & Seidl, A. M. (1999). Using public libraries to provide technology access for individuals in poverty: A national analysis of library market areas using a geographic information system. *Library & Information Science Research, 21*, 299–325.

Kang, B. S. (2009). Bridging the digital divide between urban and rural areas: Experience of the Republic of Korea [White paper]. Available: http://www.unescap.org/idd/working percent20papers/IDD_TP_09_07_of_WP_7_2_911.pdf.

Katzman, N. (1974). The impact of communication technology: Some theoretical premises and their implications. *Ekistics, 225*, 125–130.

Kearney, A. T. (2008). *The question about "doing good": Is it worth it to business?* Melbourne, Australia: Author. Available: http://www.atkearney.com.au/documents/10192/472001/The_Question_about_Doing_Good.pdf/d6556ddf-2073-42c4-840a-81a5054776c1.

Kelly, B., Phipps, L., Sloan, D., Petrie, H., & Hamilton, F. (2005). Forcing standardization or accommodating diversity? A framework for applying the WCAG in the real world. *Proceedings of the 2005 International Cross-Disciplinary Workshop on Web Accessibility* (pp. 46–54), New York: ACM.

Kelly, M. (2011). Los Angeles Public Library wins big with votes, Measure L passes. *Library Journal*. Available: http://www.libraryjournal.com.

Kelly, M. (2012). The new normal. *Library Journal*. Available: http://www.libraryjournal.com.

Kennan, M. A., Lloyd, A., Qayyum, A. M., & Thompson, K. M. (2011). Settling in: The relationship between information and social inclusion. *Australian Academic and Research Libraries, 42*(3), 191–210.

Kent, S. G. (1996). American public libraries: A long transformation. *Daedalus, 125*(4), 207–220.

Kim, A. E., & Jeong, M. K. (2010). Technological diffusion, Internet use and digital divide in South Korea. *Korea Observer, 41*(1), 31–52.

Kim, E. K. (2013, March 28). More than just books: Arizona libraries add public health nurses. *NBC News*. Available: http://www.today.com.

Kim, J. (2011). Korea's cases on collaborative governance for digital inclusion. *Presentation for ITU Asia Pacific Regional Forum on Digital Inclusion for All, 21–23 June 2011, Singapore*. Available: http://www.itu.int/ITU-D/asp/CMS/Events/2011/DigitalInclusion/S2_JiyoungKim.pdf.

Kim, Y. M. (2011). W552 billion allocated for 180 new public libraries. *Korean Herald*, January 27. Available: http://www.koreaherald.com/view.php?ud=20110126000678.

Kim, Y. S. (2006). Opening small public libraries in quiet shopping malls could boost local businesses in Goyang, Korea. *World Library and Information Congress: 72nd IFLA General Conference and Council, 20–24 August, 2006, Seoul, South Korea*. Available: http://citeseerx.ist.psu.edu/viewdoc/download?doi=10.1.1.151.452&rep=rep1&type=pdf.

Kimmelman, G. (1989). *Media ownership: Diversity and concentration*. Washington, DC: Government Printing Office.

Kinney, B. (2010). The Internet, public libraries, and the digital divide. *Public Library Quarterly, 29*(2), 104-161.

Klecun, E. (2008). Bringing lost sheep into the fold: Questioning the discourse of the digital divide. *Information Technology & People, 21*(3), 267–282.

Kliff, S. (2012). The incredible shrinking public health workforce. *Washington Post*, July 6. Available: http://www.washingtonpost.com.

Knight Commission on the Information Needs of Communities in Democracy (2009). *Informing communities: Sustaining democracy in the digital age.* Available: http://www.knightcomm.org/wp-content/uploads/2010/02/Informing_Communities_Sustaining_Democracy_in_the_Digital_Age.pdf.

Knutsson, O., Blasjo, M., Hallsten, S., & Karlstrom, P. (2012). Identifying different registers of digital literacy in virtual learning environments. *Internet and Higher Education, 15*, 237–246.

Koltay, T. (2011). The media and the literacies: media literacy, information literacy, digital literacy. *Media, Culture and Society, 33*(2), 211–221.

Kommers, N., & Rainie, L. (2002). *Use of the Internet at major life moments.* Washington, DC: Pew Research Center. Available: http://www.pewinternet.org/.

Kong, L. (2013). Failing to read well: The role of public libraries in adult literacy, immigrant community building, and free access to learning. *Public Libraries Online*, January/February. Available: http://publiclibrariesonline.org/2013/03/failing-to-read-well-the-role-of-public-libraries-in-adult-literacy-immigrant-community-building-and-free-access-to-learning/.

Koontz, C., & Gubbins, B. (Eds.) (2010). *IFLA public library service guidelines.* Berlin: De Gruyter Saur.

Kope, M. (Ed.) (2006). Understanding e-literacy. In A. Martin & D. Madigan (Eds.), *Digital literacies for learning* (pp. 68–79). London: Facet.

Korantemaa, G. (2006). Ghana: Computers for all homes: Ministry, Intel and Microsoft to implement a digital inclusion program. *Ghanaian Chronicle*, March 31. Available: http://allafrica.com/stories/200603310262.html.

Korea Tourism Organization (2013). Population of Korea. Available: http://english.visitkorea.or.kr/enu/AK/AK_EN_1_4_3.jsp.

Kramp, R. S. (1975/2010). *The Great Depression: Its impact on forty-six large American public libraries.* Duluth, MN: Library Juice.

Landoy, A., & Zetterlund, A. (2013). Similarities and dissimilarities among Scandinavian library leaders and managers. In P. Hernon & N. O. Pors (Eds.), *Library leadership in the United States and Europe: A comparative study of academic and public libraries* (pp. 93–108). Santa Barbara, CA: Libraries Unlimited.

Lang, J. P. (Ed.) (1988). *Unequal access to information resources: Problems and needs of the world's information poor.* Ann Arbor, MI: Pierian Press.

Langer, J. A. (1987). A sociocognitive perspective on literacy. In J. A. Langer (Ed.), *Language, literacy and culture: Issues of society and schooling.* New York: Norwood.

Lanham, R. A. (1995). Digital literacy. *Scientific American, 273*(3), 160–161.

LaRosa, M. J., & Mejía, G. R. (2012). *Colombia: A concise contemporary history.* Lanham, MD: Rowman & Littlefield.

LaRue, J. (2009). Tough times and eight ways to deal with them. *American Libraries.* Available: http://www.americanlibrariesmagazine.org.

LaRue, J. (2011). Keeping our message simple. *American Libraries.* Available: http://www.americanlibrariesmagazine.org.

Larsen, E., & Rainie, L. (2002). The rise of the e-citizen: How people use government agencies' websites. Washington, DC: Pew Research Center.

Larson, K. C. (2001). The Saturday Evening girls: A progressive era library club and the intellectual life of working class and immigrant girls in turn-of-the century Boston. *Library Quarterly, 71*, 195–230.

Lazar, J., & Jaeger, P. T. (2011). Reducing barriers to online access for people with disabilities. *Issues in Science and Technology, 17*(2), 68–82.

Leckie, G. J. (2004). Three perspectives on libraries as public space. *Feliciter, 50*(6), 233–236.

Leckie, G. J., & Hopkins, J. (2002). The public place of central libraries: Findings from Toronto and Vancouver. *Library Quarterly, 72*, 326–372.

Lee, S. H. (2013). 2013 National Library of Korea's digital library strategy. *Conference of Directors of National Libraries in Asia and Oceania*, Kuala Lumpur, Malaysia, March 25–29, 2013.

Leiner, B. M., Cerf, V. G., Clark, D. D., Kahn, R. E., Kleinrock, L., Lynch, D. C., Postel, J., Roberts, L. G., & Wolff, S. (2012). Brief history of the Internet. *Internet Society*, October 15. Available: http://www.internetsociety.org/brief-history-internet.

Lenhart, A., Rainie, L., Fox, S., Horrigan, J., & Spooner, T. (2000). *Who's not online: 57 percent of those without Internet access say they do not plan to log on.* Washington, DC: Pew Research Center. Available: http://www.pewinternet.org.

Lerner, F. (2009). *The story of libraries: From the invention of writing to the computer age.* New York: Continuum.

Lewis, O. (1959). *Five families: Mexican case studies in the culture of poverty.* New York: Basic.

Lewis, O. (1961). *The children of Sánchez: Autobiography of a Mexican family.* New York: Random House.

Ley 1379. (2010). *Library Act of Colombia.* Available: http://www.secretariasenado.gov.co/senado/basedoc/ley/2010/ley_1379_2010.html.

Libraries for All—ESME Project (2009). Best practices: "www.meertalen.nl" by the Dutch Public Library Association. *New Models for Intercultural Library Services.* Available: http://librariesforall.eu/en/best-practices/wwwmeertalennl-by-the-dutch-public-library-association.

Library Act of Finland (1998). Available: http://www.libraries.fi/en-GB/libraryact/.

Lievrouw, L., & Farb, S. (2003). Information and equity. *Annual Review of Information Science and Technology, 37*, 499–540.

Liff, S., & Stewart, F. (2001). Community e-gateways: Locating networks and learning for social inclusion. *Information, Communication & Society, 4*, 317–340.

Littlejohn, A., Beetham, H., & McGill, L. (2012). Learning at the digital frontier: A review of digital literacies in theory and practice. *Journal of Computer Assisted Learning, 28*, 547–556.

Livingston, G. (2010). *The Latino digital divide: The native born versus the foreign born.* Washington, DC: Pew Research Center. Available: http://www.pewinternet.org.

Livingstone, S., & Helsper, E. (2007). Gradations in digital inclusion: Children, young people and the digital divide. *New Media & Society, 9*, 671–696.

Lloyd, A. (2006). Drawing from others: Ways of knowing about information literacy performance. *Lifelong Learning Conference, June 2006.*

Lloyd, A., Kennan, M. A., Thompson, K. M., & Qayyum, A. (2013). Connecting with new information landscapes: Information practices of refugees. *Journal of Documentation, 69*(1), 121–144.

Loges, W. E., & Jung, J. (2001). Exploring the digital divide: Internet connectedness and age. *Communication Research, 28*(4), 536–562.

Logius (n.d.). Background: Creation of the Web guidelines. *Ministry of the Interior and Kingdom Relations (Ministerie van Binnenlandse Zaken en Koninkrijksrelaties).* Available: http://www.webrichtlijnen.nl/english/what-and-why/background.

Longley, P. A., & Singleton, A. D. (2009). Linking social deprivation and digital exclusion in England. *Urban Studies, 46*(7), 1275–1298.

Lorence, D. P., Park, H., & Fox, S. (2006). Racial disparities in health information access: Resilience of the digital divide. *Journal of Medical Systems, 30*, 241–249.

Lounasvuori, E., & Vattulainen, P. (1996). Internet and the Finnish public libraries. In C. C. Chen (Ed.), *9th international conference on new information technology November 11–14 1996, Pretoria, South Africa. Proceedings, November 11–14, 1996* (pp. 177–186). West Newton, MA. Available: http://web.simmons.edu/~chen/nit/NIT'96/96-177-Lounasvuori.html.

Luo, L. (2010). Web 2.0 Integration in information literacy: Instruction: An overview. *Journal of Academic Librarianship, 36*, 32–40.

Lynch, M. J. (2002). Economic hard times and public library use revisited. *American Libraries, 33*(7), 62–63.

Lyons, L. (2011). Human rights: A universal declaration. *College & Research Library News*, *72*(5), 290–293.

Machlup, F. (1962). *The production and distribution of knowledge in the United States.* Princeton, NJ: Princeton University Press.

Mack, E. A., & Grubesic, T. H. (2009). Forecasting broadband provision. *Information Economics and Policy*, *21*, 297–311.

Mackenzie, A. (2010). *Wirelessness: Radical empiricism in network cultures.* Cambridge, MA: MIT Press.

Mackey, T. P., & Jacobsen, T. E. (2005). Information literacy: A collaborative endeavor. *College Teaching*, *53*(4), 140–144.

Mackey, T. R., & Jacobsen, T. E. (2011). Reframing information literacy as meta-literacy. *College & Research Libraries*, *72*, 62–78.

Mandel, C. A., & Wolven, R. (1996). Intellectual access to digital documents: Joining proven principles with new technologies. *Cataloging & Classification Quarterly*, *22*(3/4), 25–42.

Mandel, L. H., Bishop, B. W., McClure, C. R., Bertot, J. C., & Jaeger, P. T. (2010). Broadband for public libraries: Importance, issues, and research needs. *Government Information Quarterly*, *27*, 280–291.

Manrique, M., Benjumea, S., Rodríguez, I., Nieto, B., Calfo, S. F., Botero, E. S., & Salamanca, M. (2003). Los pueblos indígenas en Colombia: Derechos, políticas y desafíos. *UNICEF.* Available: http://www.unicef.com.co/wp-content/uploads/2012/11/pueblos-indigenas-Colombia.pdf.

Mansell, R., Davies, A., & Hulsink, W. (1996). The new telecommunications in the Netherlands: Strategy, policy and regulation. *Telecommunications Policy*, *20*(4), 273–289.

Marcum, J. W. (2002). Rethinking information literacy. *Library Quarterly*, *72*, 1–26.

Mart, S. N. (2003). The right to receive information. *Law Library Journal*, *95*, 175–189.

Martin, A. (2006a). Literacies for the digital age. In A. Martin & D. Madigan (Eds.), *Digital literacies for learning* (pp. 3–25). London: Facet.

Martin, A. (2006b). A European framework for digital literacy. *Nordic Journal of Digital Literacy*, *2*, 151–160.

Martin, A. (2008). Digital literacy and "digital society." In C. Lankshear and M. Knobel (Eds.), *Digital literacies: Concepts, policies and practices* (pp. 151–176). New York: Peter Lang.

Martin, C. A. (1973). "There's more than one way to skin a cat" (The issue of heredity and anti-egalitarian research). *Journal of Negro Education*, *42*(4), 559–569.

Mason, R. O. (1986). Four ethical issues of the information age. *MIS Quarterly*, *10*(1), 5–12.

Mayhew, D. R. (2000). *America's congress: Actions in the public sphere, James Madison through Newt Gingrich.* New Haven, CT: Yale University Press.

McClure, D. (1974). *The cost of poverty: Information for action.* Frankfort, KY: Legislative Research Commission.

McCook, K. (2011). *Introduction to public librarianship* (2nd ed.). New York: Neal Schuman.

McCook, K., & Phenix, K. J. (2006). Public libraries and human rights. *Public Library Quarterly*, *25*, 57–73.

McCreadie, M., & Rice, R. E. (1999). Trends in analyzing access to information, part I: Cross-disciplinary conceptions of access. *Information Processing and Management*, *35*, 45–76.

McCulley, C. (2009). Mixing and matching: Assessing information literacy. *Communications on Information Literacy*, *3*, 171–180.

McEntyre & Associates Pty Limited (2013). *Characteristics of Australia and its public library system.* Available: http://www.mcentyre.com.au.

McIver, W. J., Birdsall, W. F., & Rasmussen, M. (2003). The Internet and the right to communicate. *First Monday*, *8*(2). Available: http://www.firstmonday.org/issues/issue8_12/mciver/.

McLoughlin, C., & Morris, A. (2004). Public libraries: Roles in adult literacy provision. *Journal of Librarianship and Information Science, 36*(1), 37–46.

McMenemy, D. (2007). Librarians and ethical neutrality: Revisiting *The Creed of a Librarian. Library Review, 56,* 177–181.

McShane, I. (2011). Public libraries, digital literacy and participatory culture. *Discourse: Studies in the Cultural Politics of Education, 32*(3), 383–397.

Meek, M. (1991). *On being literate.* London: Bodley Head.

Mehra, B., Black, K., Singh, V., & Nolt, J. (2011). What is the value of LIS education? A qualitative study of the perspectives of Tennessee's rural librarians. *Journal of Education for Library and Information Science, 52*(4), 265–278.

Menou, M. J. (1983). Mini- and micro-computers and the eradication of information poverty in the less developed countries. In C. Keren & L. Perlmutter (Eds.). *The application of mini- and micro-computers in information, documentation and libraries* (pp. 359–366). North Holland: Elsevier Science.

Meneses, J., & Momino, J. M. (2010). Putting digital literacy in practice: How schools contribute to digital inclusion in the network society. *Information Society, 26,* 197–208.

Mereku, D. K., Yidana, I, Hordzi, W., Tete-Mensah, I., Tete-Mensah, W., & Williams, J. B. (2009). ICTs in education in Africa: Ghana report. *Pan-African Agenda on Pedagogical Integration of ICT.* Available: http://www.ernwaca.org/panaf/pdf/phase-1/Ghana-PanAf_Report.pdf.

Ministerie van Economische Zaken, Landbouw en Innovatie (2011). *Digital Agenda.nl: ICT for innovation and economic growth.* Available: http://www.rijksoverheid.nl/onderwerpen/ict/documenten-en-publicaties/notas/2011/05/17/digitale-agenda-nl-ict-voor-innovatie-en-economische-groei.html.

Ministerio de Comunicaciones (2008). *National ICT plan 2008–2019/Plan nacional de tecnologías de la información y las comunicaciones.* Bogotá: Republica de Colombia. Available: http://www.eduteka.org/pdfdir/ColombiaPlanNacionalTIC.pdf.

Ministerio de Tecnologías de la Información y Comunicaciones (2013). *Plan vive digital.* Bogota: Republic de Colombia. Available: http://www.mintic.gov.co/index.php/vive-digital-plan.

Ministry of Education (2001). *Library policy 2001–2004: Committee report.* Available: http://www.minedu.fi/OPM/Julkaisut/2001/Kirjastopoliittinen_ohjelma_2001-2004?lang=sv&extra_locale=en.

Ministry of Education (2003). *Library strategy 2010: Policy for access to knowledge and culture.* Available: http://www.minedu.fi/OPM/Julkaisut/2003/kirjastostrategia_2010?lang=en.

Ministry of Education (2009). *Finnish public library policy 2015: National strategic areas of focus.* Available: http://www.minedu.fi/export/sites/default/OPM/Julkaisut/2009/liitteet/opm31.pdf.

Ministry of Education and Culture (2006). *Library development program 2006–2010.* Available: http://www.minedu.fi/export/sites/default/OPM/Kirjastot/linjaukset_ja_hankkeet/Librarydevelopmentprogram.pdf.

Ministry of Education and Sports (2006). *The Ghana information & communications technology (ICT) in education policy.* Republic of Ghana. Available: www.observatoiretic.org/documents/download/272/.

Ministry of Future Creative Science (2013). *Korea Times,* February 24. Available: http://www.koreatimes.co.kr/www/news/nation/2013/02/116_131005.html.

Miranda-Murillo, D. (2006). New immigrants centers at the Austin Public Library. *Texas Library Journal, 82*(4), 144–147.

Montagnier, P., & Wirthmann, A. (2011). Digital divide: From computer access to online Activities: A micro data analysis. *OECD Digital Economy Papers* (189). OECD. Available: http://dx.doi.org/10.1787/5kg0lk60rr30-en.

Morrongiello, G. (2013). White House vetoes public seeing Obama's thanks to librarians. *Washington Examiner,* July 3. Available: http://washingtonexaminer.com.

Mossberger, K., Tolbert, C. J., & McNeal, R. S. (2008). *Digital citizenship: The Internet, society, and participation*. Cambridge, MA: MIT Press.

Mossberger, K., Tolbert, C. J., & Stansbury, M. (2003). *Virtual inequality: Beyond the digital divide*. Washington, DC: Georgetown University Press.

Muggleton, T. H. (2013). Public libraries and difficulties with targeting the homeless. *Library Review, 62*(1/2), 7–18.

Murdock, G., & Golding, P. (1989). Information poverty and political inequality: Citizenship in the age of privatized communications. *Journal of Communication, 39*(3), 180–195.

Musman, K. (1993). *Technological innovations in libraries, 1860–1960*. Westport, CT: Greenwood.

Naficy, H. (2009). Centering essential immigrant help on the library web site: The American Place (TAP) at Hartford Public Library. *Public Library Quarterly, 28*(2), 162–175.

Nath, V. (2001). *Heralding ICT enabled knowledge societies: Way forward for the developing countries*. Available: http://www.cddc.vt.edu/knownet/articles/heralding.htm.

National Center on Education and the Economy (2012a). *The Netherlands: Instructional systems*. Available: http://www.ncee.org/programs-affiliates/center-on-international-education-benchmarking/top-performing-countries/netherlands-overview/netherlands-instructional-systems/.

National Center on Education and the Economy (2012b). *South Korea: System and school organization*. Available: http://www.ncee.org/programs-affiliates/center-on-international-education-benchmarking/top-performing-countries/south-korea-overview/south-korea-system-and-school-organization/.

National Council on Disability (2009). *National disability policy: A progress report*. Washington, DC: Author. Available: http://www.ncd.gov.

National Curriculum Information Center (2013). Available: http://ncic.re.kr/english.index.do.

National Library of Korea (2012). *The soul of Korea: The national library of Korea*. Available: http://www.nl.go.kr/servlet/contentPdf?site_code=english&file_name=133952.pdf.

National Telecommunications and Information Administration (1995). *Falling through the Net: A survey of the " have nots " in rural and urban America*. Washington, DC: Author.

National Telecommunications and Information Administration (1998). *Falling through the Net II: New data on the digital divide*. Washington, DC: Author.

National Telecommunications and Information Administration (1999). *Falling through the Net: Defining the digital divide*. Washington, DC: Author.

National Telecommunications and Information Administration (2000). *Falling through the net: Toward digital inclusion*. Washington, DC: Author.

National Telecommunications and Information Administration (2002). *A nation online: How Americans are expanding their use of the Internet*. Washington, DC: Author.

National Telecommunications and Information Administration (2004). *A nation online: Entering the broadband age*. Washington, DC: Author.

National Telecommunications and Information Administration (2010). *Digital nation: 21st century America's progress toward universal broadband Internet access*. Washington, DC: Author.

National Telecommunications and Information Administration (2011). *Digital nation: Expanding Internet usage*. Washington, DC: Author.

National Telecommunications and Information Administration (2013). *Exploring the digital nation: America's emerging online experience*. Washington, DC: Author.

NBN Co. (2013). *Homepage*. Available: http://www.nbnco.com.au/.

Nelson, J. A. (2006). Marketing and advocacy: Collaboration in principle and practice. *Public Library Quarterly, 25*(1/2), 117–135.

Neville, A., & Datray, T. (1993). Planning for equal intellectual access for blind and low vision users. *Library Hi Tech, 11*(1), 67–71.

New York State Universal Broadband Council (2011). *Digital Literacy Standards for New Yorkers*. Available: http://diglitny.org/pdfs/diglit-standards-sheet.pdf.

Newhome, T., Keeling, K., McGoldrick, P., Macaulay, L., & Doherty, J. (2008). The digital divide and the theory of optimal slack. *New Media and Society, 10*, 295–319.

Ng, K. (2009, June 4). First dedicated digital library opens in Korea. *Asia Pacific Future Gov.* Available: http://www.futuregov.asia/articles/2009/jun/04/worlds-first-dedicated-digital-library-opens-korea/.

Ngugi, C., Irungu, N., Muwonge, B., Langa, P.V., Pederson, J., Butcher, N., Hoosen, S., Moll, I., Adam, F., Backhouse, J., & Mhlanga, E. (2007). *ICTs and higher education in Africa*. Cape Town: Centre for Educational Technology (CET). Available: http://ahero.uwc.ac.za/index.php?module=cshe&action=viewtitle&id=cshe_312.

Nicholas, D., Rowlands, I., Jubb, M., & Jamali, H. R. (2010). The impact of the economic downturn on libraries: With special reference to university libraries. *Journal of Academic Librarianship, 36*, 376–382.

Nicholas, K. (2003). Geo-policy barriers and rural Internet access: The regulatory role in constructing the digital divide. *Information Society, 19*, 287–295.

Noh, Y., Ahn, I. J., & Choi, S. K. (2012). A study of changes in the library and information science curriculum with evaluation of its practicality. *Journal of Academic Librarianship, 38*(6), 348–364.

Norris, P. (2001). *Digital divide: Civic engagement, information poverty, and the Internet worldwide*. Cambridge: Cambridge University Press.

Northern Territory Government (2006). *Evaluation of the Northern Territory Library's Libraries & Knowledge Centres model*. Available: http://artsandmuseums.nt.gov.au/__data/assets/pdf_file/0006/114846/nakata_finalreport.pdf.

Northern Territory Government (2013). *Public Libraries & Knowledge Centres*. Available: http://artsandmuseums.nt.gov.au/northern-territory-library/programs-and-projects/knowledgecentres#.Uhe6fD9dCso.

Notley, T. M., & Foth, M. (2008). Extending Australia's digital divide policy: An examination of the value of social inclusion and social capital policy frameworks. *Australian Social Policy, 7*, 87–110.

Nyquist, E. B. (1968). Poverty, prejudice, and the public library. *Library Quarterly, 38*, 78–89.

Oakleaf, M. (2008). Dangers and opportunities: A conceptual map of information literacy assessment approaches. *Libraries & the Academy, 8*, 233–253.

Oakleaf, M., & Kaske, N. (2009). Guiding questions for assessing information literacy in higher education. *Libraries & the Academy, 9*, 273–286.

O'Brien, D., & Schraber, C. (2008). Digital literacies go to school: Potholes and possibilities. *Journal of Adolescent & Adult Literacy, 52*(1), 66–68.

O'Brien, K. J. (2006). Dutch found to be most computer literate in world. *New York Times*, February 21. Available: http://www.nytimes.com/2006/02/21/technology/21iht-pew.html?_r=3&.

OCLC (2012). A snapshot of priorities & perspectives: Libraries in the Netherlands. Available: http://www.oclc.org/content/dam/oclc/reports/nl-libraries/214758usb-Member-Communication-Survey-Report-Nederland.pdf.

Office for Public Management Ltd. (2008, October). *Community perspectives on digital exclusion: Qualitative research to support the development of the digital inclusion strategy*. London: Crown Copyright, Department for Communities and Local Government.

Oldenburg, R. (1991). *The great good place*. New York: Paragon House.

O'Neil, D. V., & Baker, P. M. A. (2003). The role of institutional motivations in technological adoption: Implementation of DeKalb County's Family Technology Resource Centers. *Information Society, 19*, 305–324.

Organisation for Economic Co-operation and Development (2000). *Understanding the digital divide*. Available: http://www.oecd.org.

Organization for Economic Cooperation and Evaluation & Hungarian Ministry of Education (2004). *Promoting equity through ICT in education: Projects, problems and prospects*. Available: http://www.oecd.org/edu/research/31558662.pdf.

Orman, L. (1987). Information intensive modeling. *MIS Quarterly, 11*(1), 73–84.

Orshansky, M. (1963). Children of the poor. *Social Security Bulletin, 26*(7), 3–5.

Orshansky, M. (1965). Counting the poor: Another look at the poverty profile. *Social Security Bulletin, 28*(1), 3–29.

Osu Children's Library Fund (2013). *Approach.* Available: http://www.osuchildrens libraryfund.ca/about-oclf/approach/.

Park, H. Y. (2008). *Linguistic minority children's heritage language learning and identity struggle.* PhD diss., University of Wisconsin–Madison.

Park, S. (2012). Dimensions of digital media literacy and the relationship with social exclusion. *Media International Australia* (142), 87–100.

Parker, E. B. (1970). Information utilities and mass communication. In H. Sackman & N. Nie (Eds.), *Information utility and social choice: Papers prepared for a conference sponsored jointly by the University of Chicago, Encyclopedia Britannica and the American Federation of Information Processing Societies* (pp. 51–70). Montvale, NJ: AFIPS Press.

Parker, E. B. (1973–1974). Implications of the new information technology. *Public Opinion Quarterly, 37*(4), 590–600.

Parker, E. B., & Dunn, D. A. (1972). Information technology: Its social potential. *Science, 176*(4042), 1392–1399.

Pawley, C. (2003). Information literacy: A contradictory coupling. *Library Quarterly, 73,* 422–452.

Pensa, P. (2009). Chicago Public Library starts new a new, lean chapter. *Chicago Tribune,* December 4.

Pera, M. (2013). Libraries and the Affordable Care Act. *American Libraries.* Available: http://www.americanlibrariesmagazine.org.

Perlgut, D. (2011). Digital inclusion in the broadband world: Challenges for Australia. *Conference presentation for the Communications Policy and Research Forum, November 7, 2011.* Sydney, Australia.

Phenix, K. J., & McCook, K. (2005). Human rights and librarians. *Reference and User Services Quarterly, 45,* 23–26.

Phillipson, R. (1992). *Linguistic imperialism.* Oxford: Oxford University Press.

Phillipson, R. (2009). *Linguistic imperialism continued.* New York: Routledge, Taylor and Francis.

Pitts, J., & Stripling, B. (1990). Information power challenge: To provide intellectual and physical access. *School Library Media Quarterly,* 133-134.

Poland, M. K., & Naficy, H. (2012). The American Place at Hartford Public Library: Tackling digital citizenship. *National Civic Review, 101*(4), 27–29. doi:10.1002/ncr.21089.

Powell, A., Byrne, A., & Dailey, D. (2010). The essential Internet: Digital exclusion in low-income American communities. *Policy and Internet, 2*(2), article 7.

Preer, J. (2008). Promoting citizenship: How librarians helped get out the vote in the 1952 presidential election. *Libraries & the Cultural Record, 43,* 1–28.

Prenksy, M. (2001). Digital natives, digital immigrants. *On the Horizon, 9*(5), 1–6.

Prime Minister's Office Finland (2011). *Programme of Prime Minister Jyrki Katainen's government.* Available: http://valtioneuvosto.fi/hallitus/hallitusohjelma/pdf/en334743.pdf.

Public Library Association: Goals, Guidelines, and Standards Committee (1979). *The public library mission statement and its imperative for service.* Chicago: American Library Association.

Putnam, L. (2012). Creating the library of tomorrow from the ground up. *KQED,* January 12. Available: http://blogs.kqed.org/mindshift/2012/01/creating-the-library-of-tomorrow-from-the-ground-up/.

Rainie, L. (2010). *Internet, broadband, and cell phone statistics.* Washington, DC: Pew Research Center. Available: http://www.pewinternet.org.

Rankin, V. (1992). Pre-search: Intellectual access to information. *School Library Journal,* March, 168–170.

Rantala, L., & Suoranta, J. (2008). Digital literacy policies in the EU: Inclusive partnership as a final stage of governmentality. In C. Lankshear and M. Knobel (Eds.), *Digital literacies' concepts, policies and practices* (pp. 91–117). New York: Peter Lang.

Rathenau Instituut (2013). Advisory council for science and technology policy. *Policy and Advice*. Available: http://www.rathenau.nl/en/web-specials/the-dutch-science-system/policy-and-advice/advisory-bodies/advisory-council-for-science-and-technology-policy.html.

Real, B. M., Bertot, J. C., & Jaeger, P. T. (2014). Rural public libraries and digital inclusion: Issues and challenges. *Information Technology and Libraries, 3*(1), 6–24.

Regional Access and Public Libraries (2013). Australian public libraries: Statistical report 2011–2012. *State Library of Queensland*. Available: http://nsla.org.au/sites/www.nsla.org.au/files/publications/NSLA.public_library_stats_2011-12_0.pdf.

Reinhard, N., & Macadar, M. A. (2006). Governance and management in the Sao Paulo public telework center. *Information Technology for Development, 12*, 241–246.

Reith, D. (1984). The library as social agency. In A. R. Rogers and K. McChesney (Eds.), *The library in society* (pp. 5–16). Littleton, CO: Libraries Unlimited.

Republic of Ghana (2003). The Ghana ICT for accelerated development (ICT4AD) policy. Available: http://img.modernghana.com/images/content/report_content/ICTAD.pdf.

Reuters (2010). Nearly half of elderly in U.S. will face poverty. *MSNBC.com*. Available: http://www.msnbc.com.

Richards, N. M. (2013). The perils of social reading. *Georgetown Law Review, 689*(3). Available: http://www.georgetownlawreview.org/files/2012/03/Richards.pdf.

Riecken Community Libraries (2013). Available: http://www.riecken.org/.

Ro, J. (2002). *Infrastructure development in Korea*. Available: http://unpan1.un.org/intradoc/groups/public/documents/apcity/unpan008650.pdf.

Robbins, L. S. (1996). *Censorship and the American library: The American Library Association's response to threats to intellectual freedom*. Westport, CT: Greenwood.

Roberts, P. (1993). Philosophy, education and literacy: Some comments on Bloom. *New Zealand Journal of Educational Studies, 28*(2), 165–180.

Roberts, P. (1995). Defining literacy: Paradise, nightmare or red herring? *British Journal of Educational Studies, 43*, 412–432.

Rogers, E. M. (1995). *Diffusion of innovations* (4th ed.). New York: Free Press of Glencoe.

Rommes, E. (2002). Creating places for women on the Internet: The design of a "Women's Square" in a digital city. *European Journal of Women's Studies, 9*, 400–429.

Rosenblum, M. (2013). What's a library? *Huffington Post*, May 8. Available: http://www.huffingtonpost.com.

Roy, L., Bolfing, T., & Brzozowski, B. (2010). Computer classes for job seekers: U.S. students team with public librarians to extend public services. *Public Library Quarterly, 29*(3), 193–209.

Sacchi, A., Giannini, E., Bochic, R., Reinhard, N., & Lopes, A. B. (2009). Digital inclusion with the McInternet: Would you like fries with that? *Communication of the ACM, 52*(3), 113–116.

Salvador, A. C., Rojas, S., & Susinos, T. (2010). Weaving networks: An education project for digital inclusion. *Information Society, 26*, 137–143.

Samek, T. (2001). *Intellectual freedom and social responsibility in American librarianship, 1967–1974*. Jefferson, NC: McFarland.

Sankin, A. (2013). Internet access won't fix inequality. Available: http://www.salon.com/2013/11/23/internet_access_wont_fix_inequality_partner/.

Sawhney, H. (2003). Universal service expansion: Two perspectives. *Information Society, 19*, 327–332.

Scherer, C. W. (1989). The videocassette recorder and information inequity. *Journal of Communication, 39*(3), 94–103.

Schloman, B. F., & Gedeon, J. A. (2007). Creating trails: Tool for real-time assessment of information literacy skills. *Knowledge Quest, 35*, 44–47.

Scottish Executive (2007). *Digital inclusion in partnership.* Available: http://www.scotland.gov.uk/Resource/Doc/167938/0046198.pdf.

Seale, J., Draffan, E. A., & Wald, M. (2010). Digital agility and digital decision-making: Conceptualizing digital inclusion in the context of disabled learners in higher education. *Studies in Higher Education, 35*(4), 445–461.

Sefton-Green, J., Nixon, H., & Erstad, O. (2009). Reviewing approaches and perspectives on "digital literacy." *Pedagogies: An International Journal, 4*, 107–125.

Selwyn, N. (2004). Reconsidering political and popular understandings of the digital divide. *New Media & Society, 6*, 341–362.

Selwyn, N., Gorard, S., & Furlong, J. (2005). Whose Internet is it anyway? Exploring adults' (non)use of the Internet in everyday life. *European Journal of Communication, 20*(5), 5–25.

Servon, L. (2002). *Bridging the digital divide: Technology, community and public policy.* London: Blackwell.

Sgroi, D. (2008). Social network theory, broadband and the future of the World Wide Web. *Telecommunications Policy, 32*(1), 62–84.

Shavitt, D. (1986). *The politics of public librarianship.* Westport, CT: Greenwood.

Shera, J. H. (1933). Recent social trends and future library policy. *Library Quarterly, 3*, 339–353.

Shuler, J. A., Jaeger, P. T., & Bertot, J. C. (2010). Implications of harmonizing e-government principles and the Federal Depository Library Program (FDLP). *Government Information Quarterly, 27*, 9–16.

Shuler, J. A., Jaeger, P. T., & Bertot, J. C. (2014). E-government without government. *Government Information Quarterly, 31*, 1–4.

Sigler, K. I., Jaeger, P. T., Bertot, J. C., DeCoster, E. J., McDermott, A. J., & Langa, L. A. (2012). Public libraries, the Internet, and economic uncertainty. In A. Woodsworth (Ed.), *Advances in librarianship* (Vol. 34): *Librarianship in times of crisis* (pp. 19–35). London: Emerald.

Smith, A. (2012). *46 percent of American adults are smartphone owners.* Washington, DC: Pew Research Center. Available: http://pewinternet.org/~/media//Files/Reports/2012/Smartphone percent20ownership percent202012.pdf.

Smith, D. J. (2006). *Social inclusion and early desistance from crime.* Edinburgh: Centre for Law and Society, University of Edinburgh. Available: http://www2.law.ed.ac.uk/cls/esytc/findings/digest12.pdf.

Smith, J. (2012). The best and worst master's degrees for jobs. *Forbes*, June 8. Available: http://www.forbes.com.

Smith, J. (2013). The best and worst master's degrees for jobs right now. *Forbes*, June 7. Available: http://www.forbes.com.

Snavely, L., & Cooper, N. (1997). The information literacy debate. *Journal of Academic Librarianship*, January, 9–14.

Snyder, T. (1993). *120 years of American education: A statistical portrait.* National Center for Education Statistics. Available: http://nces.ed.gov/pubs93/93442.pdf.

Soby, M. (2008). Digital competence—From education policy to pedagogy: The Norwegian context. In C. Lankshear and M. Knobel (Eds.), *Digital literacies' concepts, policies and practices* (pp. 119–149). New York: Peter Lang.

Sohn, J. (2013) Lose yourself in reading at small library. *Korea.net.* Available: http://www.korea.net/NewsFocus/Culture/view?articleId=112029.

Somashekhar, S. (2013). States find new ways to resist health law. *Washington Post*, August 28. Available: http://www.washingtonpost.com.

Sossou, M. A. (2006). The meaning of gender equality in Ghana. *Women in Welfare Education 8*(1), 37–54.

Sourbati, M. (2009). Media literacy and universal access in Europe. *Information Society: An International Journal, 25*(4), 248–254.

Spooner, T., Meredith, P., & Rainie, L. (2003). *Regional variations in Internet use mirror differences in educational and income levels.* Washington, DC: Pew Research Center. Available: http://www.pewinternet.org.

Spooner, T., Rainie, L., & Meredith, P. (2001). *Asian-Americans and the Internet: The young and the connected.* Washington, DC: Pew Research Center. Available: http://www.pewinternet.org.

Stanley, L. D. (2003). Beyond access: Psychosocial barriers to computer literacy. *Information Society, 19,* 407–416.

Starr, P. (2004). *The creation of the media: Political origins of modern communication.* New York: Basic Books.

State Library New South Wales (2013). *Homepage.* Available: http://www.sl.nsw.gov.au/.

Statistics Korea (2012). *Korea's Population: 50 million.* Available: http://kostat.go.kr/portal/english/news/1/17/1/index.board?bmode=read&bSeq=&aSeq=273104&pageNo=1&rowNum=10&navCount=10&currPg=&sTarget=title&sTxt=.

Statistics Netherlands (2013). *Homepage.* Available: http://statline.cbs.nl/StatWeb/publication/?VW=T&DM=SLEN&PA=37943eng&LA=EN.

Stevenson, S. (2009). Digital divide: A discursive move away from the real inequities. *Information Society, 25,* 1–22.

Stielow, F. (2001). Reconsidering "arsenals of a democratic culture": Balancing symbol and practice. In N. Kranich (Ed.), *Libraries and democracy: The cornerstones of liberty* (pp. 3–14). Chicago: American Library Association.

Stinnett, G. (2009). Archival landscape: Archives and human rights. *Progressive Librarian, 32,* 10–20.

Strover, S. (2003). Remapping the digital divide. *Information Society, 19,* 275–277.

Sturges, P., & Gastinger, A. (2010). Information literacy as a human right. *Libri, 60,* 195–202.

Suarez, D. (2007). Education professionals and the construction of human rights education. *Comparative Education Review, 51*(1), 48–70.

Subrahmanyam, K., & Smahel, D. (2011). *Digital youth: The role of media in development.* London: Springer.

Subramaniam, M., Ahn, J., Waugh, A., Taylor, N.G., Druin, A., Fleischmann, K., & Walsh, G. (2013). Crosswalk between the framework for K–12 science education and standards for the 21st-century learner: School librarians as the crucial link. *School Library Research, 16.* Available: http://ter.ps/2r1.

Subramaniam, M., Oxley, R., & Kodama, C. (2013). School librarians as ambassadors of inclusive information access for students with disabilities. *School Library Research, 16.* Available at: http://ter.ps/22z.

Svenonious, E. (2000). *The intellectual foundation of information organization.* Cambridge, MA: Massachusetts Institute of Technology Press.

Swanson, D. R. (1979). Libraries and the growth of knowledge. *Library Quarterly, 49,* 3–25.

Taylor, N. G., Gorham, U., Jaeger, P. T., & Bertot, J. C. (2014). IT and collaborative community services: The roles of the public library, local government, and nonprofit entity partnerships. *International Journal of Public Administration in the Digital Age.*

Taylor, N. G., Jaeger, P. T., Gorham, U., Bertot, J. C., Lincoln, R., & Larson, E. (2014). The circular continuum of agencies, public libraries, and users: A model of e-government in practice. *Government Information Quarterly.*

Taylor, N. G., Jaeger, P. T., McDermott, A. J., Kodama, C. M., & Bertot, J. C. (2012). Public libraries in the new economy: 21st century skills, the Internet, and community needs. *Public Library Quarterly, 31*(3), 191–219.

Telecommunications Act of 1996 (US), 47 USC § 225 *et seq.*

Thompson, K. M. (2008). The US information infrastructure and libraries: A case study in democracy. *Library Review, 57*(2), 96–106.

Thompson, K. M., & Adkins, D. A. (2012). Addressing information resource issues through LIS education in Honduras. *Journal for Education in Library and Information Science, 53*(4), 254–266.

Thompson, K. M., & Afzal, W. (2011). Determinants of information access: An examination of the role of culture. *OMNES: The Journal of Multicultural Society, 2*(2), 22–42.

Thompson, R. M. (2003). *Filipino English and Taglish: Language switching from multiple perspectives*. Philadelphia, PA: John Benjamins.

Tongia, R., & Wilson, E. J. (2007). Turning Metcalfe on his head: The multiple costs of network exclusion. Paper presented at the 2007 Telecommunications Policy Research Conference.

Tsatsou, P. (2011). Digital divides revisited: What is new about divides and their research? *Media Culture Society, 33*(2), 317–331.

Turner, B. (Ed.) (2012). *Statesman's Yearbook* (148th ed.). Hampshire: Palgrave MacMillan.

U.K. Department of Communities and Local Government (2008). *Digital exclusion profiling of vulnerable groups*. London: Communities and Local Government Publications. Available: http://dera.ioe.ac.uk/603/1/999909.pdf.

Umesao, T. (1963). Joho sangyo ron. *Chuo-kohron*, 46–58.

United Nations (1948). *Universal Declaration of Human Rights*. Available: http://www.un.org/Overview/rights.html.

United Nations (1986). *New information technologies and development*. New York: UN Center for Science and Technology Development.

United Nations (2012). *E-government survey 2012: E-government for the people*. Available: http://www.unpan.org/egovkb/global_reports/08report.htm.

United Nations (2013). *International human development indicators*. Available: http://hdr.undp.org/en/data/profiles/.

United Nations Office on Drugs and Crime (2011). *Global study on homicide*. Available: http://www.unodc.org/documents/data-and-analysis/statistics/Homicide/Globa_study_on_homicide_2011_web.pdf.

University of California–Los Angeles (2003). *UCLA Internet report: Surveying the digital future*. Los Angeles: Anderson Graduate School of Management. Available: http://images.forbes.com/fdc/mediaresourcecenter/UCLA03.pdf.

Urban Libraries Council (2010). *Partners for the future: Public libraries and local governments creating sustainable communities*. Chicago, IL: Author.

U.S. Bureau of Labor (2012). *International comparisons of GDP per capita and per hour, 1960–2011*. Available: http://www.bls.gov/ilc/intl_gdp_capita_gdp_hour.htm#table 04.

U.S. Census Bureau (2003). *Selected communications media: 1920–2001*. Available: http://www.census.gov/statab/hist/HS-42.pdf.

U.S. Census Bureau (2005). *USA statistics in brief*. Available: http://www.census.gov/statab/www/racehisp.html.

U.S. Census Bureau (2013). *Income, poverty, and health insurance coverage in the United States: 2012*. Washington, DC: U.S. Department of Commerce. Available: http://www.census.gov/prod/2013pubs/p60-245.pdf.

U.S. Centers for Medicare and Medicaid Services (n.d.). Table 145. Medicaid—Summary by State: 2000 and 2006. *Medicaid, program statistics, Medicaid statistical information system*. Available: http://www.census.gov/compendia/statab/2010/tables/10s0145.pdf.

U.S. Citizenship and Immigration Services (2006). *Library services for immigrants: A report on current practices*. Available: http://www.uscis.gov/USCIS/Officepercent20ofpercent20Citizenship/Citizenshipper-cent20Resourcepercent20Centerpercent20Site/Publications/PDFs/G-1112.pdf.

U.S. Department of Agriculture (2011). *About the recovery act BIP*. Available: http://www.rurdev.usda.gov/utp_bip.html.

U.S. Office of Retirement and Disability Policy (2009). *Table 2. Supplemental Security Income. Social Security Administration, Supplemental Security Record*. Available: http://www.ssa.gov/policy/docs/factsheets/cong_stats/2009/al.html.

U.S. Supplemental Nutrition Assistance Program (n.d.). *Table of participation and benefits as of October 28, 2010*. Available: http://www.fns.usda.gov/pd/34SNAPmonthly.htm.

U.S. Women, Infants and Children Program (n.d.). *Table of WIC Program: Total participation*. Available: http://www.fns.usda.gov/pd/26wifypart.htm.

van Deursen, A. J. A. M., & van Dijk, J. A. G. M. (2009). Improving digital skills for the use of online public information and services. *Government Information Quarterly*, 26(2), 333–340.

van Deursen, A. J. A. M., & van Dijk, J. A. G. M. (2013). The digital divide shifts to differences in usage. *New Media & Society*. doi: 10.1177/1461444813487959.

van Dijk, J., & Hacker, K. (2003). The digital divide as a complex and dynamic phenomenon. *Information Society, 19*(4), 315–326.

Van Sant, W. (2009). Librarians now add social work to their resumes. *St. Petersburg Times*, June 8. Available: http://www.tampabay.com/.

Vehovar, V., Sicherl, P., Hüsing, T., & Dolnicar, V. (2006). Methodological challenges of digital divide measurements. *Information Society* (22), 279–290.

W3Tech (2013). *Usage of content languages for websites*. Available: http://w3techs.com/technologies/overview/content_language/all.

Wagga Wagga City Library (2013). Homepage. Available: http://www.wagga.nsw.gov.au/library.

Waller, V. (2009). The relationship between public libraries and Google: Too much information. *First Monday, 14*(9). Available: http://firstmonday.org/ojs/index.php/fm/article/view/2477/2279.

Waples, D., Carnovsky, L., & Randall, W. M. (1932). The public library in the Depression. *Library Quarterly, 2*, 321–343.

Warren, M. (2007). The digital vicious cycle: Links between social disadvantage and digital exclusion in rural areas. *Telecommunications Policy, 31*, 374–388.

Warschauer, M. (2003). *Technology and social inclusion: Rethinking the digital divide*. Cambridge, MA: MIT Press.

Watson, L. (2010). The future of library as a place of learning: A personal perspective. *New Review of Academic Libraries, 16*(1), 45–56.

Webster, F. (2005). The end of the public library? *Science as Culture, 14*, 283–287.

Wentz, B., Jaeger, P. T., & Lazar, J. L. (2011). Retrofitting accessibility: The legal inequality of after-the-fact online access for persons with disabilities in the United States. *First Monday, 11*(7). Available: http://www.uic.edu/htbin/cgiwrap/bin/ojs/index.php/fm/article/viewArticle/3666/3077.

Whitacre, B., Gallardo, R., & Strover, S. (2013). *Rural broadband availability and adoption: Evidence, policy challenges, and options*. National Agricultural & Rural Development Policy Center. Available: http://expeng.anr.msu.edu/uploads/files/133/BroadbandWhitePaper.pdf.

White House (2009). *Vice President Biden launches initiative to bring broadband, jobs to more Americans*. Available: http://www.whitehouse.gov/the_press_office/Vice-President-Biden-Launches-Initiative-to-Bring-Broadband-Jobs-to-More-Americans.

Whitworth, A. (2009). *Information obesity*. Oxford: Chandos.

Wiegand, W. A. (1989). *An active instrument for propaganda: The American public library during World War I*. Westport, CT: Greenwood.

Wiegand, W. A. (1999). Tunnel vision and blind spots: What the past tells us about the present; Reflections on the twentieth-century history of American librarianship. *Library Quarterly, 69*(1), 1–32.

Willams, P., & Minnian, A. (2007). Exploring the challenges of developing digital literacy in the context of special educational needs communities. In S. Andretta (Ed.), *Change and challenge: Information literacy for the 21st century* (pp. 115–144). Adelaide: Auslib Press.

Williamson, M. (2000). Social exclusion and the public library: A Habermasian insight. *Journal of Librarianship and Information Science, 32*(4), 178–186.

Willingham, T. L. (2008). Libraries as civic agents. *Public Library Quarterly, 27*(2), 97–110.

Wilson, M. C. (1998). To dissect a frog or design an elephant: Teaching digital information literacy through the library gateway. *Inspel, 32*(3). 189–195.

Winkel, J. (2007). Lessons on evaluating programs and collections for immigrant communities at the Queens Borough Public Library. *Colorado Libraries, 33*(1), 43–46.

Wong, Y. C., Law, C. K., Fung, J. Y. C., & Lam, J. C. Y. (2009). Perpetuating old exclusions and producing new ones: Digital exclusion in an information society. *Journal of Technology in Human Services, 27*, 57–78.

Wood, G. S. (2004). *The Americanization of Benjamin Franklin*. New York: Penguin Press.

Woods, B. (1993). *Communication, technology and the development of people*. London: Routledge.

World Bank (2006). *eGhana Project: World Bank group approves US$40 million for implementation of Ghana's ICT program* [Press release]. Available: http://web.worldbank.org/WBSITE/EXTERNAL/NEWS/0,contentMDK:21012483~pagePK:64257043~piPK:437376~theSitePK:4607,00.html.

World Bank (2012). *eGhana: Implementation status results report*. Available: http://documents.worldbank.org/curated/en/2012/12/17076691/ghana-eghana-p093610-implementation-status-results-report-sequence-11.

World Bank (2013a). Colombia. *Data: Countries and Economies*. Available: http://data.worldbank.org/country/colombia.

World Bank (2013b). *Data: GDP per capita (current US$)*. Available: http://data.worldbank.org/indicator/NY.GDP.PCAP.CD/countries.

World Bank (2013c). *GDP ranking*. Available: http://data.worldbank.org/data-catalog/GDP-ranking-table.

World Bank (2013d). Ghana. *Data: Countries and Economies*. Available: http://data.worldbank.org/country/ghana.

World Bank (2013e). Honduras. *Data: Countries and Economies*. Available: http://data.worldbank.org/country/honduras.

World Summit on the Information Society (2003, December 12). *Plan of action*. Available: http://www.itu.int/wsis/docs/geneva/official/poa.html.

World Wide Web Foundation (2013). *Project: Ghana open data initiative (GODI)*. Available: http://www.webfoundation.org/projects/ghana-open-data-initiative-godi/.

Wresch, W. (1996). *Disconnected: Haves and have-nots in the information age*. New Brunswick, NJ: Rutgers University Press.

Xie, B., & Jaeger, P. T. (2008). Computer training programs for older adults at the public library. *Public Libraries, 47*(5), 42–49.

Yakel, E. (2004). Information literacy for primary sources: Creating a new paradigm for archival researcher education. *OCLC Systems & Services, 20*(2), 61–64.

Yang, K. H., Park, S. K., Yoon, S. N., & Kim, J. (2010). Measurement of the digital inequality in remote rural areas: Case of South Korea. *International Journal of Information Technology and Management, 9*(2), 142–161.

Yates, K. (2009). Hard economic times: A boon for public libraries. *CNN.com*, February 28. Available: http://www.cnn.com/2009/US/02/28/recession.libraries/index.html.

Yu, L. (2011). The divided views of the information and digital divides: A call for integrative theories of information inequality. *Journal of Information Science, 37*(6), 660–679.

Yu, P. K. (2002). Bridging the digital divide: Equality in the information age. *Cardozo Art & Entertainment Law Journal, 20*, 1–52.

Yuan, L., & Powell, S. (2013). *MOOCs and open education: Implications for higher education*. Available: http://publications.cetis.ac.uk/2013/667.

Zabriskie, C. (2013). Libraries in New York City: Why we give a damn and why you should too. *Huffington Post*, April 30. Available: http://www.huffingtonpost.com.

Zandvliet, E. (2009). *Regelhulp — Simplifying online applications for social services*. Ministry of Health, Welfare and Sport. Available: http://www.epractice.eu/en/cases/regelhulp.

Zickuhr, K. (2013). *Who's not online and why*. Washington, DC: Pew Research Center. Available: http://www.pewinternet.org.

Zickuhr, K., Rainie, L., & Purcell, K. (2013). *Library services in the digital age*. Washington, DC: Pew Research Center. Available: http://libraries.pewinternet.org/2013/01/22/library-services/.

Zickuhr, K., & Smith, A. (2012). *Digital differences*. Washington, DC: Pew Internet and the American Life Project. Available: http://pewinternet.org/Reports/2012/Digital-differences.asp.

Zukin, C., & Snyder, R. (1984). Passive learning: When the media environment is the message. *Public Opinion Quarterly, 48*(3), 629–638.

Index

About the Authors

Kim M. Thompson, PhD, is a lecturer in the School of Information Studies of the Charles Sturt University and an affiliate faculty member of Information Policy & Access Center (iPAC) in the College of Information Studies at the University of Maryland. Drawing upon a background spanning information studies, library science, and international consulting, her research and teaching focus is on information poverty and the physical, intellectual, and sociocultural supports for and barriers to information access. Her work primarily focuses on underserved and disadvantaged populations and is based mainly on theoretical analysis. Her articles are found in the *Journal of Documentation*, *Public Library Quarterly*, *Library Quarterly*, and *Library & Information Science Research*, among others. Implications of her research extend to improving information services in libraries and other information organizations as well as providing greater understanding of information poverty issues on an international scale.

Paul T. Jaeger, PhD, JD, is associate professor and diversity officer of the College of Information Studies and co-director of the Information Policy and Access Center at the University of Maryland. Dr. Jaeger's research focuses on the ways in which law and public policy shape information behavior, particularly for underserved populations. He is the author of more than 130 journal articles and book chapters. This is his ninth book. His other recent books are *Information Worlds: Social Context, Technology, & Information Behavior in the Age of the Internet* (Routledge, 2010) with Gary Burnett; *Public Libraries and the Internet: Roles, Perspectives, and Implications* (Libraries Unlimited, 2011) with John Carlo Bertot and Charles R. McClure; *Disability and the Internet: Confronting a Digital Divide* (Lynne Rienner, 2012); and *Public Libraries, Public Policies, and Political Processes: Serving and Transforming Communities in Times of Economic and Political Constraint* (Scarecrow, 2014) with Ursula Gorham, John Carlo Bertot, and Lindsay C. Sarin. His research has been funded by the Institute of Museum & Library Services, the National Science Foundation, the American Library Association, the Smithsonian Institution, and the Bill & Melinda Gates Foundation, among others. Dr. Jaeger is co-editor of *Library Quarterly*, co-editor of the *Information Policy Book Series* from MIT Press, and associate editor of *Government Information Quarterly*.

Natalie Greene Taylor is a research associate and doctoral candidate of the Information Policy & Access Center (iPAC) in the College of Information Studies at the University of Maryland. Her research focuses on partnerships between libraries and government agencies and roles of school libraries in meeting community needs. She received her master's of library science at the University of Maryland–College Park, specializing in e-government and school library media, for which she is certified in the state of Maryland. She has published articles in *Library & Information Science Research*, *Public Library Quarterly*, *Information Polity*, and *International Journal of Public Administration in the Digital Age*, among others.

Mega Subramaniam, PhD, is an assistant professor and associate director of the Information Policy & Access Center (iPAC) in the College of Information Studies at the University of Maryland. She conducts research on enhancing the role of school libraries in fostering the mastery of information and new media literacy so essential to the learning of science and mathematics among underserved young people. She is the co-editor of *School Library Research*, and she has published articles in *Library Quarterly*, *School Library Research*, *Library Trends*, *Journal of Librarianship and Information Science*, and many more. Her research has been funded by the National Science Foundation, Institute of Museum and Library Services, the National Library of Medicine and the Deutsch Foundation, among others.

John Carlo Bertot, PhD, is professor and co-director of the Information Policy & Access Center in the College of Information Studies at the University of Maryland. His research spans library and government agency technology planning and evaluation, information and telecommunications policy, and e-government. He is president of the Digital Government Society of North America and serves as chair of the International Standards Organization's Library Performance Indicator (ISO 11620) working group and is past chair of the American Library Association's (ALA) Library Research Round Table. John is editor of *Government Information Quarterly* and co-editor of *Library Quarterly*. Over the years, John has received funding for his research from the National Science Foundation, the Bill & Melinda Gates Foundation, the Government Accountability Office, the American Library Association, and the Institute of Museum and Library Services.

CPSIA information can be obtained at www.ICGtesting.com
Printed in the USA
BVOW07*1101110814

362148BV00002B/3/P

9 780810 892712